THE Baking ANSWER BOOK

Solutions to Every Problem You'll Ever Face

Answers to Every Question You'll Ever Ask

LAUREN CHATTMAN

Storey Publishing

*The mission of Storey Publishing is to serve our customers by
publishing practical information that encourages
personal independence in harmony with the environment.*

Edited by Margaret Sutherland and Molly Jackel
Art direction and book design by Jessica Armstrong
Text production by Liseann Karandisecky

Cover photography by Mars Vilaubi
Illustration by Alison Kolesar
Indexed by Christine R. Lindemer, Boston Road Communications

Printed in China by Regent Publishing Services
10 9 8 7 6 5 4 3 2 1

LIBRARY OF CONGRESS CATALOGING-IN-PUBLICATION DATA

Chattman, Lauren.
  The baking answer book by / Lauren Chattman.
    p. cm.
  Includes index.
  ISBN 978-1-60342-439-4 (flexibind with cloth spine : alk. paper)
  1. Baking. I. Title.
  TX763.C487 2009
  641.8'15—dc22

                                                    2009013730

Contents

Introduction

I must have been about 10 years old when I baked something on my own for the very first time: butterscotch blondies from *The Joy of Cooking*. It seemed like a magic trick: Mix together a few ingredients, put the batter in the oven, and, presto, dessert! During the next few years, I moved on to chocolate chip cookies, brownies, and apple cobbler, amazing myself and my family with my successes in the kitchen.

With these recipes under my belt, I asked my mom to buy some yeast so I could try my hand at a whole-wheat bread recipe. To my horror, the dough I had kneaded, punched down, and shaped exactly according to the recipe directions failed to rise in the slightest during baking. My finished loaf was about the size of a bar of cream cheese, and it weighed as much as a brick. What went wrong? Reviewing the recipe, I couldn't find a clue. I didn't bake bread for another 10 years.

Back in the 1970s there were very few resources for novice bakers. If you didn't have an experienced mom or grandma to offer advice, you had to learn through trial and error. Although my own mom is a fabulous cook, she lacks a sweet tooth, so until I began a professional pastry and baking program at the Institute for Culinary Education in New York City, I had no one to turn to when I ran into baking trouble.

Cooking school was wonderful. Learning kitchen science and tricks of the trade didn't make baking any less magical for me — quite the opposite. When I learned the secrets to making fluffy meringue cookies, tender layer cakes, and crisp puff pastry, I felt like a kitchen wizard, able to apply simple rules and skills to create an endless array of baked goods.

Since then, I've worked in restaurant kitchens and in my own kitchen writing cookbooks. I've had my share of puzzling moments ("Is *this* how you fold croissant dough?"), disappointments ("Wow, these scones are tough."), and outright disasters ("How did my Thanksgiving pumpkin pie get so watery and lumpy?"). But instead of burying the failures in the trash and trying to forget them, I've been able to consult with some very knowledgeable baker-mentors and I've acquired a shelf full of wonderful baking books to help me proceed when I'm not sure about a recipe's directions, or what to do when things go very wrong. When I was given the opportunity to gather together baking questions and answers into this convenient little package that could sit right beside my mixer on the kitchen counter, I jumped at the chance.

This book is organized into chapters on ingredients, equipment, and baking science, followed by chapters on different categories of baked goods. So if you are wondering whether aluminum foil or wax paper is an appropriate substitute for parchment paper, you can flip to chapter 2, **Equipment**. If you are attempting a Julia Child recipe for French apple tart, you can turn to chapter 8, **Pies, Tarts, Cobblers, and Crisps**, to find out whether Macintosh apples are a good substitute for Granny Smiths. Any question about baking that I've ever had, and any question I've imagined having, is included in this book. I hope it will give you the confidence that comes with knowing that the answers to your baking questions are close at hand.

ACKNOWLEDGMENTS

Writing this book was such a gratifying experience. Researching and organizing the information that appears here has certainly made me a better baker, and a better writer, too. From the bottom of my heart, I'd like to thank the people who helped me.

Jennifer Griffin first put me in touch with the great people at Storey publishing, so she is the first on my list. At Storey, Margaret Sutherland guided me through every step of the "Answer Book" process with extraordinary intelligence, enthusiasm, and patience. It was a real pleasure working with her, and I look forward to doing so again. Molly Jackel did a wonderful job of editing the manuscript. She made the final book as clear and readable as I hoped it would be. Kudos to illustrator Alison Kolesar, whose line drawings illustrate and clarify where words aren't adequate.

The cookbook authors whose knowledge informs the answers in this book are too numerous to list. I count on my entire baking library when I have a question in the kitchen, and it is a great comfort to know that among the hundreds of books I own there is an answer to any question I may have. But without a doubt I owe the greatest debt to several great bakers who have personally shared their knowledge with me over the years. My first teacher, Nick Malgieri, gave me the tools to make me an extremely gratifying career change 15 years ago. My ongoing collaboration with White House Pastry Chef Roland Mesnier has been one of the best professional experiences of my life. I learn something new about baking every time we talk. Most recently, Daniel Leader, a founder of the artisan baking movement in this country and a walking encyclopedia of all things bread, has shared some of his vast knowledge with me. Anything helpful I say about bread in this book can be traced back to our conversations.

Finally, I'd like to thank my family, for puzzling through some of the most difficult questions in this book with me and for sharing what comes out of the oven every day.

CHAPTER 1

Ingredients

Great baked goods begin with quality ingredients, properly handled and measured. This might seem obvious, but it's worth repeating because so many efforts by well-intentioned bakers are derailed by thoughtless substitution of baking powder for baking soda, the choice of imitation white chocolate instead of real white chocolate with cocoa butter, or the use of vegetable shortening that's been sitting on the pantry shelf for over a year.

This chapter will answer questions about ingredients: what to keep on hand so spontaneous baking is possible; how to store pantry items to keep them fresh for as long as possible; how to differentiate between the different types of flour or sugar or fat in your pantry so you know you are using the right type for a particular recipe. Secure in the knowledge that you have the right ingredients and that they are in good shape for baking, you can dive into any recipe with confidence.

Q What pantry items should a home baker keep on hand?

A This depends on how often and how ambitiously you bake. Would Scottish shortbread (just four ingredients — flour, butter, sugar, and salt) satisfy your baking urge in a pinch? Or would you like to be able to bake a loaf of whole-wheat raisin bread (you'd need whole-wheat flour, yeast, and raisins) on a snowy day without going to the supermarket? Stock your pantry and refrigerator accordingly. The following lists include items that can be stored in the refrigerator for at least a week, as well as items stored at room temperature for much longer.

The Basic Baker's Pantry

To bake simple items such as biscuits and scones, brownies, butter cookies, or a pound cake at a moment's notice, you should have the following ingredients on hand.

* **In the pantry:** all-purpose flour, granulated sugar, light brown sugar, dark brown sugar, unsweetened chocolate, semisweet chocolate chips, baking powder, baking soda, salt, vanilla extract

* **In the refrigerator:** low-fat or whole milk, large eggs

* **In the freezer:** unsalted butter, pecans or walnuts

The Intermediate Baker's Pantry

Adding the following to your store of pantry items will allow you to expand your repertoire to include fruit pies (provided you have some fresh or frozen fruit), oatmeal and peanut butter cookies, corn muffins, and a variety of quick breads.

* **In the pantry:** confectioners' sugar, cornstarch, rolled oats (not quick-cooking), cornmeal, unsweetened cocoa powder, vegetable oil, vegetable shortening, raisins, ground cinnamon, ground ginger, nutmeg

* **In the refrigerator:** cream cheese, natural peanut butter

* **In the freezer:** whole and sliced almonds

The Serious Baker's Pantry

To make tender cakes, yeast-risen breads, and pastries, and to add to your flavor palette when baking, keep the following ingredients on hand.

* **In the pantry:** cake flour, whole-wheat flour, light and dark corn syrup, dark (not blackstrap) molasses, honey, dried apricots, dried figs, dried dates, instant espresso powder, almond extract, ground cloves, allspice, mace

* **In the refrigerator:** buttermilk, yogurt

* **In the freezer:** active dry yeast, hazelnuts, pine nuts

STORAGE AND SHELF LIFE OF PANTRY ITEMS

Fresh ingredients are essential for great-tasting baked goods. Storing ingredients properly and discarding them when they are no longer fresh is the first step to successful baking. Use an indelible pen to mark boxes, bags, and jars of seldom-used items with the purchase date to keep track of how long you've had them. Items stored in the pantry should be kept in airtight containers.

The following guide will help you keep your ingredients in optimum baking condition.

What	Where	How Long
Baking powder	pantry	3 months
Baking soda	pantry	6 months
Butter, unsalted	middle of refrigerator freezer	up to 3 months up to 6 months
Chocolate, unsweetened, semisweet, and bittersweet	pantry	1 year
Cocoa powder	pantry	1 year
Cornmeal	pantry refrigerator or freezer	6 months 12 months
Cornstarch	pantry	18 months
Corn syrup	pantry	indefinite
Dried fruit	pantry	6 months
Eggs	in carton in middle of refrigerator	3 to 5 weeks
Espresso powder	pantry	1 year

What	Where	How Long
Flour, white	pantry freezer	8 months 1 year
Flour, whole-wheat	pantry freezer	2 months 6 months
Honey	pantry	1 year
Molasses	pantry	6 months
Nuts	freezer	6 months to 1 year
Oats	pantry refrigerator or freezer	6 months 1 year
Peanut butter (natural)	refrigerator	3 months
Salt	pantry	indefinite
Shortening	pantry	3 months
Spices	pantry	1 year
Sugar, brown	pantry	4 months
Sugar, confectioners'	pantry	18 months
Sugar, granulated	pantry	2 years
Vanilla and other extracts	pantry	4 to 5 years
Vegetable oil	pantry	4 to 6 months
Yeast, dry	refrigerator freezer	6 months 1 year
Yogurt	refrigerator	3 weeks

Scottish Shortbread

With only four ingredients — butter, flour, sugar, and salt — this is the ultimate minimalist cookie recipe. Buttery, crumbly, and perfectly sweet, these cookies are the distilled essence of what we love about baking.

MAKES 16 COOKIES

2 cups unbleached all-purpose flour
½ cup plus 1 tablespoon sugar
¼ teaspoon salt
1 cup (2 sticks) unsalted butter, chilled and cut into small pieces

1. Preheat the oven to 300°F (150°C).
2. Combine the flour, sugar, and salt in a large mixing bowl and beat on low with an electric mixer until combined. Add the butter and continue to beat until the dough is sandy and holds together when pinched between your fingers.
3. Transfer the dough to a 10-inch tart pan with a removable bottom and press it into an even layer with your fingertips. Work quickly so as not to soften and melt the butter.
4. Bake for 20 minutes. Remove from the oven, and, using a pizza wheel or the tip of a sharp paring knife, lightly score the dough into 16 wedges. Pierce the dough all over with the point of a skewer. Return the pan to the oven and bake until the shortbread is dry, firm, and very pale golden, 40 to 50 minutes longer.
5. Transfer the pan to a wire rack to cool completely. Remove the bottom from the pan, and cut the shortbread with a sharp knife along the scored lines. Shortbread will keep at room temperature in an airtight container for 1 week.

Q What is the difference between cake flour, all-purpose flour, and bread flour? Is all-purpose flour really "all-purpose"?

A Different types of flour have different amounts of protein. Protein provides strength and structure to baked goods. While percentages differ from brand to brand and from region to region, in general, cake flour is between 7.5% and 9% protein, all-purpose flour has a protein content of about 12%, and bread flour ranges from 13% to 14% protein. Low-protein cake flour will give white cake and other delicate cakes and biscuits a soft, tender crumb. All-purpose flour will give cookies a nice shape without adding so much protein that they become tough. The additional protein in bread flour will give strength to bread dough so it won't collapse as gases created by yeast expand inside the dough as it bakes.

SEE ALSO: Self-rising flour, page 128; cake flour, page 199.

Q How do I substitute all-purpose flour for other flours?

A With a few adjustments, all-purpose flour can be used in place of cake or bread flour. To approximate 1 cup of cake flour, use ¾ cup plus 2 tablespoons of all-purpose flour sifted with 2 tablespoons of cornstarch. Cornstarch has no protein, so adding it to the flour will add volume without adding protein.

A relatively strong all-purpose flour (a national brand like Gold Medal or a northern brand like King Arthur have more protein than Southern brands) may be substituted for bread flour, but expect a slightly less chewy and crusty product. Bread flour is able to absorb more water per cup than all-purpose flour, so use 1 cup plus 2 tablespoons of all-purpose flour for every cup of bread flour called for in a recipe.

Q What is the difference between white flour and whole-wheat flour?

A Flour is milled from wheat kernels, each one consisting of three parts: the bran, the germ, and the endosperm. The bran is the tough outer layer made up mostly of fiber. The germ is the core, packed with protein, healthy oil, and vitamins and minerals. The endosperm is the largest part of the kernel, made up mostly of starch and proteins. Flour that retains the bran and germ during milling, giving it a speckled brown and off-white color, is called

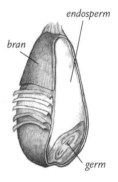

kernel of wheat

whole wheat. When the bran and germ are removed during milling, the resulting flour is white.

Color isn't the only difference between the two. The bran and germ in whole-wheat flour add nutritional value. And then there's flavor. Whole-wheat flour lends a nutty, toasted flavor and fragrance to baked goods while white flour is milder and more neutral.

Q Can I use whole-wheat flour instead of white flour for more healthful baked goods?

A The flakes of bran in whole-wheat flour can weaken the protein structure of baked goods, inhibiting their rise and giving them a heavy and dense texture. When adapting a recipe for the first time, it's best not to substitute more than one-third to one-half of the white flour called for with whole-wheat flour. This way, your product will have the structural benefits provided by white flour along with the nutritional benefits of whole wheat. Increase the proportion of whole-wheat to white flour in later attempts, if you like, seeing how high you can go without compromising the texture of your baked goods.

You may want to make other adjustments when substituting whole-wheat for white flour. Whole-wheat flour absorbs more water than white flour, so you may find that when you substitute whole-wheat flour for white you'll need to add more liquid, a tablespoonful at a time, until your dough reaches the right consistency.

It's a matter of taste, but some people add more sweetener to recipes with whole-wheat flour to balance the robust flavor of the flour.

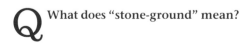

Q What does "stone-ground" mean?

A Wheat and other grains such as corn must be milled into flour or meal before they are bagged and shipped to the market. Stone grinding is an old-fashioned type of milling in which the grain is simply ground between massive stones. The result is 100% whole-grain flour or meal. Whole wheat that is stone-ground contains all of the bran and germ from the ground wheat berries. Most commercial mills today, in contrast, use large metal rollers to grind the grain quickly, stripping out the endosperm and grinding it by itself. The result is white flour.

To make whole-wheat flour, these commercial producers stir the bran back into the flour, but the oily germ, which contains the healthful oils and other nutrients, is left out to increase the flour's shelf life. (By law, flour labeled "whole wheat" need contain only 95% of the whole-wheat berry.) For the most nutritious and best tasting 100% whole-grain flour and meal, look for "stone-ground" on the label. If you can't find stone-ground grain locally, you can mail order it (see Resources). You won't be sorry.

Q What does "unbleached and unbromated" mean?

A After wheat is ground into flour, it needs to age before it is ready to be used in baking. Treating newly milled flour with bleaching agents not only gives it a pure white color, but also hurries along the aging process so the flour is ready to sell at an earlier date. Potassium bromate is another additive that hurries along aging. Most bakers now agree that flour aged naturally by exposing it to oxygen in the air rather than by adding bleach or bromate is preferable for a couple of reasons. First of all, unbleached and unbromated flour tastes better, with no bitter aftertaste that can be left behind by maturing agents. Secondly, potassium bromate is a possibly cancer-causing chemical that is probably harmless in small quantities but nevertheless must carry a warning label in some states and is outlawed in some European countries for its carcinogenic potential. So look for flour that is labeled "unbleached and unbromated" for the best, most healthful results.

Q **What exactly is organic flour and is it worth the extra money?**

A Certified organic flour is milled from pesticide-free grain grown in soil only fertilized by natural substances. Harvested grain is stored without fumigants or irradiation. All of this environmentally sensitive cultivation and handling costs money, but more and more people are willing to pay the price. Many bakers believe that organic flour produces better-tasting baked goods. Others buy organic flour because of the worry that pesticides and other synthetic agents may enter the wheat plants and be retained in flour, presenting a health risk over the course of many years. Still others support organic farming for its gentle impact on our environment.

Q I've seen other types of flour — rye, soy, buckwheat, spelt — at the supermarket and the health food store. How can I incorporate them into my baking? Are any of them a gluten-free alternative to wheat?

A Aside from being milled from different grains (or seeds or beans in the case of buckwheat and soy), and having distinctly different flavors, these flours are all much lower in gluten than wheat flour. Gluten is a substance formed when certain types of protein in wheat combine with water during mixing or kneading, resulting in long, flexible strands that stretch and then solidify as dough expands in the oven, giving bread its bubbly air pockets. Flours milled from soy and spelt have substantially less gluten than wheat flour, and buckwheat and rye have virtually no gluten at all. This is good news if you have a dietary sensitivity to gluten, but not so good if you want to bake a well-risen, crusty loaf of bread. Gluten is needed in much smaller quantities in baked goods such as cakes, cookies, biscuits, and scones.

If you are interested in incorporating specialty flours into your baking, start with recipes designed with these flours' properties in mind. When you know how they bake up on their own, you can experiment by substituting a low- or no-gluten flour for some or all of the wheat flour in your favorite recipes. Here is some information to help get you started.

Specialty Flours

* **Rye flour** is made from ground rye, of course, and is very low in gluten. Baked goods made with rye are tangy

and slightly sour. There is a long tradition in Germany, Austria, and throughout Eastern Europe of baking breads with 100% rye flour, but these heavy, dark, moist breads aren't the rye breads most Americans are familiar with. We are more likely to eat and bake breads made with no more than 50% rye flour.

* **Buckwheat flour** is ground from the seeds of a plant related to sorrel and rhubarb. It has a distinctive grayish color and earthy flavor and has no gluten at all. Traditionally used in Russia to make the crepelike blini, it can also be used in combination with wheat flour. Substitute no more than one-third to one-half buckwheat flour for wheat flour in recipes you'd like to modify, so they can gain some of buckwheat's distinctive flavor without losing structural integrity.

* **Soy flour** is made from ground dried soybeans and is very high in protein, but not the kind that creates gluten. To bake a higher-protein bread that's not dense and heavy, substitute no more than 20% to 30% soy flour for wheat flour or risk baking a loaf weighty enough to use as a doorstop.

* **Spelt** is an ancient grain first cultivated in the Middle East around 5000 BCE. Spelt is similar to wheat, with a comparable flavor, but with a much lower gluten content. Many people who have trouble digesting wheat can tolerate bread and other baked goods made with spelt.

Spelt Brownies

Spelt flour contributes to the tenderness of these low-fat brownies.

MAKES 16 BROWNIES

¾ cup unsweetened Dutch-process cocoa powder

1 tablespoon instant espresso powder

½ cup spelt flour

½ teaspoon baking powder

¼ teaspoon salt

1 cup packed light brown sugar

2 large eggs

3 tablespoons unsalted butter, melted and cooled

1 teaspoon vanilla extract

1½ cups (about 13) dried dates, pitted and finely chopped

1. Preheat the oven to 350°F (180°C). Line an 8-inch square baking pan with heavy-duty foil, making sure the foil is tucked into all the corners and there is at least 1 inch over-hanging the top of the pan on all sides. Coat with cooking spray.
2. Sift the cocoa powder, espresso powder, spelt flour, baking powder, and salt in a medium bowl.
3. Combine the sugar, eggs, butter, and vanilla in a food processor and pulse several times until almost smooth. Transfer to a large mixing bowl. Stir in the cocoa mixture until just incorporated. Stir in the dates.
4. Pour the batter into the prepared baking pan. Bake the brownies until they are just set in the center, 25 to 30 minutes. Transfer the pan to a wire rack to cool completely.
5. Grasping the foil on opposite sides of the pan, lift out the brownies and cut into 16 squares.

Raisin-Rye Muffins

Rye flour gives these muffins an intriguing aroma and a soft, cake-like texture.

MAKES 12 MUFFINS

1 cup rye flour

1 cup all-purpose unbleached flour

1¼ teaspoons baking powder

½ teaspoon baking soda

1 teaspoon ground cinnamon

½ teaspoon salt

⅓ cup packed light brown sugar

5 tablespoons vegetable oil

¼ cup dark (not blackstrap) molasses

2 large eggs

1 cup buttermilk or low-fat plain yogurt

1 cup raisins

¼ cup caraway seeds

1. Preheat the oven to 375°F (190°C). Line a 12-cup muffin tin with paper liners or coat it with cooking spray.
2. Combine the rye flour, all-purpose flour, baking powder, baking soda, cinnamon, salt, and brown sugar in a large mixing bowl. Add the oil, molasses, eggs, and buttermilk or yogurt, and stir until all ingredients are moistened. Stir in the raisins and caraway seeds.
3. Divide the batter evenly among the muffin cups. Bake the muffins until a toothpick inserted into the center comes out clean, about 20 minutes. Let the muffins cool in the pan for about 5 minutes, then invert them onto a wire rack, turning them right side up to cool completely.

Q How is confectioners' sugar different from white sugar?

A Confectioners' sugar is very finely ground white sugar, mixed with a little cornstarch to keep it from clumping. Most often it is used for sprinkling over baked cakes and cookies just before serving, or it is whisked together with water, milk, or another flavoring liquid to make a smooth and sugary icing. Occasionally, because it has added cornstarch, confectioners' sugar is used instead of granulated sugar in cookie recipes where a particularly tender result is desired. It has a similar effect to using cake flour instead of all-purpose flour, lowering the total protein content of the dough so that the baked cookies have the desired softness and fine crumb.

Q What is superfine sugar?

A Superfine sugar is finely ground granulated sugar that dissolves quickly in liquids. In England (and occasionally in American cookbooks) it is referred to as castor sugar. Although most frequently used in beverages like lemonade, superfine sugar has some baking uses. You will sometimes see it in meringue and frosting recipes. Occasionally it will be called for in cake and cookie recipes when a particularly fine-grained result is desired.

Q What is brown sugar? What is the difference between light and dark brown sugar?

A Molasses is a byproduct of the sugar refining process. Originally, brown sugar was partially refined sugar. The molasses left in the sugar colored it, gave it flavor, and kept it moist. These days, brown sugar is made by adding molasses to fully refined white sugar, so the exact percentage of molasses can be measured and consistency maintained. Light brown sugar contains about 3.5% molasses. Dark brown sugar has about 6.5% molasses.

Q I opened a box of brown sugar months ago and now it is rock hard. Should I throw it away?

A Like white sugar, brown sugar doesn't go bad, but it can become so dried out that it is impossible to use. Store brown sugar in an airtight container or resealable plastic bag to avoid finding a rocklike mass in your pantry. If your brown sugar does dry out, there are several ways to soften it. If you have some time, place it in an airtight container with a slice of apple overnight. The sugar will absorb the moisture from the apple and soften. For a quicker fix, place the sugar in a microwave-safe bowl and cover it with a damp paper towel and then with plastic wrap. Microwave on HIGH for 30 seconds to 1 minute, taking care not to melt the sugar, fluff with a fork, and use immediately.

Q Can I substitute brown sugar for white sugar in recipes and vice versa?

A You may substitute an equal amount of brown sugar for some or all of the white sugar in any baking recipe. Depending on the percentage of sugar in the recipe, you may be able to taste the molasses flavor in the end result. White sugar will work in any recipe calling for brown sugar, but the result may be a bit bland. If you find yourself without brown sugar but have white sugar and molasses on hand, you can improvise. For dark brown sugar, add a tablespoon of molasses for every cup of white sugar. For light brown sugar, add 1½ teaspoons of molasses for every cup of white sugar.

Q Is raw sugar, or turbinado sugar, similar to brown sugar?

A Turbinado sugar (sometimes called "sugar in the raw") has a golden color and a molasses flavor similar to light brown sugar, but brown sugar has more moisture than turbinado sugar, which is dry like white sugar. This is because of differences in the way the two are processed. To make brown sugar, cane juice is fully processed into white sugar, and then molasses is added back in to moisten, color, and flavor the final product. For white sugar, the cane juice is filtered, crystallized, and washed to remove molasses. Turbinado sugar is processed like white sugar, but some molasses is allowed to cling to the crystals, which are then spun dry in a centrifuge.

Demerara sugar, popular in England, is very similar in color and texture to turbinado sugar. Muscovado sugar, also used in England, has a much more pronounced molasses flavor. Any of these sugars can be substituted for white sugar or brown sugar, making allowances for their differences in flavor and understanding that turbinado sugar won't add moisture to baked goods the way brown sugar does.

Q I see light, dark, and occasionally blackstrap molasses on the supermarket shelf. Which molasses is the best kind for baking?

A Light and dark molasses can be used interchangeably, like light and dark brown sugar, depending on taste. Unless directed, avoid blackstrap molasses, which has a bitterness not welcome in most baked goods.

Q Is honey more healthful than sugar? Can I substitute it for sugar when I'm baking?

A Even though its production is much more picturesque than sugar's (compare a hive in a field of flowers to a belching smokestack adjacent to a field of burned sugar cane), honey, like table sugar, is a simple carbohydrate, with almost no additional nutritional value. Honey is a little bit sweeter than sugar, and obviously has more moisture, so if you'd like to substitute honey for sugar, you'll have to take this into account. Use ⅞ cup honey for every cup of sugar, reducing the liquid in the recipe by 3 tablespoons for every ⅞ cup of honey used. Conversely, to use sugar in place of honey, use 1¼ cups of sugar for every cup of honey, adding an extra ¼ cup of liquid for every 1¼ cups of sugar added.

Q What is the difference between light and dark corn syrup?

A Light corn syrup is colorless and is flavored with salt and vanilla. Dark corn syrup is flavored with molasses and caramel flavor and color — thus its brown color. They can be used interchangeably in recipes, but dark corn syrup will add a bit of molasses flavor.

Q In the past I've reserved maple syrup for pancakes and waffles. Is it possible to use maple syrup instead of sugar in baking?

A Maple syrup is less sweet than sugar, so if you want to substitute it for sugar you'll have to use more of it to sweeten your baked goods. To give your baked goods a mild maple flavor, substitute 1½ cups of maple syrup for every cup of white sugar, and reduce the liquid by 1½ cups.

Q Can I substitute salted butter for unsalted butter in a recipe if I use less salt than is called for?

A The salt content of butter varies from brand to brand and from batch to batch. Salted butter can contain as little as ¼ teaspoon of salt per stick or as much as ¾ teaspoon, and there is no way to know exactly how much salt your butter contains. For the most consistent results, it is better to use unsalted butter and add the precise amount of salt specified in a particular recipe.

Q What is the difference between European and regular butter? Can they be used interchangeably?

A European and European-style butters contain more butterfat (about 83%) than supermarket butter (about 80%) and less water. In baking, this translates into cakes and pastries with lighter and flakier textures and extra-rich flavor. Many professional pastry chefs will use nothing else. For the home baker, regular butter is perfectly fine, since most recipes for home cooks are developed using regular butter. But European butter can easily be substituted, in many cases with markedly superior results. In general, European butters are more expensive than supermarket brands (although many of them are now sold not only at gourmet and specialty food stores but also at supermarkets alongside their commercial counterparts), so it's most economical to reserve them for recipes in which butter takes center stage, such as puff pastry, pound cake, and shortbread. Be aware that imported butter is often sold in tubs or blocks, not tablespoon-marked sticks, so you'll have to weigh or measure it to use it for baking.

Q How do vegetable oil and vegetable shortening differ from butter? What about margarine? Why do some recipes call for butter and others call for oil or shortening?

A Vegetable oil, shortening, and butter all have places in baking, but shouldn't be substituted for one another without care. In baked goods where the fat's primary function is flavor, as in shortcrust doughs, American-style layer cakes, and many cookies, you'll do best with butter.

When creamed with sugar, butter and solid vegetable shortening become leaveners, giving cakes and cookies a higher rise than they would get with baking powder or baking soda alone. Vegetable oil won't do this. For the same reason, butter or solid shortening must be used in puff pastry and Danish and croissant dough. The solid fat, when incorporated into the dough, melts in the oven to create air pockets, which translate into extreme flakiness. Solid fat is also essential for flaky piecrust. Vegetable shortening incorporated into flour creates more air pockets as the crust bakes than butter, but won't give piecrust any flavor. Many bakers prefer a combination of vegetable shortening and butter for a flaky and tasty crust.

Vegetable oil lends moisture and tenderness to baked goods, but won't help them rise. It is used in chiffon cakes, where abundant whipped egg whites give the cake a light texture and the oil makes it moist but not greasy. Vegetable oil is also used in vegetable-based quick breads and cakes such as zucchini muffins and carrot cake, where the flavor of the butter would compete with the flavor of the other ingredients. Canola oil is a good choice for its neutral flavor.

Long believed to be a more healthful alternative to butter, margarine's health benefits have been largely discredited in recent years. And because "butter-flavored" margarine tastes nothing like butter, it is best to stick with real butter when a recipe calls for it.

Q **What is best for greasing a pan so my baked goods don't stick?**

A Butter, cooking spray, and vegetable shortening may each be used for greasing a baking pan. The choice will depend on personal preference, with consideration of what you are baking. Butter has a great flavor (cooking spray and shortening are flavorless) and promotes browning, but at high temperatures or for prolonged baking times can overbrown. Neither cooking spray nor vegetable shortening will burn. Cooking spray gives great coverage, so there's no danger of missing a nook or cranny of an elaborate Bundt pan. Sometimes a recipe will call for greasing and then flouring a pan, because a thin layer of flour provides extra insurance against sticking. In this case, vegetable shortening is a better choice than cooking spray, which sits on the surface of a pan in little beads and can absorb clumps of flour, which then stick to the surface of the baked cake in an unappetizing and unattractive way. Or use a cooking spray that already contains flour, such as Baker's Joy, which will work the same way but in one easy step.

Q Will it make a difference if I substitute skim milk for whole milk or nonfat sour cream for full-fat sour cream in a recipe?

A Dairy products containing fat contribute to a cake's or cookie's tenderness and moisture. In some cases, substituting a lower-fat version won't be disastrous. Low-fat (1% or 2%) milk contains enough fat to adequately moisten a cake batter, although skim milk, which contains no fat, won't work as well. In the case of sour cream or cream cheese, it is essential to use full-fat when specified, because baked goods rely on these ingredients for their fat content.

Q My family drinks skim milk exclusively, although I buy half-and-half for my coffee. To avoid buying whole milk just for a baking recipe, can I add a splash of half-and-half to my skim milk?

A It's all about the percentages, and you can certainly mix the two to approximate whole milk. Skim milk has no fat at all. Whole milk is about 3.5% butterfat. Half-and-half is about 10% butterfat. Heavy cream is about 35% butterfat. So you can substitute 3 or so tablespoons of half-and-half for 3 tablespoons of skim milk in every cup, or 1 tablespoon of heavy cream for 1 tablespoon of skim milk. If your mind boggles at the math then, yes, just add a splash of half-and-half or cream to your skim milk and you will likely have added sufficient fat to enrich your batter or dough.

Q What is buttermilk? Why is it so popular with bakers?

A Buttermilk is a cultured dairy product, like yogurt. Harmless bacteria are added to milk and then the milk is heated, in the process converting some of the milk's sugars into acids. The acids give buttermilk its characteristic zing, valued by bakers because it adds a pleasantly tangy flavor to everything from pancakes and biscuits to chocolate cakes. If you don't have buttermilk on hand or doubt that you will use a quart of it when the recipe you are following requires only a cup, you can sour regular milk by stirring 1 tablespoon of white vinegar or lemon juice into 1 cup of milk. Let it stand for 5 to 10 minutes before adding it to your recipe.

SEE ALSO: Buttermilk in pastry dough, page 98; buttermilk in scones, page 147.

Q Can soymilk be substituted for regular milk in baking?

A Many people prefer soymilk for health reasons: Richer in protein and higher in fiber than cow's milk, it also contains isoflavones, chemical compounds that have been linked to the prevention of cancer, heart disease, and other serious illnesses. People who are lactose intolerant or allergic to cow's milk can drink soymilk without ill effects. Although soymilk doesn't naturally contain calcium, many brands are enriched with enough calcium to make it milk's nutritional equal. Soymilk, which is made by soaking, grinding, cooking, and then squeezing dried soybeans, can be substituted for milk in most baking recipes, where its flavor, which differs significantly from milk, won't be noticeable. Soymilk isn't recommended in recipes such as pudding or custard, where milk is a primary ingredient.

Q What are some basic rules for handling eggs safely?

A A very small number of eggs may contain salmonella bacteria, which when consumed raw may cause serious illness, especially among the elderly, the very young, pregnant women, and anyone with a compromised immune system.

Egg Safety

* **Buy only uncracked eggs** that have been properly stored in a refrigerated case, because bacteria proliferate quickly if the shells are cracked, and especially at higher temperatures.

* **Don't wash your eggs.** During processing they have been sanitized and sprayed with a natural mineral oil to protect them from contamination. Washing them will leave them more vulnerable to bacteria.

* **Refrigerate eggs immediately**, in the coldest part of the refrigerator. Don't store your eggs on the door shelf, which can be warmer than the interior. Use them within 3 to 5 weeks. Refrigerate unused shelled eggs and use within 2 days.

* **Use warm, soapy water** to wash hands, utensils, and work surfaces that have come in contact with raw eggs.

* **Most important, eggs should never be consumed raw**, although the possibility of contracting salmonella this way is remote. Because bacteria are destroyed when eggs are cooked to a temperature of 160°F (71°C), salmonella is usually a nonissue for bakers as virtually all baked goods reach or exceed this temperature in the oven. After pies are topped with meringue, they should be baked for at least 15 minutes in a 350°F (180°C) oven to reach a safe temperature. Use an instant-read thermometer to check the temperature of custard fillings and sauces, which should also be cooked to a safe temperature of 160°F (71°C).

Q Why do recipes often specify "large" eggs?

A Successful baking requires precise measuring, so good recipes specify egg size to ensure consistent results. Eggs are packaged according to weight. If you know the weights of different size eggs, you can make substitutions. A medium egg weighs 1¾ ounces, a large egg weighs 2 ounces, an extra-large egg weighs 2¼ ounces, and a jumbo egg weighs 2½ ounces. So, for example, you can substitute 4 jumbo eggs for 5 large eggs.

Q What is meringue powder? Is it the same as powdered egg whites? How do I substitute either one for fresh egg whites?

A Both powdered egg whites and meringue powder are made with egg whites that have been pasteurized, and thus are safe to consume when uncooked. Bakers use the two products when they'd rather not use raw eggs — in cake frostings and cookie icings that will be consumed at an event where the crowds may include the elderly, children, or pregnant women, for whom salmonella bacteria can be particularly dangerous.

Powdered egg whites are just that — dehydrated egg whites pulverized into a powder. Whisk 2 teaspoons of powdered egg whites plus 2 tablespoons of warm water to make the equivalent of 1 fresh egg white. Powdered egg whites can be found in the baking aisle of the grocery store.

Meringue powder is a combination of dried egg whites, sugar, and gum. It will add more shine and stability to your frostings and icings than powdered egg whites will, but is more difficult to locate. You'll probably have to go to a baking supply store or purchase it online (see Resources). Otherwise, simply substitute powdered egg whites. There is no need to add more sugar if using plain egg whites.

Q What is the difference between baking soda and baking powder?

A Baking soda is a chemical leavener. When it comes in contact with acids, the reaction produces carbon dioxide, a bubbly gas that causes baked goods to rise. Baking soda works with an acidic ingredient such as lemon juice, sour cream, or buttermilk to prompt this reaction, but many baked goods don't contain acidic ingredients. To get a similar rise in these cases, bakers use baking powder, which is baking soda combined with a little acid and some cornstarch to keep the two ingredients dry and non-reactive until moistened.

Q Why do some recipes call for baking powder *and* baking soda?

A Using both baking powder and baking soda is extra insurance that your baked goods will rise. Baking powder is a very reliable leavener, containing a perfectly balanced mixture of bicarbonate of soda and acid. The bubbles it produces won't dissipate as quickly as the bubbles produced by baking soda. So sometimes, even if a recipe contains an acidic ingredient like buttermilk, it will call for baking powder and a little bit of baking soda. The baking soda neutralizes the acids in the batter or dough, allowing the baking powder to do the work of leavening.

MAKING YOUR OWN BAKING POWDER

Some bakers complain of a slight off-flavor that commercial baking powder supposedly gives to baked goods, although I have not experienced this in my own baking. Perhaps it is the sodium aluminum sulphate, one of the acids added to baking soda to create baking powder, that imparts a hint of metal. If this is a problem for you, or if you find yourself out of baking powder at an inconvenient moment, you can make your own baking powder by combining ¼ teaspoon baking soda, 1 teaspoon cornstarch, and ½ teaspoon cream of tartar (an acid) for every teaspoon of baking powder called for. Don't try to mix large quantities to keep in the pantry. Remember that because homemade baking powder is not "double-acting," it will begin to release its carbon dioxide when it comes in contact with liquid, so if you are mixing a dough or batter with it, get your cookies or cake in the oven as soon as you are through with mixing.

Q Can table salt, kosher salt, and sea salt be used interchangeably?

A Table salt dissolves easily in baked goods and is the choice of most bakers. Kosher salt may be substituted, but is only about half as salty. Be sure to add twice as much for the same effect: If a recipe calls for ¼ teaspoon of table salt, add ½ teaspoon of kosher salt. Sea salt is quite expensive (especially for French fleur de sel or Malden sea salt from Great Britain; see Resources) and its flavor is indistinguishable from table salt in baked goods. Save sea salt for sprinkling onto finished dishes where its pure flavor and crunchy texture can be appreciated.

kosher salt

table salt

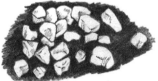
sea salt

Bittersweet Chocolate Cookies with Sea Salt

Here's a baking recipe in which sea salt makes sense, used as a finishing touch sprinkled on top of the balls of cookie dough. Fleur de sel or any other good quality sea salt will work, but Malden salt from England is especially good, because the large flakes provide some crunch to the soft cookies as well as a salty contrast to the sweetness and trufflelike consistency of the cookies.

MAKES 24 COOKIES

4 ounces unsweetened chocolate, finely chopped

2½ cups bittersweet chocolate chips

½ cup (1 stick) unsalted butter, cut into 8 pieces

½ cup unbleached all-purpose flour

½ teaspoon baking powder

2 teaspoons sea salt

4 large eggs

1½ cups packed light brown sugar

2 teaspoons vanilla extract

1. Preheat the oven to 350°F (180°C). Line baking sheets with parchment paper.
2. Combine the unsweetened chocolate, 1½ cups of the chocolate chips, and the butter in a microwave-safe bowl and heat on HIGH until just melted, 30 to 90 seconds, depending on the power of your oven. Whisk until smooth. Set aside to cool slightly.

3. Combine the flour, baking powder, and ½ teaspoon of the sea salt in a small bowl.
4. Combine the eggs and brown sugar in a large mixing bowl. Using an electric mixer set on high speed, beat until the batter falls in thick ribbons when lifted from the bowl with the beaters, about 5 minutes. Stir in the melted chocolate mixture and the vanilla on low speed. Stir in the flour mixture until just combined. Stir in the remaining 1 cup chocolate chips.
5. Transfer the bowl to the refrigerator for 15 minutes (or up to 6 hours) to chill the dough.
6. Drop the batter onto prepared baking sheets by heaping tablespoonfuls, about 3 inches apart. Sprinkle a generous pinch of sea salt on top of each cookie. Bake until the tops are cracked and shiny, 10 to 12 minutes. Carefully slide the parchment sheet with the cookies to a wire rack to cool completely. Store in an airtight container for up to 3 days.

Q What kinds of chocolate should I have on hand?

A Different types of chocolate are used to get various results in baked goods.

Chocolate Varieties

* **Unsweetened chocolate**, often called baking chocolate, contains cocoa solids and cocoa butter but no sugar. It has a chalky rather than smooth texture and a bitter flavor, but when baked into brownies, cakes, and cookies, it imparts a deep chocolate flavor and fudgy texture. It is commonly sold in boxes of eight 1-ounce squares for easy measuring, although large blocks may be purchased at gourmet stores and online from baking supply purveyors, in which case you will have to chop and weigh it yourself.

* **Bittersweet (or dark) chocolate and semisweet chocolate** are made by combining unsweetened chocolate with sugar and refining it further. The difference between the two is in the percentage of sugar. Bittersweet chocolate averages about 46% sugar while semisweet is about 57% sugar. An equivalent amount of one of these will impart less chocolate flavor to a cake than unsweetened chocolate would. Sweeter and less bitter than unsweetened chocolate, bittersweet and semisweet chocolate are used in recipes such as flourless chocolate cake that don't contain a lot of sugar and that benefit from this type of chocolate's complex flavors.

* In addition to sugar, milk solids and vanilla are added to **milk chocolate**, giving it a very mild chocolate flavor. It isn't often used in baking, because this flavor becomes diluted to the point of muteness when mixed with other ingredients. Reserve milk chocolate for chocolate chunk cookies and sweet chocolate frostings.

* **White chocolate** is not officially chocolate because it contains no chocolate solids. It gets its richness and muted chocolate flavor from cocoa butter. Delicate and subtle, it won't have much impact when added to baked goods. It's best reserved for mousselike cake fillings.

* **Chocolate chips** have less cocoa butter than blocks or bars of eating chocolate, so they won't completely melt when baked into cakes and cookies. Of course, they can be melted in a microwave or on top of the stove, and come in handy when you need just a few ounces of chocolate to drizzle over a cake or cookies as a garnish. For richer ganache frostings and fillings, it's best to stick with bittersweet or semisweet chocolate.

* **Cocoa powder** (see page 37 for more information) is made by removing the cocoa butter from processed and ground cocoa beans and grinding what is left into a fine powder. This powder, when added to doughs and batters, adds intense chocolate flavor. Simple cakes and cookies made with cocoa powder, enriched with butter and sweetened with sugar, can be remarkably fudgy and delicious.

Q I understand that specific types of chocolate are better in certain recipes than others. But is there a way to substitute, say, semisweet for unsweetened?

A It's best to use the type of chocolate specified in a recipe, but, in a pinch, a careful substitution will work. Use the following conversions:

CHOCOLATE SUBSTITUTIONS

1 ounce bittersweet chocolate =	½ ounce unsweetened chocolate + 1 tablespoon sugar
1 ounce semisweet chocolate =	½ ounce unsweetened chocolate + 1½ tablespoons sugar
6 ounces bittersweet chocolate =	½ cup plus 1 tablespoon unsweetened natural cocoa powder + ½ cup sugar + 3 tablespoons unsalted butter
1 ounce unsweetened chocolate =	3 tablespoons unsweetened natural cocoa powder + 1 tablespoon unsalted butter
3 tablespoons unsweetened natural cocoa powder =	1 tablespoon unsweetened chocolate; reduce fat in recipe by 1 tablespoon
3 tablespoons Dutch-process cocoa powder =	3 tablespoons unsweetened natural cocoa powder + ⅛ teaspoon baking soda
3 tablespoons Dutch-process cocoa powder =	1 ounce unsweetened chocolate + ⅛ teaspoon baking soda; reduce fat in recipe by 1 tablespoon

Q What is the difference between Dutch-process and regular cocoa powder?

A Dutch-process (or alkalized) cocoa powder has been processed with an alkali to reduce acidity, making it milder tasting and giving it a darker color. Non-alkalized cocoa powder has a slightly more bitter taste, but is also more intensely chocolaty. The difference between the two is not only in taste and color, however. Because of their different pH levels, alkalized and non-alkalized cocoas interact differently in recipes calling for baking powder or baking soda. Recipes calling for Dutch-process cocoa powder use baking powder, which is essentially baking soda with added acid, as a leavener. Baked goods containing non-alkalized cocoa don't need the extra acid in baking powder, and will rise well with only baking soda.

Q How is an extract made? Is pure vanilla extract better than other vanilla extracts?

A An extract is a concentrated flavoring that can be made from either natural or artificial ingredients. Extracts, including almond, coffee, maple, lemon, mint, and most commonly, vanilla, give depth and balance to baked goods. Vanilla extract is made by macerating chopped vanilla beans in a solution of alcohol and water until the liquid takes on the flavor of the beans. Artificial vanilla, which has a similar flavor profile, is made from wood pulp. Most bakers and pastry chefs agree that pure vanilla extract gives baked goods a more intense flavor and aroma than the artificial variety.

CHAPTER 2

Equipment

There are some pieces of equipment that are absolutely essential if you want to bake. You can't make cookies without a baking sheet, or a cake without a cake pan. Good luck to you if you don't own a set of measuring cups and spoons! And then there are items that you can certainly live without, but make baking a pleasure and a joy. I'm thinking of my lovely yellow KitchenAid stand mixer and my fancy Silpat baking mat, imported from France. The questions and answers in this chapter will help you assess the equipment you already own, make decisions about purchasing tools that you may still need, and make sure you're perfectly equipped to bake whatever your heart desires.

BAKING PANS: A BAKER'S DOZEN

Here are 13 pans, listed loosely in order of usefulness. The items at the top may see daily or weekly use. Toward the bottom you'll find pans that are nice to have, if only for the couple of times a year you make madeleines or a soufflé.

Baking sheets. Equip your kitchen with several rimmed and rimless baking sheets to accomplish a multitude of baking tasks, from baking cookies, jelly rolls, and focaccia to toasting nuts and coconut in the oven.

Square and rectangular baking pans. An 8-inch square pan and a 9- by 13-inch pan will allow you to make small and large batches of brownies and bar cookies as well as snacking cakes and sheet cakes.

Layer cake pans. 9-inch round cake pans are standard, but sometimes a recipe will call for 8-inch pans. You'll need 2 or sometimes 3 pans to make one recipe. Buy them in matched sets, so your layers will match exactly. And choose pans with sides at least 2 inches high, to accommodate batters from a multitude of recipes.

Muffin tin. Necessary for cupcakes as well as muffins, a 12-cup tin is the most useful. If you are only making six cupcakes or muffins, place batter in every other cup of a 12-cup tin and fill the empty cups with water to prevent buckling.

Loaf pan. For quick breads and sandwich loaves. A 9-inch loaf pan is most common, but an 8-inch one is also handy. They can also be used to assemble ice cream and frozen mousse terrines. Mini-loaf pans are less essential, but fun to have if you want to make small loaves for gift-giving or a bread basket.

Bundt pan. A tube pan with fluted sides is used to make coffee cakes and other casual cakes. Sometimes these cakes have sticky streusel toppings and fillings, making them difficult to unmold. That is why most Bundt pans now on the market have a nonstick surface, for a clean release. The standard size is 12 cups.

Pie plate. Glass produces a nicely browned crust and is nonreactive (unlike metal) so it won't affect the flavor of acidic fruit fillings over time.

Tart pan with removable bottom. A 9-inch pan will make a tart that serves six; an 11-inch pan will serve ten.

Springform pan. Cakes that can't be removed from a regular pan, such as cheesecake or flourless chocolate cake, must be baked in a springform pan. A spring-loaded hinge releases the sides of the pan from the bottom, and the cake is left standing on the bottom of the pan, ready to serve. Nine inches is standard for most recipes, but springform pans come in a variety of sizes, including 3 and 4 inches for individual cakes.

Tube pan. Necessary for making an angel food cake. Look for one with feet that elevate the pan as the cake cools, allowing for air to circulate under the cake once you've overturned it.

Soufflé dish. Large (1½ to 2 quart) dishes will hold hot soufflés as well as a variety of frozen mousses and semifreddo desserts. Small ceramic ramekins (4-ounce, 6-ounce, and 8-ounce sizes) are necessary for making pot de crème, crème caramel, crème brûlée, and individual molten chocolate cakes and bread puddings.

Madeleine molds. You can bake madeleine batter in mini-muffin tins, but these traditional shell-shaped molds give these simple sponge-type cookies the optimum crust-to-cake ratio.

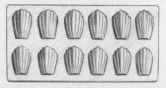

Flan and cake rings. Although professional bakers use cake rings (basically cake pans without bottoms) to bake cakes directly on parchment-lined baking sheets, home bakers will find them most useful for assembling neatly layered cakes. A cake ring will give shape to a cake layered with mousse, pastry cream, and ice cream, containing the fillings until they can set up in the refrigerator or freezer.

Q What should I look for when shopping for baking sheets?

A The best baking sheets, rimless or not, are made of heavy-duty aluminum, which conducts heat beautifully so that the bottoms of your cookies brown but don't burn, and won't warp over time the way flimsier pans will. It's better to use parchment paper or a Silpat to render the surface of the sheet nonstick than to buy a baking sheet with a dark nonstick surface, because small items like cookies tend to overbrown on darker sheets. For the same reason, avoid French steel baking sheets if you are using them primarily for cookies. Of course, if you are using your baking sheets specifically for intense browning, such as roasting vegetables, then nonstick and French steel may be just right for you.

Q Do I need both rimmed and rimless baking sheets?

A If your kitchen activities are limited to baking cookies, then you will need only rimless sheets, which will allow you to slide cookies right from the sheet onto a wire rack for cooling, minimizing the chance that the hot, soft cookies will break during transfer. A rimless sheet also comes in handy for getting pizza or bread into the oven if you don't own a pizza peel. Line the baking sheet with a piece of parchment paper, shape your pizza dough or bread dough on top of the parchment, and then slide the parchment from the sheet to a preheated baking stone as you would with a pizza peel.

Rimmed baking sheets, also called jelly-roll pans, are preferable to rimless ones for the many other times when it is important to keep your batter or whatever else you are placing on your sheet within the confines of the pan. This includes a jelly roll, of course, which is made by first spreading cake batter evenly across the bottom of the pan, before baking it, cooling it, spreading it with filling, and then rolling it up. Rimmed pans are also great for containing a mess, for example, when drizzling a cake with a glaze. Place your cake on top of a wire rack inside the pan. Your glaze will drip down the sides of the cake and onto the pan, not the counter.

Q **What effect will insulated baking sheets have on the way my cookies bake?**

A Cookies baked on insulated baking sheets, which have a cushion of air between two sheets of metal, are less likely to burn on the bottom. By the same token, they may not be as crisp and caramelized on their tops as you might like. Choosing insulation is a matter of what effect you are going for and, to some degree, personal preference. Cookies often take a minute or two longer to bake through on an insulated baking sheet, so if you are using one in a recipe that doesn't specifically call for it, you may have to increase the baking time.

If you have two rimmed baking sheets, you can improvise an insulated sheet by nesting them one on top of the other. The thin pocket of air between the two sheets will result in the same type of baking.

Q Will nonstick cake pans burn my cakes?

A Cakes will darken when baked in nonstick pans, though not as dramatically as cookies will when baked on nonstick baking sheets. It's really a matter of personal preference. If you like the caramelized flavor of a deep golden crust and appreciate a sturdier surface for applying frosting, then a nonstick pan may be right for you. If you don't like such a marked difference in color between your cake and your crust, then go with a light-colored pan. The best are made of aluminum.

Q Do nonstick pans need to be greased?

A Manufacturers will tell you no, but to be safe you should always grease and flour even a nonstick cake pan to guarantee a clean release. If a recipe calls for lining a pan with parchment paper, do this also. There are few things more distressing than the sight of half of your cake stuck to the bottom of your pan after you have unsuccessfully attempted to flip it onto a wire rack or cardboard cake circle.

Q What about glass and ceramic baking dishes? How do they rate on browning (or burning) baked goods?

A Glass and ceramic are on opposite ends of the spectrum. Clear glass, like dark metal, absorbs heat rather than reflecting it, resulting in darker crusts. A glass pie plate is a good choice for a juicy fruit pie, because it promotes browning and crisping which will prevent the bottom of the pie from becoming damp and soggy. Glass is not a good choice for a crustless dessert like a crumble or crisp, because there is a risk that the fruit on the bottom would scorch and burn. In this case, ceramic, which is slower to absorb heat, is preferable, as it cooks the fruit more gently.

Nor is glass a good choice for quick breads, pound cakes, and bar cookies, because of the potential for burning. There are a lot of pretty ceramic and stoneware loaf pans and baking dishes out there that will do this job if you prefer them to metal. But be aware that ceramic and stoneware generally produce baked goods that are lighter in color than those baked in aluminum and especially nonstick pans.

Q I'm intrigued by the flexible nonstick silicone bakeware I see everywhere. How does it compare to conventional metal and glass?

A Manufacturers claim that bakeware made of silicone (the same flexible nonstick material used in Silpats) is easier to clean and offers a better nonstick surface than any other material. But in my experience there are some distinct disadvantages to using it in baking. First of all, the pans, which now come in every shape imaginable, from madeleine molds to muffin tins to kugelhopf pans, are flexible to the point of floppiness. You will need to place your pan on top of a baking sheet and then carry the baking sheet to the oven to avoid spills, but be aware that baking anything on top of a baking sheet will lengthen baking time.

Dense, heavy batters such as fruitcake or gingerbread can cause the sides of a silicone baking dish to bulge, resulting in misshapen baked goods. It's better to bake these batters in rigid pans that will give the finished cakes a good shape.

Silicone won't produce a caramelized crust that's so desirable on cakes and muffins. On the plus side, it's good for items that require gentle heat in a cooler oven, such as crème brûlée. Also heed manufacturers' instructions not to use these pans in an oven hotter than 425°F (220°C), at which point the silicone will begin to smoke and produce a foul odor.

Q When a recipe specifies a pan size (9-inch pie plate, 8- by 4-inch loaf pan) how are the pans measured? My loaf pan, for example, is narrower on the bottom than the top.

A All pans are measured across the top, not the bottom. In the case of fluted tart, Bundt, or brioche pans, measure from the outermost part of the top edge of one side to the outermost part of the top edge of the other side.

BAKING PAN VOLUME GUIDE

Consult the following list for pan substitutions and approximate
metric equivalents. Make sure the pan you want to use is of
the same volume as the pan specified in a recipe.

Dimensions	Volume
6" × 2" round	4 cups
8" × 1½" round	4 cups
8" × 4" × 2½" loaf	4 cups
8" × 2" round	6 cups
9" × 1½" round	6 cups
7½" × 3" Bundt pan	6 cups
8" × 8" × 1½" square	6 cups
11" × 7" × 2" rectangle	6 cups
8½" × 4½" × 2" loaf	6 cups
9" × 2" round	8 cups
8" × 8" × 2" square	8 cups
9" × 9" × 1" square	8 cups
9" × 5" × 3" loaf	8 cups
8" × 2½" heart-shaped	8 cups
9" × 3" Bundt pan	9 cups
8" × 3" tube pan	9 cups
9" × 2½" springform	10 cups
9" × 9" × 2" square	10 cups
10½" × 15½" × 1" jelly-roll	10 cups
10" × 2" round	11 cups
10" × 3½" Bundt pan	12 cups
9" × 3" tube pan	12 cups
9" × 3" springform	12 cups
10" × 2½" springform	12 cups
12½" × 17½" × 1" jelly-roll	12 cups
13" × 9" × 2" rectangle	14 cups

Q My cake recipe calls for two 8-inch round baking pans but I have only two 9-inch round pans. Is it a mistake to bake the layers in bigger pans?

A If you bake what are supposed to be 8-inch-round sponge cake layers in 9-inch pans, your layers will of course be thinner (which could be a problem if the recipe later calls for you to split them in two), and will bake more quickly than if they had been baked in smaller pans. Perhaps more important, your cake's texture and rise may be affected, as changing pan size may alter these qualities. When baking a delicate cake, use the size of pan specified in the recipe for the best outcome.

Less delicate baked goods — butter and pound cakes, bar cookies, brownies, and quick breads — won't suffer from the change as much. When substituting pans, do try to use one of equivalent volume (see page 47). You won't be able to adequately fill a much larger pan, and a much smaller pan may overflow with excess dough or batter. You will also need to adjust the baking time, decreasing it if you are using a shallower pan and increasing it if you are using a deeper one.

Q How many mini muffins will a recipe for regular size muffins yield?

A Muffin tins come in a variety of sizes these days. Each cavity in a mini-muffin tin holds about 1½ tablespoons of batter. Each cavity in a standard-size muffin tin holds about

½ cup. There are also jumbo muffin tins, whose cavities hold 1 cup, and muffin-top tins with shallow craters that will hold ½ cup of batter. So a recipe for standard-size muffins with a yield of 12 will get you the same number of muffin tops, six jumbo muffins, or close to two dozen mini muffins. Remember to adjust baking times. Jumbo muffins will need an extra 10 to 12 minutes in the oven; mini muffins will bake 10 minutes faster; and muffin tops will be done 8 to 10 minutes sooner than standard-size muffins.

Q What can I make if I own only a hand-held mixer? Which baking tasks require a stand mixer?

A A hand-held mixer will whip egg whites or heavy cream and mix muffin and cake batters. The heavy-duty (and more expensive) hand-held models are up to mixing stiff cookie doughs. These models have thin wire beaters rather than old-fashioned beaters with metal shafts down the center, which tend to get clogged with dough. A hand-held mixer costs a fraction of the price of a stand mixer, so for bakers on a budget, forgoing a stand mixer can make good sense.

That said, devoted home bakers who invest in a good-quality stand mixer such as a KitchenAid rarely regret the decision over the course of the many years they enjoy their purchase. A stand mixer will whip egg whites or cream in half the time of a hand-held mixer. It will blend ingredients with almost no effort on the part of the baker, its paddle clearing the sides and bottom of the bowl without the need to stop the machine and scrape. Many stand mixers come with dough hooks for kneading stiff bread doughs, and are built with powerful motors that can run for upwards of 20 minutes without overheating or burning out.

Q If I'm going to make the investment in a stand mixer, should I go for the largest one on the market?

A KitchenAid mixers, which set the standard for all other stand mixers, come in several sizes, the smallest of which, the Artisan, has a 5-quart bowl and a power output of 325 watts, making it large and powerful enough to mix bread dough for two loaves or cake batter for 24 cupcakes. Most home bakers won't need anything more. If you are thinking of starting a cupcake business out of your kitchen, you might take a look at the KitchenAid 6-quart, 575-watt Professional-series mixer that can handle recipes with up to 12 cups of flour. Whichever model you choose, make sure you like the color, because you will be living with it for a long time. My friend Roland Mesnier, who was the pastry chef at the White House for 25 years and used his machine for many hours a day during that time, ordered a backup mixer about 10 years into his tenure, thinking he'd be in trouble if the old one broke down. When he retired, both the old mixer and the new one were still going strong.

You can save yourself some money by buying the smallest (which is by no means cheap) rather than the largest KitchenAid mixer. But I do recommend investing in an extra mixing bowl, which comes in handy when you need your mixer twice for one recipe (egg whites to be folded into cake batter, for example). This way you won't have to stop to wash and dry your bowl in the middle of your baking.

Q **Can I use a food processor instead of a mixer to mix my doughs and batters?**

A Many bread and pastry doughs can be mixed in a food processor instead of a mixer, in seconds rather than minutes. But the food processor's great power and speed can ruin dough as quickly as it can mix it if precautions aren't taken. Here are some tips for adapting recipes.

Food Processor Mixing Tips

* **Bread recipes** often call for adding warm water or another liquid to the dry ingredients, but when using a food processor you might consider using a cooler liquid, because the powerful motor will heat the dough as it kneads it. Fully kneaded dough should be at a temperature between 77 and 82°F (25–28°C). Use an instant-read thermometer the first few times you make bread dough in the food processor to be sure you are in this range.

* **Hand-kneaded bread**, or bread kneaded in a mixer with a dough hook attachment, usually requires minutes of kneading time, but a food processor will produce a smooth and elastic dough in a minute or less. Take care not to overknead your dough in the food processor,

which will destroy its elasticity and prevent it from rising to its full potential in the oven. Run the machine just until the dough forms into a ball. If you feel the dough requires more kneading, hand-knead it on the countertop for a minute or two to finish it off.

* **The food processor motor** generates heat that can be an issue when making pie and pastry doughs. It is essential to begin with very cold butter or vegetable shortening (consider cutting it into bits and freezing it for 15 to 30 minutes before beginning) and to use ice water. The idea is to have tiny pieces of solid fat well-distributed throughout the dough, so as it bakes in the oven the fat will melt, creating air pockets that will give the crust a flaky texture. You don't want the heat of the food processor to liquefy the fat before it is incorporated into the flour and heated in the oven.

* **Add the ice water** carefully. There is a danger to adding it to the processor with the motor running. The water tends to clump together with just a portion of the flour and fat mixture, accumulating in a wet and sticky mass around the blade and leaving much of the flour at the bottom of the bowl. It's better to open the bowl and evenly sprinkle the ice water over the fat and flour mixture before processing. Pulse a few times, just until the dough comes together instead of crumbling when pinched between your fingers. It should feel cool to the touch. Remove the dough from the bowl and press it into a disc. Work quickly, before the heat of your hands

can melt any of the fat. Wrap the disc in plastic and refrigerate it until it is well chilled and the gluten that has formed during mixing has had time to relax, making the dough easy to roll into a thin sheet.

Q Which is better — a rolling pin with or without handles?

A Either type of rolling pin will do the job. It's really a matter of personal preference. Chances are if you learned to roll pie dough in your mother's kitchen, you will feel comfortable with an American rolling pin, a hardwood cylinder with handles on either end and a steel shaft down the center that gives it a smooth rolling action. If you learned about dough at cooking school or a bakery, you probably will prefer the French-style pin, which is simply a hardwood cylinder with no handles and no shaft. Many professional bakers choose a French-style pin because it lets them feel the thickness of the dough as they roll. If you have small hands, you might consider a tapered rolling pin, a variation on the French-style pin but with slimmer ends that make it easy to grasp.

American rolling pin

French-style pin

tapered rolling pin

Food Processor Pizza Dough

Good pizza dough is wet and sticky. It's difficult to knead by hand, and can take a toll on your electric mixer's motor. But it comes together beautifully in the food processor.

MAKES TWO 14-INCH PIZZA CRUSTS

1 envelope (2½ teaspoons) active dry yeast

1¾ cups tepid water

4 cups unbleached all-purpose flour

1½ teaspoons salt

2 tablespoons olive oil

1. Stir to dissolve the yeast in the water.
2. Combine the flour and salt in the food processor and pulse once or twice to combine.
3. With the motor running, pour the water, yeast mixture, and the olive oil into the feed tube and process until the dough forms a smooth ball, 30 seconds to 1 minute.
4. Coat the inside of a large mixing bowl with olive oil. Shape the dough into a rough ball, cover the bowl with plastic wrap, and let stand in a warm, draft-free spot until it has doubled in size, 1 hour to 1 hour 30 minutes.
5. Transfer the dough onto a work surface, cut in half with a bench scraper, lightly dust with flour, drape each piece with plastic wrap, and let it rest for 20 minutes.
6. Use the dough as directed in any pizza recipe, or place each piece in an airtight container and freeze for up to 2 months. Defrost in the refrigerator overnight before using.

Food Processor Pie Dough

Keep your ingredients (including your flour!) as cold as possible, to ensure that the butter and shortening don't melt as they are processed.

MAKES 1 DOUBLE OR LATTICE-TOP PIECRUST

2½ cups unbleached all-purpose flour, chilled
½ teaspoon salt
½ cup vegetable shortening, chilled
½ cup (1 stick) unsalted butter, cut into 1/4-inch pieces and chilled
6 tablespoons ice water, plus more if necessary

1. Combine the flour and salt in the food processor and pulse several times to blend.
2. Add the shortening and pulse 8 to 10 times until the mixture resembles coarse meal. Add the butter and pulse another 8 to 10 times until the mixture again resembles coarse meal.
3. Sprinkle the water over the flour mixture. Pulse 5 to 7 times, until the dough just begins to come together in large clumps. If it doesn't come together, sprinkle another table-spoon of water over the mixture and pulse again. Remove the lid of the food processor and press some dough between your fingers. If it is still very crumbly, process once or twice more.
4. If it holds its shape, press it into two 5-inch discs. Wrap it in plastic and refrigerate for at least 2 hours and up to 2 days before using.

Q Are there any other electronic items that are essential for baking?

A A microwave oven is nice to have for melting chocolate and butter, but you can also do this on the stovetop. A blender is useful for puréeing fruit or grinding graham crackers, but a food processor will do almost everything a blender can. I would say that the only other electronic item that's absolutely essential for serious baking is an electronic scale.

Professional bakers have always preferred weighing ingredients to measuring them by volume, to ensure uniform results batch after batch. Measuring by volume is necessarily imprecise. Ingredients like flour may settle. Small differences between sets of measuring cups may mean that your 1-cup measure holds slightly more flour than someone else's measure. More and more frequently, cookbook authors and food writers are including weight along with volume measurements in ingredient lists, so that home cooks can get the same reliable results as professionals.

Mechanical scales, while less expensive, are less precise and more difficult to read than electronic scales. Look for an electronic scale that will hold at least 5 pounds, with a large digital display and an automatic shut-off to save batteries. Scales with a flat surface will allow you to place your own mixing bowl on top, rather than being limited to a bowl that comes with the scale. A scale with a switch that will allow you to weigh ingredients in both ounces and grams is nice for bread bakers, because so many bread recipes supply metric measurements in addition to English measurements for the sake of precision.

Q What are dry and liquid measures and how should I use them?

A Dry and liquid measures of less than a pint both hold the same quantities of ingredients by volume (a 1-cup dry measure will hold 1 cup of flour, as will a 1-cup liquid measure) but they are designed differently so as to measure either liquid or dry ingredients as precisely as possible. At the 1-pint point, a dry measure is larger than a liquid measure by a little over 16% (a liquid pint 473 milliliters and a dry pint is 551 milliliters).

Dry measuring cups are designed to be filled using the "dip and sweep" method. To accurately measure 1 cup of flour, dip a 1-cup dry measure into your flour canister and then use a knife to sweep any flour above the rim back into the canister. For an accurate measure, your cup should be filled to the brim.

Liquid measuring cups are made of clear glass or plastic, with pour spouts to neatly transfer measured liquids from cup to mixing bowl. Incremental measures are printed on the sides of the cup. To use one of these cups, pour your liquid into it and then look at the lines at eye level to be sure that you have filled it just to the right line.

By these descriptions, you can understand how difficult it would be to accurately measure a cup of flour in a 1-cup liquid measure (how would you smooth out the top surface evenly enough to know that you had exactly 1 cup?) or to measure 1 cup of milk in a dry measure (even if you dared to fill the measure to the brim, would you be able to transfer it to your bowl without spilling?). Success in baking depends first of all on accurate measurements, so it is very important to have these two sets of measuring cups and to use them with care.

Q How important is parchment paper for baking?

A I personally could not bake without parchment, which is paper that has been impregnated with silicone to make it nonstick. Rolls of parchment are inexpensive and easy to find in any supermarket (look on the shelf next to the aluminum foil). Precut sheets can also be purchased in bulk from baking supply stores or online (see Resources). If you bake a lot, I highly recommend buying it this way so you don't run out. Bleached parchment is better than unbleached, because it is more flexible and won't become brittle at high temperatures and shatter when it comes out of the oven.

Primarily, parchment paper is used to line baking sheets and cake pans to prevent baked goods from sticking and to hasten cleanup. But there are dozens of other reasons to keep it handy in the kitchen.

Parchment Paper Uses

* **To line a pizza peel** before shaping bread or pizza; then you can just slide the dough, still on the parchment, right onto your preheated baking stone without fear that it will stick to the peel.

* **To cut a stencil** for sifting confectioners' sugar or cocoa powder over the top of cakes, cupcakes, and cookies.

* **To trace fancy piping patterns** for cake decorations.

* **To fold and roll into tiny cornets** for piping chocolate or icing onto cakes and cookies.

* **To roll icebox cookie dough into logs**; keep the dough wrapped in the parchment in the refrigerator for up to 1 day until ready to use and it will unwrap beautifully without sticking.

* **To roll out sticky pie and pastry dough,** gingerbread, and anything else that might stick to your countertop; place the dough between two sheets and then roll without fear.

* **To wrap around soufflé dishes** and ramekins to create nonstick collars that will support your soufflés as they rise.

Q Can I substitute wax paper or nonstick aluminum foil for parchment in a pinch?

A Most recipes will instruct you to prepare your pans before you begin to mix your batter or dough, so chances are you will realize you are out of parchment before you are too far along with your cake or cookies. But if you realize your recipe calls for parchment too late, you can judiciously substitute wax paper or nonstick foil. Wax paper is fine for lining cake pans, because it will be covered by cake batter. But don't use it to line baking sheets, because when it is exposed to oven temperatures above 300°F (150°C) it will begin to smoke and burn. If you are making extremely delicate and sticky cookies such as tuiles, which need to bake on a very slippery surface, you can use nonstick foil, which has been treated with a food-safe nonstick coating. (Please note that while some baked goods can be peeled off of regular aluminum foil, cookies made with super-adhesive ingredients like jam or caramel will stick to regular foil like superglue.) You can also use a Silpat or other silicone baking mat.

Q I see that a Silpat is quite expensive. How exactly would I use one? Is it worth the investment?

A Silpat is the brand name of a French baking mat that professional bakers and many home cooks use instead of grease or parchment paper to line baking sheets, guaranteeing a nonstick surface. Although pricey, it is reusable up to 3,000 times, making it cheaper in the long run than parchment paper. Aside from lining baking sheets, the Silpat also comes in handy during other baking and pastry tasks. You can use it as a nonstick work surface for rolling out dough, as you would a sheet of parchment (although using a sharp knife or pastry cutter to trim dough still sitting on the mat is a bad idea, as sharp edges will damage the nonstick surface). You can pour hot caramel or pipe melted chocolate directly onto the mat, and easily remove either when cooled.

Even if you invest in a Silpat, however, there will still be times when you'll need parchment. A Silpat can't be cut to fit into a cake pan. Nor can it be used to make a cornet or a stencil. So the answer is, a Silpat is well worth the price if you bake often, but it won't obviate the need for parchment.

Q What is a cardboard cake circle?

A Professional bakers use cardboard circles (or squares or rectangles) as bases on which to build their cakes. If a cake is built and decorated on top of one of these circles, it can then be transferred from the countertop to a serving platter with ease. Cake circles are great for two reasons. Frosting a cake can get messy. Doing it on top of a cake circle instead of directly on a platter allows you to lift your cake from the messy countertop onto a pristine platter rather than trying to clean up errant frosting from the platter itself. Using a cake circle as a base will also allow you to transport a cake easily and safely inside a cake keeper, so it can be transferred to a serving platter when you reach your destination.

Cardboard cake circles are available at baking supply stores and online, but you can always make your own by tracing the outline of your cake pan onto a piece of sturdy cardboard and then cutting it out. If you do so, remember to cover your circle with foil, especially if your cardboard spells out "Pampers" or "Budweiser" in big letters.

Q I see many recipes these days recommend testing doneness with an instant-read thermometer. Is this really necessary? What is the best type of thermometer to buy? Do you have any tips for getting an accurate reading?

A Experienced bakers working with a familiar recipe will be able to judge by sight and touch whether or not their cake or loaf of bread is done. But for less experienced bakers or even for old hands trying something new, an instant-read thermometer, which takes the internal temperature, provides proof that it's time to pull an item from the oven. It's especially important to use an instant-read thermometer for recipes in which overbaking or underbaking would be disastrous and the visual signs of doneness are ambiguous, as in the case of cheesecake or crème brûlée. A reading of the internal temperature in these cases is really the only way to know that your custard has baked enough to hold together but not so much that it is curdled.

An instant-read thermometer is essential for tempering chocolate, because proper tempering requires heating and then cooling and then reheating the chocolate with exactitude. (To give you an idea: First, the chocolate is brought to a temperature of between 100 and 105°F [38–41°C]; then it is cooled to a temperature of between 75 and 80°F [24–27°C]; then it is slowly brought back up to 88°F [31°C].) And don't forget to use your thermometer when egg safety is an issue, as when making 7-minute frosting, pastry cream, and other recipes with gently heated eggs and whites.

Digital and dial-face thermometers are available in cookware shops and online. I prefer a digital thermometer, which is easier to read. To get an accurate reading, insert the thermometer into your cake, custard, or loaf of bread, angling it toward the middle. Some thermometers will give you a reading in 10 seconds; some will take up to 30 seconds.

DONENESS AND INTERNAL TEMPERATURE

Here are some useful numbers to know when testing for doneness with an instant-read thermometer.

Soft white breads like challah or Pullman loaves	190°F (88°C)
Crusty artisan breads	210°F (99°C)
Layer cakes	190°F (88°C)
Cheesecake	150°F (66°C)
Crème brûlée	175°F (79°C)
7-minute frosting	160°F (71°C)
Lemon curd	170°F (77°C)
Crème anglaise	180°F (82°C)
Swiss meringue	130°F (54°C)

Q How is an instant-read thermometer different from a candy thermometer?

A An instant-read thermometer has a sharp probe that can be inserted into the interior of a loaf of bread or a cake to measure its internal temperature. Instant-read thermometers are not ovenproof, so after 10 to 30 seconds, when you've gotten your reading, you must remove the thermometer from the food. An instant-read thermometer will measure temperatures from 0 to 220°F (18–104°C). In addition to baked goods, the thermometer can be used to measure the temperature of, say, a crème anglaise to see if it is sufficiently chilled to go into the ice cream maker.

oven thermometer

candy thermometer

instant-read thermometer

A candy thermometer (sometimes called a fry thermometer) is designed to measure the temperature of very hot liquids such as boiling sugar or oil. This type of thermometer attaches to the side of the pan and stays put so you can monitor the temperature of your liquid as it heats. Its gauge goes from 100 to 400°F (38–204°C).

Q Do I really need an oven thermometer, as so many baking books suggest?

A Because every oven has a dial or digital display for setting the temperature and also some kind of display to let you know when your oven has reached that temperature, buying an oven thermometer might seem superfluous. But the fact is, many if not all ovens will give inaccurate readings unless they are routinely calibrated by a technician. An inaccurate temperature gauge will adversely affect your baked goods. Baking biscuits in a too-cool oven will inhibit them from rising adequately. Baking a cake in a too-hot oven will cause it to overbrown while leaving the interior uncooked.

HOW TO COOK SUGAR

Cooked sugar, which has been heated to above 212°F (100°C), is necessary in recipes for fruit preserves, fudge and other candy, cooked meringues, nougat, caramel, praline, and many others.

It sounds simple: Heat sugar with a little water until the sugar dissolves, insert a candy thermometer, and remove the pot from the heat when the water has evaporated and the sugar has reached the proper temperature.

The difficulty is in getting the sugar to melt into a smooth liquid without crystallizing and becoming grainy during the process or as it cools. Crystallization can occur when even just 1 grain of sugar that has failed to dissolve comes into contact with the melted sugar solution, causing a chain reaction in which the sugar that has been dissolved reverts back to its former crystal form. So it is important to make sure that no sugar crystals remain stuck to the sides of the pan, threatening to fall into the solution and set off the crystallization process.

There are several ways to keep errant sugar granules from sticking to the sides of your pot: You can use a pastry brush moistened with water to brush the sides of the pot clean. If you do this, be sure that the brush itself is clean. Any impurity introduced into the sugar solution may cause crystallization.

Another method is to moisten your hands and wipe the sides of the pot with wet fingers. This way, you can feel whether granules remain. Something I've found very effective is to bring my solution to a simmer and then cover the pot for a minute, allowing the water condensing inside the pot to wash the sides clean.

Molten sugar is an extremely sensitive and unstable solution, and any jostling or stirring can cause the sugar to crystallize. So even after you have successfully melted your sugar into a smooth caramel, you must be sure to treat it gently, resisting the urge to stir, which might cause a disastrous change at the molecular level. Most likely, your sugar will cook unevenly because of the uneven heat of the cooktop burner. If one spot starts to brown before the rest, gently tilt and swirl the contents of the pot until the sugar is evenly colored.

When the water has evaporated, the sugar will cook — and burn — quickly. Watch your pot and your thermometer carefully. It's best to remove the pot from the heat as soon as it reaches the low range of the temperature recommended in the recipe. Residual heat will continue to cook the sugar, and you don't want to risk burning it. Some people take the precaution of plunging the bottom of the pan into a bowl of ice water to stop the cooking quickly.

Many pastry chefs like to cook sugar on its own, without any water, because there is less risk of the water splashing some of the granules onto the sides of the pan, and because it saves time. But precisely because it is so fast, the "dry" method is a good way for a less experienced cook to burn a pot of sugar. The sugar will transform from a clear syrup to a very dark caramel in a matter of seconds. Using water slows down the process and gives you more control.

Rich Caramel Sauce

This is a good excuse to practice sugar cookery. This rich, gooey sauce is delicious on ice cream or as a warm dip for fresh fruit. I've had good luck in avoiding crystallization with the no-stir method, but feel free to use any of the tricks on pages 66 and 67 to keep the sides of your pan sugar crystal-free.

MAKES ABOUT 2 CUPS

1½ cups sugar
½ cup water
1 cup heavy cream
6 tablespoons dark rum (optional)

1. Combine the sugar and water in the pan, gently stirring until all of the sugar is moistened, and being careful not to touch the spoon against the sides of the pot.
2. Bring to a simmer over medium heat, cover, turn the heat to low, and cook for 1 minute to allow the condensing water to wash down the sides of the pot.
3. Remove the lid, increase the heat to medium, and bring to a boil. Lower a candy thermometer into the syrup, clipping it onto the side of the pot and making sure that the

sensor is submerged in the syrup but not touching the bottom of the pot. Boil until the sugar turns a light amber color and the thermometer registers 340°F (171°C). Do not stir. If part of the syrup is turning darker than the rest of the syrup, gently tilt the pan to even out the cooking.

4. When the syrup is a uniform amber color, remove the pan from the heat and stir in the heavy cream with a long-handled wooden spoon. Be careful, because the cream will bubble up. When the bubbling has subsided, stir in the rum, if using.

5. Transfer the mixture to a heatproof bowl and let stand until warm. Serve immediately or transfer to an airtight container and store at room temperature for up to 1 week, reheating in a microwave or on the stove before serving.

Q How many spatulas does a baker need?

A A baker can't have too many spatulas. At the minimum, have three rubber spatulas in small, medium, and large sizes. I like spatulas made of heatproof silicone, which won't melt when used to scrape the insides of a hot pan. For removing cookies from a baking sheet, removing the first brownie from a pan, or turning pancakes, you'll need a spatula with a wide (about 3-inch), sharp blade made of metal or nylon. Finally, both a small (4-inch) and large (10- to 12-inch) offset spatula, which is a metal spreader angled from a wooden handle, are indispensable. Use them to spread frosting, smooth cake batter, and to slide under pie and pastry doughs so they don't stick to a countertop.

rubber spatula   *wide spatula*   *offset spatula*

Q What is the best implement for removing zest from citrus fruit?

A Zest is the outer yellow rind of the lemon, lime, or orange that contains the fruit's fragrant oils and perfumes. The inner white rind, called the pith, has a harsh and bitter flavor and should not be used in baking. Citrus zest is used as a flavoring or a garnish in a variety of baking recipes. Choose your zesting implement depending on how you intend to use the zest.

If you want the zest to disappear into a dough or batter, you should grate it as finely as possible. The small holes of a box grater will accomplish this, but then it will be up to you to pick at the zest, which remains stubbornly stuck on the sides of the grater, with a toothpick, skewer, or tip of a paring knife. Less frustrating and much more efficient is a Microplane grater. A tool originally sold in hardware stores for rasping wood, it easily removes fine shreds of zest from fruit and deposits it onto your work surface (just as the rasp deposits sawdust on the floor), leaving behind the bitter white pith.

For fine strands of zest to use as a garnish, use a citrus zester, a handheld device with five tiny holes that will remove the zest in delicate strands. A citrus stripper or shredder is another utensil with a sharp-notched edge that removes the zest in ¼-inch-wide strips. If you want even thicker strips of zest, to make candied lemon peel or to create a custom garnish, use a sharp vegetable peeler, taking care to leave behind as much of the bitter white pith as possible.

Q I have 15 minutes and $150 dollars to spend on baking odds and ends. What should I put in my shopping cart?

A Aside from the basics I've already mentioned, here is a list of relatively inexpensive items you might pick up if you don't already own them.

Useful Baking Utensils

* **Bench scraper**. A stainless steel straight-edge blade with a wooden handle, this handy tool will divide sticky bread dough with ease and scrape the countertop clean. King Arthur Flour Company (see Resources) sells a silicone scraper with a straight edge and a rounded side that can scrape cookie dough from the inside of a mixing bowl as well. (The catalog claims that this scraper can clean ice off your windshield, but I can't say I've put mine to this use.)

* **Biscuit cutter**. You can always use a juice glass to cut biscuits, but a stainless steel biscuit cutter with a sharp edge and a handle makes the job easier. They are sold in nesting sets of 4, ranging in size from 1½ to 3 inches in diameter.

* **Citrus reamer**. Made of plastic or wood, this implement quickly and efficiently extracts juice from a lemon, lime, or orange.

* **Fine mesh strainer**. Essential for rinsing fruit, straining sauces, and sifting dry ingredients. Choose a fine gauge or double-mesh strainer with a handle and sturdy feet for stability.

* **Glass bowls**. A set of glass nesting bowls will help you to organize your ingredients as you get ready to bake. These are also essential if you plan on melting chocolate or butter in the microwave.

* **Ice cream scoop**. A spring-loaded scoop that holds a generous tablespoon of cookie dough will let you portion out uniform and beautifully shaped cookies. It is a joy to have if you bake a lot of drop cookies.

* **Pastry bag and tips**. To start off, buy a canvas pastry bag with a small set of tips (star, leaf, basket weave, plain or writing) as well as a coupler so the tips can be interchanged without emptying the bag. If you enjoy using several colors of icing, it's more practical to buy a box of disposable plastic pastry bags instead of washing the bag each time you want to switch colors.

* **Pastry brush**. Indispensable soft-bristled brushes will help you grease pans, brush excess flour from rolled pastry and cookie dough, cover pies and pastries with glaze or egg wash, and so much more. I don't recommend silicone brushes for baking, because their bristles are too thick and rough for delicate doughs. Pastry brushes can retain flavors and odors, so keep a separate set for brushing barbecue sauce on your chicken.

* **Pastry cutter**. The fluted edges of this wheel will give your lattice pie top its attractive finished look.

* **Stainless steel bowls**. A set of nesting bowls will come in handy for mixing and organizing. Stainless steel bowls can also be used to gently heat delicate ingredients like chocolate and eggs over a pan of simmering water in lieu of a double-boiler.

* **Whisk**. A 10-inch balloon whisk will help you add volume to cream or egg whites. A flat-style whisk is better for whisking a sauce in a pan (such as crème anglaise) so that it doesn't stick and clump as it heats. Either one will work to blend dry ingredients.

* **Wire racks**. Have at least two of these, for cooling cakes, cookies, muffins, and many other items as they come out of the oven. Look for sturdy racks with wires set close enough to each other so that small items won't slip through and delicate ones will be adequately supported when still soft.

CHAPTER 3

What Happens When We Bake
Science for Bakers

For many bakers, the transformation of a liquid cake batter into a solid cake is magical and mysterious. This attitude of wonderment is fine when the result is a cake with an even, tender crumb and a beautifully browned crust. But when your cake is as heavy as a brick or riddled with large tunnels and bubbles, you might lose faith in the magical properties of butter, eggs, and flour.

A little bit of knowledge about how ingredients interact will take some of the mystery out of baking, giving you more control over the outcome of your baked goods and helping you bake with confidence.

HOW BAKED GOODS RISE

Baked goods rise when air bubbles incorporated into them expand in the heat of the oven. There are several different ways of getting those bubbles to form. Sometimes a single technique or leavener is used; sometimes they are used in combination. Here is a rundown of the five different ways rising occurs.

1. Steam. Steam can be a powerful leavener, working in concert with other leaveners but sometimes raising baked goods on its own. Puff pastry is an example of the power of steam in the absence of any other means of raising dough. Puff pastry is made by wrapping a sheet of dough around a large slab of chilled butter, then rolling and folding it until it consists of many hundreds of layers of solid butter and pastry. When the pastry is placed in a very hot oven, the water contained in the butter turns to steam, expanding and pushing the layers of dough away from each other and upward. An oven temperature of at least 425°F (220°C), is necessary to create the greatest amount of steam quickly, before the pastry hardens into its characteristic crisp flakes and sets.

puff pastry dough layers

*steam pushing apart
layers of puff pastry*

2. Creaming. Many recipes call for the creaming together of butter (or sometimes shortening) and sugar before any eggs or chemical leaveners are added to the batter or dough. Creaming is a mechanical method for creating air bubbles, during which granules of sugar trap air between molecules of fat. A lot of recipes will specify "softened" or "room temperature" butter because rock-hard butter will be difficult to beat into a smooth mixture and will resist the incorporation of air bubbles. But it is equally important that your butter not become too warm. Butter melts at a temperature of about 70°F (21°C), at which point its molecules change shape and won't trap as much air. The result may be a heavy and greasy cake. Even cool butter will melt quickly if the air in your kitchen is warm, so take care when baking in a warm room to start with butter that is closer to 65°F (18°C), and to chill your bowl and beaters in the refrigerator for 15 minutes before using them.

Creaming together shortening and sugar presents no such difficulties, because shortening maintains an optimum consistency for incorporating air (in addition to already having been aerated with nitrogen during processing) at a wide range of temperatures.

3. Chemical leaveners. Recipes for drop cookies, muffins, and quick breads, the batters and doughs of which are generally dense and heavy, usually call for a powerful chemical leavener: either baking soda or baking powder. When moistened, these leaveners release bubbles of carbon dioxide into the dough or batter. The bubbles expand in the heat of the oven, causing the baked goods to rise.

The leavening power of baking soda is activated only in the presence of acid. So it is used in recipes that contain ingredients such as lemon juice, buttermilk, or non-alkalized cocoa powder, all of which will work with baking soda to produce those bubbles when liquid is added to the mix.

For recipes without acidic ingredients, baking powder is required. Baking powder is a mixture of baking soda, acids, and a little bit of cornstarch to keep the ingredients dry and thus forestall the production of carbon dioxide until needed. It works exactly the same way as baking soda, but on its own instead of in the presence of an additional acidic ingredient.

Baking soda will begin to release carbon dioxide bubbles as soon as it comes in contact with a liquid, and these bubbles will pop, the gas dissipating, in a matter of minutes. So it is important to mix your batter or dough and get it into the oven quickly, before this happens and the baking soda loses its leavening power. With baking powder you have a little more time because of the way it is formulated. It contains two acids (thus the label "double-acting"), one of which begins to produce carbon dioxide immediately, and one of which reacts only in the heat of the oven.

Baking soda is more powerful, proportionately, than baking powder. In general, for every cup of flour in a recipe, you will need ¼ teaspoon of baking soda or 1 teaspoon of baking powder. Once you know these proportions, and the way baking soda and baking powder react with acids and liquids, you can see that there are ways to substitute one for the other.

Say you want to make biscuits with buttermilk instead of milk. If your recipe calls for 2 teaspoons of baking powder and ¾ cup of milk, you can adapt it by using ½ teaspoon baking soda and ¾ cup of buttermilk. Or say you realize that your recipe calls for Dutch-process cocoa, whose acids have been neutralized, and baking powder, but you only have natural cocoa powder, which does contain acids. Replace the baking powder with one quarter of the amount of baking soda for an equivalent result.

4. Yeast. Bread and many sweet breads and pastries such as babka, croissants, and Danish rely on yeast for rising. Yeast is a microorganism that feeds on starches in flour, producing carbon dioxide as a byproduct. The carbon dioxide, which fills air cells in the dough created by kneading, expands in the oven, causing the dough to rise.

While many bakers understand yeast's function in bread making, they may not realize that yeast can't raise dough on its own. It works only in the presence of gluten, the protein aggregate that develops into stretchy, elastic strands as wheat flour is mixed and kneaded with water or another liquid.

During mixing and kneading, the proteins in flour organize themselves into a webbed cell structure made of gluten strands. As the dough rests after kneading, the yeast proliferates, and the carbon dioxide it produces as it multiplies fills the gluten cells. That's why bread dough rises on the countertop as well as in the oven. Once in the hot oven, these gases will expand, stretching those gluten cells. The well-developed gluten expands to accommodate the gases, until the protein solidifies at a certain temperature.

The open crumb of an artisan bread is a sign that the yeast was lively and productive, producing plentiful carbon dioxide, and the gluten in the flour was well-developed and was able to stretch and contain the gas. At a certain temperature, rising ceases because the proteins will coagulate, eventually becoming the glossy crumb and crisp crust of a well-baked loaf or pastry.

5. Eggs and air. Many cake and cookie recipes will direct you to beat eggs into creamed butter and sugar. Doing so will incorporate yet more air into your batter. But these recipes are still relying primarily on creaming and chemical leaveners to create air bubbles.

Other cake recipes, however, rely more strongly on eggs, both whole and separated, for a good rise. There are several ways to handle eggs so that they will function this way. Sometimes, a butter cake recipe will direct you to beat only the egg yolks into a mixture of creamed butter and sugar, then whip the whites in a separate bowl and fold them into the batter. Incorporating additional air into the whites will give a butter cake extra lift when a lighter texture is desired.

Recipes for French-style sponge cake, or génoise, will direct you to beat whole egg yolks and sugar over simmering water until they are warm and the sugar is dissolved, and then continue to beat them off-heat until they're pale yellow and reach the "ribbon" stage. This takes between 3 and 5 minutes and produces a mixture that is pale yellow and thick, and when lifted by the beaters falls back into the bowl in thick "ribbons." As with creaming, air is incorporated into the eggs. Warming the mixture softens the fat in the yolks, which makes the egg and sugar mixture more elastic and able to hold more air. The dry ingredients are sifted over the yolk mixture and very gently folded in, sometimes along with a small amount of butter.

The cake must be baked immediately, before the foamy batter starts to deflate.

American-style sponge cake has a lighter, dryer texture than génoise, not only because it doesn't contain any butter to weigh it down and moisten it, but because whipped egg whites are folded into the batter just before baking. The protein in egg whites, when properly whipped, unwind and link up with each other, similar to the way proteins coagulate when cooked, but stay moist and elastic. Air beaten into them expands in the oven until the proteins set at a certain temperature.

The lightest style of cake, angel food cake, contains no egg yolks or butter and is leavened solely with egg whites. This type of cake must be baked in an ungreased pan for two reasons. Any kind of fat will destroy the structure of whipped egg whites, dissolving it and ruining the cake's chances of rising. In addition, when the low-protein (because it has no yolks) cake is removed from the oven, it needs to cling to the sides of the pan as it cools, allowing it to solidify before it can collapse in on itself. For the same reason, to protect its high but fragile rise, an angel food cake should be inverted straight out of the oven and cooled upside down in the pan, so that gravity can preserve the rise until the proteins in the cooked whites solidify.

Baking Experiment

The Half-Pound Cake recipe on the following page is an example of how cake can be raised by creaming alone.

Half-Pound Cake

Pound cake is a traditional English recipe dating back to the early eighteenth century, famous for its easy-to-remember ingredients: 1 pound each of butter, sugar, eggs, and flour. A 4-pound cake, however, is a bit large for most households, so I've adapted the traditional recipe to a more modest size and, like most modern versions, for a lighter, more tender cake.

Most recipes today call for a little bit of baking powder or baking soda as insurance, but it is fun to make this cake without relying on either one, just to prove that creaming (along with the added leavening power of eggs) does really work. Baking the cake at a moderate temperature allows the air bubbles time to expand before the cake sets, for an optimum rise.

Note that the butter should be soft but not warm — if you are relying on creaming alone you will want your butter to hold as much air as possible, and it will do so only if it doesn't melt. Chill your mixing bowl for 15 minutes before beginning to cream, as a precaution against melting. Lightly beating the eggs before adding them will help incorporate them into the creamed butter and sugar. The extra egg yolks help the batter hold onto the air beaten into it.

SERVES 8 TO 10

3 large eggs plus 2 large egg yolks, at room temperature
1 tablespoon vanilla extract
1½ cups cake flour
¼ teaspoon salt
½ pound (2 sticks) unsalted butter, softened but still cool
1⅓ cups sugar

1. Preheat the oven to 325°F (160°C). Chill a large mixing bowl in the freezer for 15 minutes. Coat the inside of a 9- by 5-inch loaf pan with cooking spray and dust it with flour, knocking out any excess.

2. Combine the eggs, yolks, and vanilla in a glass measuring cup and lightly beat. Combine the flour and salt in a medium mixing bowl.

3. Remove the large bowl from the freezer and add the butter and sugar. Cream with an electric mixer on medium-high until fluffy and almost white, about 3 minutes, scraping down the sides of the bowl as necessary.

4. With the mixer on low, add the egg mixture in a slow, steady stream, stopping to scrape down the bowl at least once. Turn the mixer to medium-high and beat for 30 seconds longer. Add the flour, about ½ cup at a time, until fully incorporated, scraping down the bowl after each addition. After the last addition, mix on medium-high for 30 seconds.

5. Scrape the batter into the prepared pan, smooth the top with a spatula, and bake until a toothpick inserted into the center comes out clean, about 1 hour 15 minutes. Let the cake cool in the pan for 10 minutes and then transfer to a wire rack to cool completely. This cake will keep at room temperature, wrapped in plastic, for up to 3 days or refrigerated for up to 1 week.

Q What happens when egg whites are whipped?

A Egg whites consist of tightly wound but separate strands of protein that uncoil and link together with each other during whipping, forming a weblike network that traps and holds air. It is crucial when making an egg white foam capable of raising a cake or soufflé not to overwhip the whites. You want them to stay soft, moist, and flexible, so they can stretch along with the trapped air as it heats in the oven. Overwhipping will separate the protein from the moisture in the egg whites, leaving you with lumpy whites made of dry, stiff, and set protein that's been separated from the water molecules in the egg. When overwhipped egg whites are folded into a cake or soufflé batter, they do nothing to help the cake or soufflé rise, since they are incapable of expanding.

Q What is the difference between "soft peaks" and "stiff peaks" and when is one preferable over the other?

A The longer you beat whites, the more air you will incorporate into them and the more rigid the proteins will become. Egg whites whipped to soft peaks will flop over

soft peaks

stiff peaks

over-whipped

slightly when a whisk is pulled up from the bowl. Whipped to stiff peaks, the whites won't flop over. Egg whites whipped to soft peaks are good in soufflés, where moisture and maximum flexibility are important. Whipped to stiff peaks, they are better in meringues, angel food cakes, and other recipes where maximum volume is desired.

Q Why do recipes emphasize the need for a clean bowl and beaters when beating egg whites?

A Oil or grease on the surface of an improperly cleaned bowl or beater will corrupt an egg white foam, coating the proteins and inhibiting their ability to link up with each other to form the flexible web needed to trap air bubbles.

Q What happens if you accidentally spill a little bit of yolk into the bowl with your whites before whipping?

A Egg yolks contain fat. Even a speck of yolk can prevent a bowl of egg whites from whipping properly, so if some yolk winds up in your whites you should discard the contents of the bowl, wash it scrupulously, and start again. To prevent waste and bother, separate your eggs one at a time in a small bowl, transferring each successfully separated white to a larger mixing bowl as you go. This way, if a little yolk gets into one of your whites as you work, you can simply throw away one white instead of discarding the whole bowl.

Q Why do room-temperature whites whip better than cold ones?

A The coiled proteins in egg whites will relax slightly as they warm up, so that whipping them will take less time. Egg whites straight out of the refrigerator can achieve the same volume, but it will take longer.

Q Why are old egg whites better than very fresh ones for whipping?

A Egg whites that are 3 or 4 days old whip to greater heights than very fresh ones because the coiled proteins will relax over the course of several days. If you are using eggs from the supermarket, they will most likely be at least a week old by the time you purchase them. But if you are lucky enough to have a source for fresh eggs, let them sit for a few days before whipping.

Q Why is cream of tartar sometimes called for in recipes for whipping egg whites?

A Cream of tartar or another acidic ingredient, such as lemon juice or vinegar, is often added to egg whites before whipping because the acid encourages the egg proteins to uncoil more quickly to trap air bubbles. It also strengthens the protein in whipped whites, making them more stable and less likely to deflate during baking. Similarly, whites beaten in a copper bowl are made more elastic due to their contact with the element, which makes the whites flexible so they can expand more in the oven.

Q What is the effect of sugar on egg whites during whipping? When and how should sugar be added?

A Sugar whipped along with egg whites dissolves and coats the proteins so they don't dry out and harden. It creates a glossy, thick foam that is more stable and less likely to deflate than a foam made with egg whites alone. Sugar will slow down the incorporation of air into the mixture, so it's best to whip the whites by themselves at least until they reach a foamy, almost-soft peak stage before adding the sugar. Then, add the sugar in a very slow stream as you whip the egg whites. Waiting too long to add the sugar is a mistake, the danger being that the egg whites will already have begun to dry out, and won't be able to take advantage of sugar's protective capabilities.

Q How do baked goods keep their shape?

A The short answer is just one word: protein. See the following pages for a longer explanation of the two different sources of protein — in eggs and in flour — that bakers rely on to keep their cakes and other creations from crumbling to pieces.

HOW EGG PROTEINS HELP BAKED GOODS KEEP THEIR SHAPE

The protein in eggs and flour is what holds baked goods together. Eggs, both the yolks and the whites, are high in protein, which goes from liquid to solid as it cooks. Anyone who has scrambled an egg knows this.

Here is how it happens: Uncooked protein consists of small, individual, tightly coiled strands. Heating these proteins causes them to unravel (or denature) and then link together with each other, forming a solid mass, or, more precisely, separate solid curds. If you stir uncooked eggs into a cake batter, the proteins will do the same thing, linking up with each other to hold your cake together and give it a solid structure.

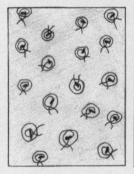

uncooked protein strands

heated unraveled protein

relinked protein strands

Eggs work the same way in cookies. Think about the difference in texture between a chocolate chip cookie, which contains eggs and becomes a solid, chewy mass when baked, and a shortbread cookie, which contains no egg and has an extremely crumbly, fragile texture.

The same denaturing process is at work in baked custards, but a little more caution must be used so that you wind up with a smooth rather than a cottage cheese–like result. In the case of crème anglaise, a mixture of milk, sugar, and eggs is gently heated until it thickens into a smooth sauce at about 160°F (71°C). Constant stirring is necessary to break up clumps of coagulating protein and care must be taken not to overheat the mixture or no amount of stirring will prevent the formation of clumps. In the case of a custard that isn't stirred, like cheesecake or crème brûlée, it is especially important to heat the custard gently until it sets into a smooth mass. Custards are often baked in a water bath, which protects them from heating too quickly and to too high a temperature.

HOW FLOUR HELPS BAKED GOODS KEEP THEIR SHAPE

Gluten development is key to the structure and texture of baked goods, even those made without yeast. As when making bread dough, during the mixing of other doughs and batters, the proteins in flour organize themselves into a webbed cell structure made of gluten strands. Whichever method of leavening a recipe employs, this webbed cell structure works in a similar way to trap air. As the flexible walls of the cells expand to accommodate expanding gases, or water turning to steam, the baked goods rise.

Compare a slice of tender pound cake to a slice of chewy artisan bread. The differences in texture are significant, for two reasons: First, the cake calls for a low-protein cake flour. This type of flour will develop just enough gluten to support the cake, which will rise just enough to give it a light texture and delicate crumb. In contrast, high-protein bread flour will be able to produce much more gluten than cake flour, for an extremely strong and extensible dough that can support the bread's lofty rise.

The way flour is handled also has a significant impact on a product's structure and texture. Compare directions for mixing biscuits with mixing bread dough. For biscuits, the dough is handled as little as possible, mixed just until all dry ingredients are moistened, to avoid overdevelopment of the gluten, which can lead to toughness. For bread dough, the opposite is true. Vigorous, prolonged kneading is required to develop the gluten to its utmost, so it can support the dough as it rises in the oven.

Q What happens to sugar when it caramelizes? Why does the crust of a bread or muffin taste so good?

A Caramelization is a chemical reaction that occurs when sugar is heated until its molecules break apart and recombine into a variety of compounds with a diversity of flavors and aromas ranging from sweet to sour to bitter. These compounds account for the complex taste of caramel.

Q How do baked goods get their caramelized crusts?

A Sugar on the surface of baked goods, exposed to the heat of the oven, caramelizes. The resulting sweet crustiness provides a delicious contrast to the yielding interior of most cakes and pastries. Even breads with no added sugar can sport caramelized crusts, thanks to starches that convert into sugars in reaction to yeast during fermentation.

Q Aside from sweetening, tenderizing, and browning, does sugar serve other functions in baking?

A Sugar also raises the temperature at which a batter will change from fluid to solid by delaying the coagulation of proteins. A little sugar added to bread dough will have a similar effect, delaying protein coagulation and giving the gluten more time to stretch before it sets.

Q What role does salt play in baking?

A Primarily, salt plays the same role in baking that it does in cooking. It enhances the flavors of the other ingredients in the recipe, making brownies more chocolaty and corn muffins more redolent of corn. It brings out the earthy flavors of stone-ground whole wheat in bread. Without a pinch of salt, your cookies, cream puffs, and crème caramel will taste flat and bland. Salt even makes sugar cookies taste more pleasantly sweet than they would without salt. The proportion of salt to other ingredients is minute in most baked goods, and presents little risk to people trying to watch their salt intake. So unless you are on a strict no-salt diet, use the recommended amount of salt for optimum flavor results.

In addition to enhancing the flavor of bread, salt plays a crucial role in crafting tall and beautifully browned loaves. Salt strengthens gluten, tightening the webbing of proteins that give bread dough the structure to expand without collapsing. It also acts to slow fermentation in yeast breads. Slow fermentation prevents yeast breads from bubbling up too quickly, allowing gluten to develop as the dough rests, which contributes to a yeast dough's high rise in the oven. In addition, when yeast is allowed to proliferate too quickly, it gobbles up all of the sugars in the dough, sugars that, ideally, caramelize and give the crust a rich brown color. Without enough salt, your bread may be dense and pale instead of tall and deliciously dark golden.

SEE ALSO: Fermentation in yeast breads, page 312

WHAT MAKES BAKED GOODS TENDER?

A rundown of basic baking ingredients and techniques will give you a good idea of how each one contributes to the tenderness of baked goods.

When flour is mixed with a liquid, a webbed network of proteins called gluten develops, which provides structure for all baked goods as they rise. Different types of flour contain different amounts of protein.

In general, the most tender baked goods are made from flour with a low protein content. Thus, yellow cake, biscuits, and madeleines often call for very soft cake flour, which will develop relatively little gluten and thus contribute to the tenderness of the finished product. Conversely, an abundance of gluten is desirable in items such as French bread, which has a bubbly and open crumb along with a thick, chewy crust. High protein bread flour makes sense in these recipes, where tenderness isn't important but a strong structure is. Using cake flour in a baguette recipe would be a disaster, because the dough would lack the strong gluten structure to support it as it rose in the oven, resulting in a flat, soft bread with a close crumb.

Supermarkets, natural foods stores, and baking catalogs have an array of flours of different protein contents. Remember that protein content can vary from season to season (wheat grown at certain times of year is lower in protein than at others) and by brand. Processing impacts protein content — bleached all-purpose flour is weaker than unbleached. The way a flour is labeled can also vary by region. Because of regional baking traditions and tastes,

Southern brands of all-purpose flour will have less protein than national and Northern brands.

Following is a chart of how much protein each type of flour generally contains, to help you choose the right ones for your particular baking needs.

Fat, whether from butter, oil, shortening, or egg yolks, contributes to tenderness by coating the proteins in flour so they can't easily link together to form gluten. This is why yeast breads that contain butter or other fat, such as croissants and brioche, are much more tender than fat-free baguettes. For fat to work most effectively as a tenderizer, it is added to the flour before any liquid is added, to coat the protein strands. "Shortened" baked goods — piecrust, biscuits, scones — are ones in which the butter is cut into the flour in this way, very effectively coating the proteins with fat and thus "shortening" the gluten strands that do manage to develop.

Sugar is also a tenderizer. During mixing, sugar absorbs liquid in a dough or batter, preventing a portion of it from combining with the flour in protein and thus preventing some gluten from forming. Thus, sweeter doughs and batters will generally be more tender than doughs and batters with little or no sugar.

It's not just ingredients, but how they are handled that will affect the tenderness of baked goods. In general, gentle handling results in less gluten formation, which results in a more tender product. This is why a biscuit recipe will instruct you to mix until the dough "just holds together," rather than until it is a "smooth, round ball." It's also why experienced bakers, who are able roll pie dough in just a few motions, wind up with a more tender crust than novices who roll over the dough dozens of times, thus strengthening the gluten and toughening the crust.

Protein Content of Flours		
Cake flour	7.5 to 8.5% protein	Tender cakes and biscuits
Southern all-purpose flour	7.5 to 9.5% protein	Tender cakes and biscuits
Bleached all-purpose flour	9.5 to 12% protein	Piecrusts, cookies, muffins, cakes
Unbleached all-purpose flour	10 to 12% protein	Piecrusts, cookies, muffins, cakes, softer yeast breads such as Pullman loaf or challah, yeasted cakes and pastries
Bread flour	11.5 to 12.5% protein	Thick-crusted artisan breads, pizza

Apple Tart with Cream Cheese Crust

Acid, fat, and sugar are a recipe for tender pastry. Acidic cream cheese, along with a generous amount of sugar and a load of butter, gives this simple dough exceptional tenderness. The dough is sticky and soft because it contains so much fat, so it is best to roll it out on parchment paper before sliding it into the tart pan.

SERVES 6

1 cup unbleached all-purpose flour

¾ cup sugar

⅛ teaspoon salt

½ cup (4 ounces) chilled cream cheese, cut into small pieces

½ cup (1 stick) chilled butter, cut into small pieces

2 large, tart apples such as Granny Smiths

¼ teaspoon ground cinnamon

3 tablespoons apple jelly

1. Preheat the oven to 400°F (200°C). Flour a 12-inch square of parchment paper.
2. Combine the flour, ½ cup of the sugar, and the salt in a medium bowl and beat with an electric mixer on low speed until just combined. Add the cream cheese and butter and mix on low until the dough just comes together in a ball.
3. Press the ball of dough into a 6-inch circle on the parchment. Flour the top of the dough. Roll out to an 11-inch circle, sliding an offset spatula under the dough as you roll to keep it from sticking to the parchment.

4. Slide the dough from the parchment into a 10-inch tart pan with a removable bottom, gently pressing it into the sides of the pan. Run the rolling pin over the top of the pan to trim the excess dough. Place the pan in the freezer for 15 minutes.

5. Peel, halve, and core the apples. Cut each apple half into ¼-inch-thick slices. Combine the sliced apples, the remaining ¼ cup sugar, and the cinnamon in a bowl, tossing to coat. Let it stand, stirring occasionally, until the sugar is dissolved.

6. Arrange the apples in concentric circles on top of the chilled shell. Bake until the crust is browned and the apples are golden, about 35 minutes. Transfer to a wire rack.

7. Heat the jelly on the stove or in the microwave until liquid. Brush the hot jelly over the hot apples. Cool slightly and serve warm.

Q What effect does an acidic ingredient like lemon juice or buttermilk have on a pastry dough or batter?

A Acidic ingredients like lemon juice, buttermilk, and sour cream are called for in recipes as various as piecrust, biscuits, coffee cakes, and cookies for the tangy flavor they add.

Acidic ingredients also affect the texture of baked goods. Acids break down strands of protein created when flour is mixed with liquid, helping to prevent toughness in biscuits and cakes. In fact, cake flour will make a more tender cake than all-purpose flour not only because it has a lower protein content, but because it has been bleached, which makes it slightly acidic.

Bread and pastry doughs need enough acid for flavor and tenderness, but not enough to compromise structural integrity. The classic example is sourdough bread, which gets its name from the acids that build up in a culture of natural yeast used to raise it. The yeast raises the bread, and the acids contribute flavor. It is a delicate balance, because if too much acid builds up, it will begin to kill off the yeast, inhibiting the rise of the bread. Periodically, fresh water and flour must be added to a sourdough culture to keep its acidity in balance.

Q Flakiness is a valued characteristic in many baked goods — croissants, puff pastry, piecrust. What are the ingredients and techniques responsible for flakiness?

A Flakiness depends upon how butter or another solid fat is incorporated into dough. To achieve flakiness, relatively large and unevenly sized pieces of unmelted fat have to be distributed throughout the dough. Then, when the fat melts in the oven, space is created for expanding gases (from the steam evaporating from the butter or from the reaction between a chemical leavener and the liquid in the recipe), which create the large air pockets associated with flakiness.

There are degrees of flakiness. Piecrust and biscuits depend on the uneven distribution of butter or shortening for flakiness. When the butter is distributed too evenly, it coats the flour and prevents it from absorbing liquid, resulting in a crumbly and tender (because of the shortened gluten strands) rather than flaky texture. Making baked goods of this type is, in fact, a balancing act: Do you prefer your biscuits and crust more on the flaky side or more on the tender side? If flaky, then be careful to leave both large and small pieces of butter unevenly distributed throughout the flour before adding the liquid; if tender, then a more even distribution of fat is required. Finding the right balance will take practice.

Croissants and puff pastry are defined by their flakiness without the same consideration for tenderness. In fact, the repeated rolling and folding required in these recipes encourages gluten formation, so much so that many recipes instruct you to refrigerate the dough between rolling sessions, not only to keep the butter cold but to let the proteins relax temporarily for easier rolling. It is very important at every step to keep the butter from melting (not a concern when working with shortening), because the flaky effect depends on the fat remaining solid. Melted butter will soak into the dough, so there will be no distinct layering, and thus no large air pockets between layers.

Q What is the difference between solid and liquid fats? What are their different uses in baking?

A All fats, solid or liquid, add moisture and tenderness to baked goods and prolong their shelf life by helping them retain moisture after baking. Beyond this, solid and liquid fats can add flavor to baked goods. Butter will give baked goods that incomparable fresh cream taste, but certain oils such as hazelnut, walnut, and even olive oil can lend their own aromatic flavors to both sweet and savory baked goods.

Butter and shortening, which are solids, can aid in leavening, while liquid fats can't. They can be creamed with sugar to retain air, helping cakes rise. They can be cut into flour to make flaky pastries. They can be layered with a dough made of flour and liquid to make puff pastry and other super-flaky doughs. Liquid fats (including melted butter) can't retain air so they can't be used for any of these purposes.

Q Why do baked goods get stale?

A Water will evaporate from finished breads, cakes, and cookies as they sit over several days, leading to dryness. Fats lend moisture to baked goods and won't evaporate over time. That's why rich baked goods generally keep longer than lean products. A pound cake, well-wrapped, will keep for several days at room temperature, while a baguette will be hard as a rock after 24 hours.

But loss of moisture is just a part of the reason why baked goods stale. According to experiments described by Harold McGee in *On Food and Cooking*, even when a loaf of bread is hermetically sealed to prevent loss of water, it still becomes hard over time. Interestingly, these same experiments show how reheating the bread to a temperature of 140°F (60°C) restores its fresh texture. So what is going on?

Starch gels at 140°F (60°C). When baked goods cool, water molecules migrate from these gelated starch granules, rendering the bread or cookies hard.

Some water migration is good. When cookies are very hot right out of the oven, they will fall apart if you try to pick them up. Cooling them on a baking sheet for 5 minutes allows some of the starches to harden, making the cookies easier to handle. But as the cookies cool completely and then sit at room temperature, the starches continue to harden until the cookies are no longer chewy, but hard instead. The same thing happens to bread, cake, and any other baked goods containing starch. If you have stored your baked goods in airtight containers or wrapped in plastic, so that they retain their water, reheating them can restore some of their freshness. Reheating will cause the water molecules to reinsert themselves in between the starch molecules, making your bread, cake, or cookies tender once again.

Staling occurs most quickly at temperatures just above freezing, but very slowly below freezing. So refrigeration is actually worse for most baked goods than freezing. (Baked goods with a lot of butter should be refrigerated if being kept for more than a few days, to avoid rancidity.) The best defense against staling is to freeze your uneaten baked goods when possible. Wrap them tightly in plastic before freezing so that air from the freezer won't come in contact with the surface of the baked goods and affect their flavor, and moisture from the freezer won't form ice crystals on their surface. Bring frozen bread and refrigerated baked goods to room temperature and then reheat to restore freshness.

Q Why do commercial baked goods have such a long shelf life?

A Commercial baked goods contain preservatives such as sulfur dioxide to inhibit the growth of mold. Most home-baked breads, cakes, cookies, and pastries disappear pretty quickly and become stale before they would grow mold, so home bakers don't have to worry too much about this. Food scientist and author Shirley Corriher recommends adding some softened ground raisins (which are themselves treated with sulfur dioxide) to inhibit the growth of mold if it is something that you are worried about.

Commercial baked goods stay squeezably soft for weeks or even months also because they contain emulsifiers, substances that help two difficult-to-mix ingredients, fat and water, come together into a smooth mixture. Emulsifiers are molecules that have one water-friendly end and one oil-friendly end. When mixed with oil and water they bring the two together. Emulsifiers keep water where it needs to be to maintain bread's softness or a cookie's pleasant chewiness.

CHAPTER 4

Know Your Oven

No book about baking would be complete without a discussion of ovens — gas, electric, convection, and microwave. Herewith are questions and answers about getting the most out of your oven, however quirky it may be, caring for it, and accessorizing it with the latest in oven thermometers, oven mitts, and nonstick liners.

Q What are the differences between gas and electric ovens? Is one better for baking?

A Conventional wisdom has it that gas is better for stovetop cooking for the control it allows the cook (the heat coming from a gas burner can be adjusted instantly upward or downward, while adjustments on an electric burner take longer) while electric is better for baking (because electricity will heat an oven's interior more evenly than gas). But the reality is that much depends on the quality of your oven, whatever its heat source. There are plenty of poorly built electric ovens with dangerous hot and cool spots, as well as a lot of high-end, wonderfully engineered gas ovens that maintain even temperatures front to back and side to side. With the help of an oven thermometer and some experience, you will be able to determine how evenly your gas or electric oven cooks, and how to respond if you do have hot spots or if your oven's temperature is lower or higher than what its gauge indicates.

Q How is a convection oven different from a conventional oven? Is it good for baking?

A Conventional ovens, whether fueled by gas or electricity, feature a heating element on the bottom with racks above. With some exceptions, most baked goods must sit on the middle rack during baking to avoid the direct heat of the element, leaving the lower and upper racks empty. A convection oven has three separate heating elements, on the top, bottom, and in back, and uses a fan to circulate hot air throughout the oven, heating the entire space evenly so that food can be placed on the lower and upper racks as well as the middle without fear of burning or undercooking.

Convection ovens cook foods more efficiently than conventional ovens. When adapting most recipes for a convection oven, you should reduce the cooking time by 25 percent and reduce the oven temperature by 25°F (4°C). A convection oven will not only save you time by allowing you to bake multiple batches of cookies at once — it will also save considerable fuel by cooking all of your food with less heat and in less time than a conventional oven.

In addition to making more efficient use of the oven's interior and the energy output of the heating elements, the forced air of a convection oven helps brown foods beautifully. When hot air blows across the surface of cakes, cookies, breads, and pies, it draws away excess moisture, hastening the crustiness and caramelization valued in many of these items.

a convection oven's fan circulates hot air

Q What is the difference between a convection oven and the new "speed ovens" I've seen written up in food magazines recently? Do speed ovens produce good baked products?

A These super-fast ovens, which can bake up to 15 times faster than conventional and convection ovens, were developed for commercial use in high-volume food service settings like ballparks and fast-food restaurants. The ovens use a combination of high-speed convection for browning and controlled bursts of microwave energy for even cooking of the interior. Recently, several appliance companies including GE, Electrolux, Sharp, and most notably Turbochef have introduced models for the home cook.

I've seen the Turbochef in action and must say that its ability to produce a soufflé in 2 minutes and a crusty artisan loaf in less than 10 is impressive. (It also cooks a mean roast chicken in under 15 minutes.) Whether or not your time is worth this much money is a question you'll have to answer for yourself.

Q What are the rules for positioning oven racks before baking different items?

A If you are not using a convection oven, you should keep in mind that items will bake very differently depending on where in the oven they are placed. For even baking, the middle of the oven is best. Some recipes will direct you to position the rack in the middle. If no direction is given, assume that your items should be baked here. Items that require an especially browned bottom should be baked in the lower third of the oven. Overall baking time will be the same as when baked in the middle, but the pan or baking sheet's proximity to the heating element will promote browning on the bottom. A fruit pie requiring an especially crisp bottom crust that won't get soggy from prolonged contact with a juicy filling should be baked in the bottom third of the oven. Placing items in the upper third of the oven will promote browning on top. This is the place to bake your meringue-topped pie so it gets good color quickly and without heating up the lemon curd underneath.

Sometimes you'll have more than one pan that you'd like to bake at once. Ideally, both pans should be baked in the middle of the oven unless otherwise directed. Two 9-inch cake pans can be placed side by side and then rotated at some point during baking after the cakes have begun to set (you don't want to move them while they're still in a liquid state and risk damaging their developing structure). If both pans won't fit, as with two baking sheets of cookies, it's possible to bake one on the top rack and one on the bottom rack, keeping an eye on them and rotating the pans halfway through baking to prevent overbrowning on either the top or the bottom. I recommend this only for items like cookies that require a relatively short baking time. With longer-baking items, the risk of burning is greater and not worth the savings in time.

Q How long does it take to preheat an oven?

A The time it takes to preheat an oven will vary depending on your particular oven, how efficiently it heats, and how well it holds the heat. If it were only a question of reaching the desired temperature for baking a cake or a batch of cookies, I would advise you to turn on your oven before beginning to assemble your ingredients, as most recipes direct, resting assured that in the 15 to 20 minutes minimum that it would take you to prepare your batter or dough, your oven would be preheated. But now that many of us have a growing desire to save energy, I've started to think of preheating in terms not only of getting ready to bake, but also in terms of using the least amount of energy necessary for a successful outcome.

Some environmental advocates have suggested that it isn't worth the energy to preheat an oven, since opening the oven door causes it to lose so much heat. They argue that while putting food in a cold oven will add a few minutes to cooking time, the savings in energy over the long run will be well worth the time lost.

I am more persuaded, however, by studies showing that it takes more energy to get an oven up to temperature when it is cold than to return it to preheated temperature once it has already been heated. Casual experiments with my own oven have convinced me of this. According to the thermometer that hangs inside my oven, it takes my Thermador about 12 minutes to reach 350°F (180°C). After opening the oven for 30 seconds and closing the oven door, it takes only 3 or 4 minutes for the temperature to rise again to 350°F (180°C).

Furthermore, many baked items rely on contact with an initial blast of hot air to jump-start the process. While starting off in a cold oven may make sense when you are making baked beans, or in other cases where baking is simply a method for reaching a desired temperature that indicates doneness, with baked goods it is a different story. Bread dough won't have any "oven spring" (see page 343) if it is placed in a cold oven; the baking powder in biscuits would lose its power if the biscuits didn't immediately start to bake. If you are interested in energy efficiency, get to know your oven and how quickly it heats up. Then figure out at what point in the recipe you will need to turn it on so it is just hot enough at the moment you are ready to bake.

One suggestion for saving energy that may make more sense for bakers than starting with a cold oven is to turn off the heat without opening the oven door 5 or 10 minutes before baking is done. Most newer ovens will stay hot for at least this long, baking with residual heat. If this idea appeals to you, test your oven's ability to hold onto its heat by placing an oven thermometer inside, preheating the oven, turning off the heat, and checking the temperature after 5 or 10 minutes to see whether or not there has been a significant drop.

Cold-Oven Coffee Cake

Traditionally, cold-oven cake recipes were developed to save money on fuel. Why have the oven on, the reasoning goes, when there's nothing baking in it? It turns out that there are other reasons to start certain cakes in a cold oven. Doing so with a pound cake results in a wonderfully high rise (cakes have a longer time to rise before they set in an oven that starts cool) and a pleasantly chewy crust (a hotter oven will evaporate moisture on the surface of the cake before it has time to interact with starch, forming a crust).

In the following recipe, starting this very simple yeasted coffee cake in a cold oven allows the rapid-rise yeast, which needs only one rise, to actually ferment in the oven rather than during a separate rise on the countertop. Putting the cake in a hot oven would kill off the yeast in a matter of minutes, but starting it in a cold oven, where the temperature rises gradually, actually helps the dough rise at a faster rate than it would on the countertop in a cool kitchen, before baking it.

SERVES 8

¾ cup whole milk

4 tablespoons unsalted butter

2 envelopes (1½ tablespoons) rapid-rise yeast

1¾ cups unbleached all-purpose flour

2 tablespoons granulated sugar

½ teaspoon salt

½ cup raisins

½ cup light brown sugar

⅓ cup dark corn syrup

1 teaspoon ground cinnamon

½ cup finely chopped walnuts

1. Spray an 8-inch square baking pan with cooking spray.
2. Heat the milk and 2 tablespoons of the butter in a small saucepan until the butter is melted and the milk is very warm to the touch.
3. Pour the milk mixture into a large mixing bowl and whisk in the yeast to dissolve it. Stir in the flour, granulated sugar, and salt. Beat the dough with an electric mixer on medium-low until smooth. Stir in the raisins until incorporated. Pat the dough into the prepared pan.
4. Melt the remaining 2 tablespoons butter. Combine the brown sugar, corn syrup, cinnamon, and melted butter in a medium bowl. Smooth this mixture over the dough and sprinkle with the walnuts.
5. Transfer the pan to a cold oven. Set the oven to 350°F (180°C). Bake until the cake is golden and set in the center, 25 to 30 minutes. Let cool slightly and serve warm.

Q Why do my baked goods always seem to burn before they are baked through, even though I'm following the recipe directions?

A If your baked goods overbrown consistently, you might inadvertently be baking at a higher temperature than you mean to, if your oven runs hot. Test it by putting an oven thermometer inside and using that as a guide rather than your oven's gauge. If things seem to be baking unevenly — cakes burning on one side or 6 out of 12 muffins rising higher than the rest — then you may have a hot-spot problem.

Q What are hot spots?

A Ideally, the cookies on your baking sheet should bake at the same rate whether they are on the right, left, or middle of the baking sheet. In reality, many ovens have hot spots, even on the middle rack, making it necessary to rotate your baking pans for even cooking.

To test for hot spots, heat your oven to 350°F (180°C) and place slices of baguette on either side in the back, on either side in the front, and in the middle. Wait 10 minutes and compare how the bread slices have browned. This will give you a good idea of how evenly your oven bakes and where it bakes more quickly. Some people recommend using a baking stone at all times in the oven, because the stone will absorb the heat of the oven and then radiate it evenly, minimizing hot spots. But be sure if you try this to test the oven temperature with an oven thermometer with the baking stone in place. These stones are so effective at absorbing heat that they may cause your oven to run 25 to 50°F (4–10°C) hotter than it would without a stone.

Q If my oven heats unevenly, will installing a HearthKit oven insert help?

A Made of the same ceramic material as baking stones, the HearthKit is a 3-sided oven insert that distributes heat throughout the oven evenly, similar to the way the walls of a brick oven work. If your oven heats unevenly, with hot spots, the HearthKit will solve this problem, producing evenly baked cakes and cookies with no pan rotation at all. It is an expensive solution, but may be worthwhile if you are also devoted to baking hearth breads and pizzas regularly. Note that the insert takes up quite a lot of space and will have to be removed when it's time to bake a very large item on the bottom rack, such as a Thanksgiving turkey or a Christmas roast.

HearthKit
insert

Q Do I always need to rotate my pans?

A Pan rotation is necessary only if your oven isn't the same temperature back to front, side to side. Unfortunately, most ovens don't maintain a uniform temperature throughout their interiors, making pan rotation necessary for most of us. If you are one of the lucky few with a perfectly even oven or if you use a convection oven that circulates air to maintain even temperature throughout, then don't worry about rotating your pans. If you know you have hotter and cooler spots, then rotating is a good idea.

It's never a good idea to overload your conventional oven (convection ovens can handle many more pans), because too many pans will inhibit the circulation of hot air, causing uneven baking. But most ovens can handle two or three pans at once, with proper rotation to ensure even baking. Make sure that pans have at least an inch of clearance between each other and the walls of the oven. If you are baking on two different racks, try to stagger the pans so that one isn't sitting directly below another, blocking the heat.

It's important not to rotate your pans too early during baking. Before baked goods have begun to set, their structure is fragile and their rise provisional. Air bubbles that are still expanding in the heat of the oven may shrink on contact with the cold air rushing in. Shaking a pan of unset batter even gently in the first minutes of baking may cause it to collapse. So wait until your baked goods have begun to set but are not yet brown before rotating.

In general, the back of the oven is hotter than the front. If you have only one pan in the oven, rotate it 180 degrees once during baking. If you have two pans on the same shelf, rest one on the oven door while you rotate the other and shift it to the other side of the oven. Then rotate the first pan and place it on the side opposite from where it was. If the pans are in the bottom and top thirds of the oven respectively, don't forget to rotate them 180 degrees when you switch their positions.

Some people like to bake two batches of cookies at once. To do this, place the racks in the top of the lower third and the bottom of the upper third of the oven before preheating. Stagger the baking sheets so they are not directly on top of one another.

Q I'd like to winnow my collection of potholders and oven mitts. How many do I really need?

A Generally speaking, oven mitts provide more protection of the hands and arms than potholders, while potholders provide some versatility, functioning as trivets for hot pans on the countertop. At the minimum, I'd have a pair of mitts and two potholders. Although not essential, a heatproof handle cover is nice to have for times when you are transferring a hot handled pan to the oven. Remember, however, that heatproof handle covers should be removed before you close the oven door. To avoid burns, it's definitely a good idea to go through your collection periodically and get rid of any fire-damaged or threadbare ones.

Q I'm in the market for new potholders and oven mitts. Which ones are the best — silicone, Kevlar, leather, or good old padded cotton terry?

A A confusing array of high-tech, expensive potholders and oven mitts have recently come onto the market. Are they worth the money? As far as protecting hands from heat, inexpensive padded cotton will allow you to hold a hot pan long enough to get it from the oven to a cooling rack. (Avoid thin cotton potholders, though, as they won't offer any more insulating protection than a folded kitchen towel.)

Potholders made of more expensive materials offer more. Silicone provides superior and extended protection from heat. With a pair of silicone mitts, you could hold a very hot pizza pan for minutes on end without feeling a thing. The question is, do you really need to hold a hot pan for minutes on end?

Silicone mitts can also come into contact with an open flame for several seconds without catching fire. Silicone is also easier to keep clean than traditional cotton, since it can be thrown into the dishwasher and comes out looking like new. Many bakers, however, object to silicone's relative inflexibility. The material is so heavy and stiff that it is sometimes difficult to feel whether or not your hands are in contact with the pan. Its bulk may present a problem when you are transferring delicate or small items — a thin tart baked in a pan with a removable bottom, for example — if it bumps up against them without your feeling it.

Padded Kevlar, the material used to make bulletproof vests, is an intriguing material for oven mitts, and works very well in protecting against heat. Like silicone, it won't burn after brief contact with flames. Mitts and potholders made of padded Kevlar are machine washable, but will become stained after months or years of use.

Leather and suede might look handsome and durable, but they offer less protection from heat than silicone, Kevlar, or heavy padded cotton. I got rid of a pair after a few burns and spills. Although the pair of leather potholders I purchased said they were machine washable, they bled dye even after repeated washings.

Q I just baked a fruit pie that bubbled over and made a real mess on the bottom of my oven. What is the best way to clean it?

A The cleaning method will depend on the type of oven you own. If possible, follow the manufacturer's instructions for cleaning. If the previous tenants failed to leave you with the oven manual, don't panic. First determine if you have a self-cleaning, textured, or non-self-cleaning oven, and then proceed according to the following instructions.

Most newer ovens have a self-cleaning feature. When in use, the oven door will automatically lock, and then the oven will heat to 900°F (482°C), burning off any leftover spills. No chemicals are necessary. The cleaning doesn't take long, but to protect owners from burns the oven door remains locked for about three hours, until the oven cools to a less dangerous temperature. If you have a particularly messy oven spill, you should wipe it up with a damp sponge when the oven cools. If you don't do this, there may be some smoke during the self-cleaning cycle. To save on energy and time, use the self-cleaning feature right after baking, making use of the residual heat.

Other ovens are "textured" or "continuous cleaning." This means they are lined with a rough-textured porcelain layer that spreads out and burns off food residue during regular baking. Continuous cleaning ovens do a good job with greasy and fatty messes, but may not burn off sticky sugar as effectively as self-cleaning ovens. You should still avoid using abrasives such as scouring pads and oven cleaners, which will destroy the textured layer. Instead, wipe away remaining food stuck to the bottom and sides with a damp cloth when your oven is cool.

If you have a regular old non-self-cleaning, non-continuous-cleaning oven, you'll need some oven cleaner and a little elbow grease. First, remove the oven racks and place them in soapy water to soak. Then follow the instructions on your oven cleaner. Some will direct you to preheat the oven to 200°F (95°C), turn off the oven, spray the interior, let stand, and then wipe with a damp sponge and dry with a clean cloth. Some will work overnight in a cool oven. Many home cooks, environmentally aware and bothered by the fumes given off by commercial oven cleaners, use a homemade paste of baking soda and water to clean their ovens. Spread the paste over the dirty surfaces, avoiding the heating elements, let stand overnight, and use a sturdy metal spatula to remove the dried paste in chunks. Wipe with a sponge and then a soft, dry cloth.

Q Cleaning my oven is such a pain! Should I invest in an oven liner before I bake another messy pie?

A Teflon-coated mats that fit on the bottom rack of an oven, catching spills, can be put through the dishwasher for easy cleaning. Follow the instructions on the package for placing the mat correctly. They normally rest on the floor of the oven, catching spills and crumbs, but, in some cases, the manufacturer will recommend placing the mat on the lower rack. Or you could simply do what my mother did before Thanksgiving or whenever she knew she'd be baking or roasting something messy: Place a sheet of heavy-duty aluminum foil on the bottom rack of the oven, tossing it and replacing it with a fresh one as necessary.

Microwave Sticky Toffee Pudding Cake

This traditional English dessert is the perfect cake to make in the microwave, because it is supposed to be sticky on the surface, rather than crisped or browned. Unlike conventional ovens, which perform similarly when set at the same temperature, microwave ovens can perform quite differently from each other. Depending on an oven's manufacturer, size, power, age, and a host of other variables, this cake can take anywhere from 3 to 8 minutes to bake. Use visual clues rather than a timer to judge its doneness: The surface of the cake should appear dry, and a cake tester inserted into the center will come out with just a few crumbs clinging. The cake will continue to bake with residual heat as it rests.

SERVES 6 TO 8

FOR THE SAUCE:

1¾ cups heavy cream

10 tablespoons packed dark brown sugar

¼ cup (½ stick) unsalted butter

½ teaspoon salt

FOR THE CAKE:

½ cup (1 stick) unsalted butter

½ cup packed light brown sugar

2 large eggs

1 cup unbleached all-purpose flour

2 teaspoons baking powder

¼ teaspoon salt

6 dried dates, pitted and chopped

1. To make the sauce, combine the cream, brown sugar, butter, and salt in a small saucepan. Bring to a boil over medium-high heat, stirring frequently. Turn down the heat to medium low and simmer until reduced by half, about 15 minutes. Set aside.

2. To make the cake, grease a 6-cup microwave-safe bowl. Cream the butter and brown sugar in a large bowl until fluffy, scraping down the sides of the bowl as necessary. Add the eggs and beat until smooth. Stir in the flour, baking powder, and salt; stir in the dates.

3. Scrape the batter into the prepared dish and cover with plastic wrap. Microwave on HIGH until just set, 3 to 8 minutes. Remove from the microwave and let stand 5 minutes. Overturn onto a serving platter, pour the sauce over the cake, and serve.

Q Is it possible to make real baked goods in a micro-wave oven?

A Most bakers completely reject the microwave oven for "real" baking, relegating it to prep tasks like melting chocolate and butter. If you've tried to bake a cake in the microwave, you know why. Because of the way a microwave oven heats food, doughs and batters don't develop a delicious outer crust enclosing a tender interior. Instead, a cake batter baked in a microwave will set up, but its surface will remain moist and sticky while its interior becomes spongy.

It helps to know a little bit about how a microwave cooks to understand this unpleasant effect. Contrary to popular belief, the microwave oven does not simply cook foods "from the inside out." Rather, it emits microwaves that are absorbed by the food. The energy contained in the microwaves causes molecules inside the food to start spinning, producing friction, which produces heat. This heat, generated by the food itself, is responsible for the cooking. Conventional ovens, in contrast, have a heat source of their own. The heat from the heating element gradually heats food through, evaporating surface moisture as it penetrates to the interior of a cake and produces the exterior browning valued in most baked goods.

If you are intent on baking in your microwave, stick to recipes that don't rely on browning. Probably your best bet is a pudding cake, which can be simply a very soft cake encasing some molten batter that becomes a sauce when the surface is broken with a spoon, or a spongy confection covered by a gooey sauce that's made separately on the stove.

122

CHAPTER 5

Quick Breads, Muffins, Scones & Biscuits

Recipes for quick breads were developed in the nineteenth century to make use of newly invented chemical leaveners. Breads made with these leaveners were remarkably easy to make, requiring no kneading and no rising time, and relatively little baking time compared with yeast breads. At the time, baking soda and baking powder were seen as signs of great progress, and some bakers thought these leaveners would replace yeast entirely before the century was over. Although baking with yeast has hardly become obsolete, quick breads have remained popular because of their simplicity and versatility. In this chapter, we'll clear up any questions you might have about making the best quick breads, muffins, scones, and biscuits.

Q Why are quick breads, muffins, biscuits, and scones always grouped together?

A They are all quick to make because they use baking soda, baking powder, or a combination of the two for a quick rise in the oven. Within this category are a wide range of baked goods with various shapes, flavors, and textures. They can be large (soda bread) or small (mini muffins), sweet (chocolate chocolate-chip muffins) or savory (cheddar cheese and chive scones), light and fluffy (angel biscuits) or moist and dense (zucchini bread).

SEE ALSO: Baking soda and baking powder, pages 29 and 30.

Q What are the biggest differences between them?

A I would divide quick breads, muffins, biscuits, and scones into two categories: Quick breads and muffins start as batters; biscuits and scones start as doughs. Batter is semiliquid while dough is thick and stiff. In a quick-bread batter, the ratio of flour to liquid is generally about three to two. Quick-bread doughs have a ratio of about three to one. Quick breads and muffins don't require any shaping because the batter is just scraped or spooned into a loaf pan or muffin tin before baking. Scones and biscuits need at least minimal shaping before baking. But most scones and biscuits are remarkably easy to shape, so this extra step shouldn't inhibit beginning bakers from trying those recipes.

A GLOSSARY OF QUICK BREADS

Here are the most common types of quick breads, with simple definitions.

Banana bread. A popular quick bread utilizing an often-wasted countertop item: overripe bananas.

Bannock. Scone dough that is pressed into a circle but baked in one large piece rather than cut into triangles before baking.

Biscuit. An American quick-bread classic. The plainest biscuits are made with flour, baking powder, butter, and milk. Buttermilk and baking soda give them a higher rise and a slightly tangy flavor. Cream biscuits skip the butter and get their fat from heavy cream. Biscuits can be varied by adding flavorings like herbs, spices, cheese, or bacon, or by substituting cornmeal, oats, whole-wheat flour, or other grains for some of the flour.

Baking-powder doughnuts. Sometimes called cake doughnuts, they contain chemical leaveners instead of yeast. To make them, you have to roll and cut quick-bread dough into doughnut shapes and then deep fry.

Beer bread. A quick bread leavened with baking powder but with a surprisingly yeasty flavor from beer.

Boston brown bread. A traditional whole-grain Northeastern quick bread flavored with molasses and baked in a coffee can to give it its distinctive shape.

Coffee cake. Right on the fine line between quick bread and cake is coffee cake. The richest and sweetest of quick breads, it can still be classified as such because the batter comes together so quickly, by incorporating the liquid ingredients into the dry, and the rising often relies solely on chemical leaveners.

Combination biscuit. Biscuit dough made with a combination of yeast and chemical leaveners. Also called angel biscuits.

Corn bread. Two regional styles define this quick bread. In the North, corn bread is made with yellow cornmeal, some sugar for sweetness, and a good dose of chemical leavening for a high rise and cakelike texture. In the South, white cornmeal predominates, and the corn bread tends to be less rich and more crumbly in texture.

Dumplings. A biscuit-type dough that is steamed in liquid rather than baked.

Fry bread. A Native American bread, leavened with baking powder and deep-fried in oil or lard.

Gingerbread. A spicy and aromatic quick bread with a springy texture, sweetened with molasses.

Hushpuppy. A small cornmeal dumpling, fried in oil or lard.

Irish soda bread. Originally a quick bread made of flour, baking soda, salt, and buttermilk, American versions often include eggs, sugar, butter, currants, and caraway seeds.

Johnnycake. Cornmeal griddlecake cooked on a griddle or in a pan on the stove, rather than in the oven.

Muffin. An individual-size quick bread made with batter and baked in a muffin tin. More moist than scones or biscuits from extra liquid, muffins also have a finer and more cakelike texture because of added eggs.

Pancakes, griddle cakes, and waffles. All are made with quick-bread batters, but baked in a stove-top pan, on a griddle, or in a waffle iron.

Popovers. Although not raised with chemical leaveners, popovers are still considered quick breads because they rise without the benefit of yeast. A simple batter made with milk, eggs, flour, salt, and melted butter expands in the oven, inflating into a balloonlike shape with a crispy outer shell and a moist interior. Although popovers can be made in a muffin tin, they will rise highest in a specially designed tin with straight-sided cups that push the batter upward.

Quick bread. This can be a blanket term for any number of baked goods raised with chemical leaveners, as it is used for this glossary's title. But it can also refer to a loaf-shaped sweet bread, similar to a cake but with less sugar and fat, often containing fruit and nuts for moisture and richness.

Scones. Lightly sweetened quick-bread pastries that can be dropped, rolled, or cut into triangle shapes.

Zucchini bread. A vegetable-based quick bread that can be either sweet or savory, especially popular in the late summer months when zucchini is at its most abundant.

Q My supermarket doesn't carry cake flour. Will all-purpose flour make good biscuits?

A To lower the protein content of all-purpose flour, replace 2 tablespoons of every cup of all-purpose flour with 2 tablespoons of cornstarch. This will make a "softer" flour, similar to low-protein cake flour. Be sure to whisk the cornstarch and flour together well before stirring the dry ingredients into the wet.

Q I see that many recipes in this category call for self-rising flour. What is this?

A Self-rising flour is a baking mix consisting of a lower-protein white flour (about 8% protein, as compared to all-purpose flour, which has 11%) with added baking powder and salt, which is why recipes calling for this type of flour don't include baking powder and salt. Self-rising flour makes quick bread and related recipes that much quicker to prepare.

Q If I run out of or can't find self-rising flour, what should I do?

A Largely passed over in favor of all-purpose and cake flour in many parts of the country, self-rising flour is still a key ingredient in the Southern baker's pantry. If you can't find self-rising flour in your supermarket, this doesn't mean you have to pass on recipes calling for it. To make 1 cup of self-rising flour, use 1 cup of cake flour (which also has a low protein content) whisked together with a teaspoon of baking powder and ¼ teaspoon of salt. (See Resources to order from the manufacturer.)

Q Is there a secret to tender, light-textured muffins? Whether I'm baking corn, blueberry, or bran muffins, they always come out too tough for my taste.

A As with other quick bread batters including those for loaf breads, pancakes, and waffles, muffin batter requires a "light hand." This means that after whisking the dry ingredients in one bowl and the wet ingredients in another, mix the two together very gently and quickly — less than 30 seconds with a wooden spoon is best. Longer than this and the gluten in the flour will begin to develop, leading to tough, rather than tender, muffins.

Q What can I do so that my muffins won't have large air bubbles and tunnels inside them?

A When you beat too much air into a batter, you create the large air bubbles that expand in the oven, leaving holes in the crumb of your muffins. Use a light hand, mixing the dry ingredients into the wet just until everything is moistened and a few lumps remain, and you should eradicate this problem.

Q How can I get the tops of my muffins to rise into tall peaks, instead of the slight mounds I always seem to wind up with?

A There are a couple of ways to encourage your muffins to rise to greater heights. Assuming that you are using the quick-bread method of mixing (mixing the wet ingredients in one bowl, the dry ingredients in another, and then combining the two), you can beat more air into your batter by whisking the eggs and sugar together by hand for a minute or two before whisking in the butter or oil and any other liquid.

Another way to encourage height is to preheat the oven to a very high temperature — about 500°F (260°C). When you put your muffins in the oven, close the door and turn the heat down to the recommended temperature (muffins usually bake at 375 to 400°F [190–200°C]). The initial burst of high heat will let the chemical leaveners in the batter work most efficiently. If you do this, be sure to shave a few minutes off the baking time to compensate for the high heat at the beginning of baking.

flat muffin

well-risen muffin

Q My muffins are always soggy instead of soft and cakelike. What am I doing wrong?

A Make sure you are measuring your ingredients correctly. Even just a tablespoon too much liquid can throw a recipe off, leaving the interior of your muffins damp instead of moist. Beyond that, check your oven temperature and baking time. Perhaps your muffins just need a few extra minutes in the oven to dry out sufficiently. Finally, unless you are instructed in the recipe to let the muffins cool in the pan, invert them onto a wire rack right out of the oven. When hot muffins sit in a muffin tin too long, they'll steam and become soggy.

Q Help! My blueberry muffins turned green in the oven!

A The baking soda in your recipe reacted with the alkali in the berries, tinting your batter green. You can prevent this from happening by mixing your berries with a little bit of flour before adding them to the batter.

Q I want to bake a small batch of 6 muffins, but my muffin tin has 12 cups. Can I just fill half of them?

A You can use a 12-cup muffin tin to bake 6 muffins, but put ½ cup water in the empty cups. Because of the efficient way a metal tin conducts heat, muffins baked in a tin with empty cups tend to burn before they are baked through, and the empty cups may buckle.

Q I have mini, regular, and jumbo muffin tins, and like to mix and match my recipes and tins. Is there a rule of thumb for adjusting cooking times depending on the size of your muffin tin?

A Exact times will vary depending on your recipe ingredients and your oven, but in general, shave 5 to 7 minutes off the recommended baking time if you are making mini muffins instead of the regular size. Add 8 to 12 minutes if you are using jumbo muffin tins. And of course, when in doubt, judge doneness with your eyes (muffin tops should look dry), your fingers (surface should spring back to the touch), and a cake tester (which should come out dry when inserted into the center of a muffin).

Q What's the best way to portion out muffin batter so all of my muffins come out the same size?

A Professional bakers rely on ice cream scoops for uniformly sized muffins. These scoops, come in various sizes, and can be used to scoop out perfect portions of cookie dough as well as muffin batter. Scoops marked with a number 20 or 24 will fill standard muffin cups about three-quarters full, just right for most muffin recipes.

Q Can I freeze leftover muffins? What about muffin batter?

A Leftover muffins can be wrapped individually in plastic wrap, placed in a resealable plastic bag, and frozen for up to 1 month. Let them thaw out on the counter for 30 minutes, and then reheat in a 350°F (180°C) oven for 5 to 8 minutes to refresh them. I actually prefer freezing batter to freezing baked muffins. It's simple and you can't beat the fresh-baked flavor and texture. To freeze muffin batter, line a muffin tin with foil liners, scoop batter into the liners, and freeze until firm, about 1 hour. Then transfer the batter, still in the liners, to a resealable plastic bag. When ready to bake, transfer them straight from the freezer to the muffin tin and oven, adding on an extra 8 to 10 minutes of baking time.

Q Can I substitute whole-wheat flour and other whole grains for some of the flour in my muffin and quick-bread recipes?

A Whole-wheat flour will give your muffin and quick-bread recipes a heartier flavor and a heavier texture. If these changes in the character of your recipe appeal to you, then go ahead and replace up to one-third of the white flour in your recipe with whole-wheat flour.

SEE ALSO: Whole-wheat flour, page 8.

Q Is there a difference between quick breads and muffins made with butter and those made with oil? Can I substitute one for the other?

A Butter and oil both moisten and enrich these batters. Butter adds its unique and wonderful flavor, while oil gives quick breads and muffins a longer shelf life. If you are relying on the creaming method to mix your batter and give your bread or muffins an extra lift, then you will have to substitute vegetable shortening, another solid fat, for softened butter, because a liquid oil won't hold air bubbles the way solid butter or shortening will. If using the quick-bread method of mixing, in which the dry ingredients are combined in one bowl while the wet ingredients are combined in another, before one bowl is dumped into the other, you can use oil or melted and cooled butter interchangeably, according to your preference.

SEE ALSO: Oil versus butter, page 22.

Q My zucchini bread recipe seems to work about half of the time, and the other half of the time my bread sinks in the middle toward the end of baking or minutes after I pull it out of the oven. What's going on?

A I am guessing that sometimes your zucchini contains more water than at other times. Too much liquid in a quick bread recipe can cause the bread to cave in, because it adds weight to the interior crumb that the gluten and egg structure can't support. For a more uniform result, seek out a recipe that instructs you to squeeze out the water from the grated zucchini before adding it to the batter.

Q Are there ways to cut the fat from a muffin or quick-bread recipe?

A Adapting a recipe to make it lower in fat is a process of trial and error. It's sometimes difficult to tell just by looking at an ingredient list which substitutions will be most successful. But there are a few general rules to follow. Simply reducing the quantity of fat in a muffin recipe will surely result in a tough, dry, and not terribly tasty product. Swapping egg whites for egg yolks will give you something dry and rubbery, because yolks add moisture and whites are a drying agent. The trick to successful low-fat baking is to leave some fat — one egg yolk, a few tablespoons of oil — in the recipe while replacing the rest with another ingredient that will add tenderness, moisture, and flavor to your quick breads and muffins. Some of the best low-fat recipes use fruit purées to replace most of the oil in standard recipes. Applesauce and mashed bananas work well. Prune purée, available in the kosher foods section of the supermarket, works well in chocolate muffin recipes. You can use these guidelines not only to adapt your own recipes, but to identify low-fat quick-bread and muffin recipes that will work.

Low-Fat Wheat-Bran Muffins

This recipe uses all the tricks of the trade to get the lowest possible fat content with the least loss of moisture and flavor. Instead of two eggs, I use one whole egg and two whites. I swap ¼ cup of vegetable oil for ¼ cup of applesauce. Nonfat buttermilk moistens the batter without added fat. Raisins add sweetness, but also calories, so if that's a concern just leave them out.

MAKES 12 MUFFINS

1 cup unbleached all-purpose flour
1 cup wheat bran
1¼ teaspoon baking powder
½ teaspoon baking soda
½ teaspoon salt
¼ cup sugar
2 tablespoons vegetable oil
¼ cup applesauce

¼ cup dark (not blackstrap) molasses
1 large egg
2 large egg whites
1 teaspoon vanilla extract
1 cup nonfat buttermilk
¾ cup raisins (optional)

1. Preheat the oven to 375°F (190°C). Line a 12-cup muffin tin with paper liners or coat it with cooking spray.
2. Combine the flour, wheat bran, baking powder, baking soda, salt, and sugar in a large mixing bowl. Add the oil, applesauce, molasses, egg, egg whites, vanilla, and buttermilk. Stir just until all the ingredients are moistened. Stir in the raisins.
3. Divide the batter evenly among the muffin cups. Bake until a toothpick inserted into the center comes out clean, 20 to 22 minutes. Let the muffins cool in the pan for 5 minutes, transfer to a wire rack to cool completely.

Q
Any other tips for using fruits and nuts in quick breads?

A
Fresh and dried fruits and nuts add moisture and flavor to quick breads. Here are some suggestions to help you get the most out of your fruits and nuts.

Fruit and Nut Tips

* **Take the time to toast your nuts** to bring out their flavor. Spread the nuts on a baking sheet and bake in a 350°F (180°C) oven until fragrant, 8 to 10 minutes. Let them cool completely before chopping them and mixing them into your batter (nuts that are still warm from the oven may heat up your batter, with adverse consequences for your finished bread).

* **For banana bread,** it is imperative that you use very brown, overripe (my children call them rotten) bananas for real banana flavor. Bright yellow bananas may taste great on their own, but mashed into quick bread batter they will be tasteless compared to much sweeter brown bananas.

* **For blueberry muffins,** smaller berries are better. Very large berries may sink to the bottom of the muffin cups. Even if they don't, as they bake they will give off large amounts of liquid, creating watery pockets in the finished muffins.

* **Frozen blueberries and cranberries** can be as good as fresh. When using frozen berries, add them to your batter straight from the freezer. If allowed to defrost, they will shed liquid, coloring your batter a strange blue or red (or green — see page 131).

* **Dried fruit should be moist,** soft, and pliable. If it isn't, it will draw moisture from the batter to rehydrate itself, making your quick bread or muffins dry. Purchase dried fruit only from a market where the turnover is high and care is taken with its storage. Individual airtight packages guarantee freshness. Open bins of dried fruit, sometimes found at natural-food stores, are the enemy of the fruit's moisture. If you have leftover fruit, place it in a resealable plastic bag and squeeze out as much air as possible before sealing. To bring desiccated dried fruit back to life, soak it in very hot tap water for 1 hour, drain, and pat dry before using.

* **Drain or cook off moisture** before adding fruits and vegetables to a batter. Carrots and zucchini can be grated, mixed with a little sugar, and set in a colander for 30 minutes to drain away excess liquid. Apples and pears can be grated and then squeezed between layers of paper towels, or sautéed with a little butter and sugar to cook off some of their moisture. This extra step will give your baked goods a better texture.

Q No matter what kind of quick bread I bake in my loaf pan, there is always a deep fissure down the middle of the finished bread. Did I do something wrong?

A The crack running from end to end of your bread is a normal result of baking. The surface of the bread has set before the interior batter is finished rising, so as this rising continues, the top splits open. Consider the crack a rustic decoration and a sign that your loaf is well-risen.

a well-risen loaf

Q What is Irish soda bread?

A The answer you get will depend on where you are asking the question. In the Unites States, Irish soda bread is a slightly sweet quick bread, enriched with a little butter, moistened with buttermilk, and flavored with raisins and caraway seeds. In Ireland, soda bread is a much leaner affair, a plain bread made with flour, baking soda and salt, and a cupful of buttermilk. Either way, the dough is shaped into a round, either tall or slightly flattened, with a cut in the shape of a cross as a religious symbol but also allowing for the characteristic splitting of the loaf into quarters as it bakes.

Q My quick-bread loaf is golden-brown on top, but the interior is underbaked. What should I do?

A If you've discovered this by inserting a cake tester into your loaf right out of the oven, simply return it to the oven, loosely tenting the top with foil so it won't burn, and continue to bake it until the cake tester comes out clean. If you've discovered this only after your cake has begun to cool, then there's not much you can do except try again after reading on.

Assuming that you are working from a well-written and reliable recipe, there are a few explanations for this uneven baking. First, you might check your oven temperature. If your oven runs as little as 25°F (4°C) warmer than what its setting indicates, your bread will bake too quickly on the outside without baking through on the inside. Check the temperature with an oven thermometer and adjust your dial accordingly.

Even if your oven is displaying an accurate temperature reading, it may be heating unevenly, with the air in the top half of the oven hotter than the air in the lower half. This won't affect the internal temperature of your bread, but it may cause the crust to brown too rapidly. Check on your loaf 10 minutes before it should be done. If the top looks very brown already, loosely tent it with foil to prevent burning.

And remember that even a slightly different pan size will alter the way a quick bread bakes. If your recipe calls for a 9-inch loaf pan and you're using an 8-inch loaf pan because that's all you have, your loaf will be thicker than the one the recipe author had in mind, and it will take longer to bake.

Q What is stone-ground cornmeal?

A Whichever color cornmeal you prefer, you are sure to like it even better if it is stone-ground rather than put through a commercial roller mill. In stone-grinding, water-powered mills grind corn between stones, retaining some of the nutritious hull and germ. In contrast, steel roller mills remove almost all of the hull and germ. Oils contained in the germ give stone-ground cornmeal its wonderful flavor and aroma, but the oils also give stone-ground cornmeal a shorter shelf life than commercial meal. Store it in the refrigerator or freezer in an airtight container and use it within four to six months of purchase. Look for stone-ground cornmeal in natural-food stores and in many supermarkets.

Q Can yellow and white cornmeal be used interchangeably in corn bread recipes?

A The biggest difference between yellow and white cornmeal is the color of the corn from which the meal was ground. Yellow cornmeal is ground from yellow corn and white is ground from white corn. In my opinion, yellow cornmeal tastes more like corn, and that's why I use it when making my own corn bread and muffins. But countless bakers, especially in the South where white cornmeal predominates, prefer white to yellow in baking.

Basic Corn Bread

Corn bread is one of the most versatile quick breads, and can be endlessly adapted according to taste and occasion. Use the following basic recipe, and then choose from the add-on ingredients listed on the next page to customize your corn bread.

SERVES 8

¾ cup unbleached all-purpose flour
1¼ cups yellow cornmeal
1 tablespoon sugar
2 teaspoons baking powder
1 teaspoon salt
6 tablespoons unsalted butter, melted and cooled
1 large egg
1¼ cups whole milk

1. Preheat the oven to 375°F (190°C). Coat the inside of an 8-inch square baking pan with cooking spray.
2. Combine the flour, cornmeal, sugar, baking powder, and salt in a medium bowl.
3. Whisk the butter, egg, and milk in a large mixing bowl. With a wooden spoon, stir in the flour mixture until just combined. Stir in any add-on ingredients (see the next page, if using).
4. Pour the batter into the prepared pan. Bake the corn bread until it is golden and a toothpick inserted into the center comes out clean, about 30 minutes. Let the corn bread cool for 5 minutes in the pan and serve it warm.

Corn Bread Add-ons	
INGREDIENT	AMOUNT
Double corn	1 cup fresh or frozen corn kernels
Cheddar, pepper jack, or smoked mozzarella cheese	1 cup shredded cheese
Parmesan cheese	⅔ cup grated cheese
Scallions	1⅓ cups chopped scallions
Jalapeño pepper	1 to 2 fresh peppers, seeded for a mild chile flavor, unseeded for spicy
Roasted red pepper	½ cup drained and chopped bottled peppers
Sun-dried tomatoes	½ cup drained and chopped oil-packed tomatoes
Bacon	8 ounces sliced bacon, cooked until crisp, drained, and crumbled
Lemon	Increase sugar to ½ cup; add 1½ tablespoons grated lemon zest
Blueberries or raspberries	Increase sugar to ½ cup; add 1½ cups berries, washed and picked over

Q How long will quick breads stay fresh? Can they be frozen?

A Lean quick breads such as Irish soda bread, and breads that don't have added dried fruits and nuts for moisture and richness, like corn bread, will get stale quickly and are best eaten on the day they are made. It's difficult to toast these breads because of their crumbly texture, and, unlike yeast breads, which become refreshed when reheated, quick breads dry out even more. Use stale leftover breads like these to stuff a chicken or a Thanksgiving turkey.

Moist, rich breads like banana bread or date-nut bread will keep for several days, wrapped in plastic, in the refrigerator. In some cases, they'll taste even better the day after baking, when the flavors have had a chance to meld. These breads also freeze well, so you might think about baking them two at a time, cooling them completely, and saving one for later by wrapping it in plastic, placing in a resealable plastic bag, and freezing for up to one month. Defrost on the countertop for a few hours and then rewarm in a 350°F (180°C) oven for 5 to 10 minutes before serving.

Q How is a scone different from a biscuit? How are they similar?

A If you live in the United States, the difference is simple. These two items are closely related, but biscuits generally don't have eggs or more than a spoonful of added sugar, while scones tend to contain one or both and are sweeter and more cakelike. Americans will serve biscuits with dinner, in place or rolls or bread. Biscuits sometimes contain cheese, chopped ham or bacon, and/or herbs, making them even more savory. We usually enjoy scones at breakfast or as a snack when we crave something a little sweet. Our scones can contain raisins, currants, or other dried fruits.

Of course, there are examples of sweet biscuits and savory scones in the United States, and in England the terminology is a little different. A scone will more often than not resemble an American-style biscuit, with or without currants or other chopped dried fruit but little added sugar. Ask for a "biscuit," and you'll get a cookie.

But their differences are not as important as their similarities. Biscuits and scones use the same mixing method, in which cold butter is cut into the dry ingredients before the addition of liquid, to encourage a high rise. Both doughs should be kneaded as gently and quickly as possible for a tender result. And both are best warm from the oven, as they will become hard and dry in a matter of hours.

Q Is there a secret to baking tender, light scones?

A Make sure your butter is well chilled, don't overmix the dough, and bake the scones in a very hot oven until just cooked through.

Scottish Oat Scones

These scones contain two parts flour to one part rolled oats, which gives them a balance between light and pleasantly chewy. I suggest 1 stick of butter, but you can reduce the amount to 4 tablespoons or increase it to 10 depending on how lean or rich you like them.

Substituting one egg for ¼ cup of the milk in most scone recipes will make your scones less crumbly.

MAKES 12 SCONES

2 cups unbleached all-purpose flour

1 cup old-fashioned (not quick-cooking) oats

⅓ cup sugar

1 tablespoon baking powder

½ teaspoon salt

½ cup (1 stick) unsalted butter, cut into bits and chilled

¾ cup whole or low-fat milk

1 large egg, lightly beaten

1. Preheat the oven to 425°F (220°C). Coat a baking sheet with cooking spray or line it with parchment paper.
2. Combine the flour, oats, sugar, baking powder, and salt in a large mixing bowl. Add the chilled butter and, with an electric mixer on low speed or with your fingers, work the butter into the dry ingredients until the mixture resembles coarse meal. Using a wooden spoon, stir in the milk and egg and mix just until the dry ingredients are moistened. Do not overmix.
3. Transfer the dough onto a lightly floured work surface and divide it in half. Shape each half into a 6-inch disk. With a sharp chef's knife, cut each disk into six wedges.
4. Place the wedges ½ inch apart on the prepared baking sheet. Bake until golden, about 15 minutes. Let cool for 5 minutes and serve warm.

Q Are scones always cut into triangle shapes?

A Traditionally, scone dough is patted or rolled into a disk, and then the disk is cut into quarters or sixths, resulting in triangle-shaped pastries. But almost as often in England and throughout the United Kingdom, scone dough is rolled and cut into rounds just like American-style baking-powder biscuits. And there is no law against dropping mounds of scone dough onto a baking sheet for more rustic-looking, irregularly shaped scones.

Q Why do so many biscuit and scone recipes contain buttermilk?

A Originally a byproduct of churned butter, today buttermilk is made the way yogurt and sour cream are, by fermenting milk with a bacterial culture. When buttermilk combines with baking soda in a quick bread batter, the result is the creation of many carbon dioxide bubbles, which expand in the oven, giving the bread a particularly light and fine texture. This texture, along with a pleasant tang and welcome moisture, are buttermilk's gift to quick breads. Regular milk and baking powder may be substituted for buttermilk and baking soda (see pages 29 and 30 for using baking powder in place of baking soda), but the result won't have that old-fashioned flavor that comes from buttermilk.

Q Is "Southern" flour best for biscuits?

A Southern brands of flour, such as White Lily or Martha White, have a lower protein content than all-purpose flour from national and Northern producers such as Pillsbury, Gold Medal, and King Arthur, and will produce biscuits with a more tender crumb and a moister interior than those baked with all-purpose flour. If these are characteristics that you value in a biscuit, you can either seek out one of these specialty flours (see Resources), or make your own lower-protein flour by substituting cake flour for half of the all-purpose flour in your recipe.

Q What about fat? Will shortening make flakier biscuits, as with piecrust?

A Shortening will produce slightly flakier biscuits, because of its leavening power. In addition, biscuits made with shortening will stay fresher longer than those made with butter. But swapping butter for shortening will result in a great loss of flavor, a loss that in my opinion is definitely not worth the small gains of flakiness and shelf life. If you are devoted to designing your own perfect biscuit recipe, it might be fun to play with various combinations of butter and vegetable shortening (25:75; 50:50; 72:25) to see if you agree.

And remember, fat isn't the only thing that affects flakiness. Technique plays a large role in turning out flaky biscuits and scones. For super-flaky biscuits and scones, try folding the dough as you would a sheet of puff pastry. Gently roll it out to a thickness of ⅜ inch, fold it in half, and gently roll it out again. The layers you've folded in will result in flaky layers inside your biscuits.

Q Why is it so important to use cold butter when making biscuits and scones?

A The idea is to keep the butter from melting as you put together your biscuit or scone dough, so that it melts inside the oven, leaving the steam pockets and layers that characterize good biscuits and scones. With this in mind, it's a good idea to keep all of your ingredients cold, which will help keep the butter cold. Not only should you freeze your butter before you begin — it should be so cold that it chips when you cut it into pieces — but your milk or buttermilk should be icy cold, too. Don't stop there: Why not put your mixing bowl into the freezer for 10 minutes as extra insurance against melting? Attention to these details will pay off in superior biscuits and scones.

Q What is the difference between using milk, buttermilk, and cream in biscuit dough? Is one better than the others?

A Biscuits made with baking powder and milk are wholesome, delicious, and above all convenient, since most people will have on hand the ingredients — flour, milk, baking powder, salt, and a little bit of sugar — every day of the week. Many bakers prefer buttermilk for the slightly tangy flavor it gives to biscuits, but also because the acid in buttermilk reacts explosively with the chemical leaveners, giving these biscuits the highest rise. In recipes for cream biscuits, cream stands in for both milk or buttermilk and butter, eliminating the need for cutting the butter into the flour. The resulting biscuits are fluffy and tender, but without the characteristic flakiness of either baking powder or buttermilk biscuits.

MAKE YOUR OWN BUTTERMILK

Most quick bread, biscuit, and scone recipes don't call for more than 1 cup of buttermilk. If you use buttermilk infrequently, you might want to skip buying it a quart at a time and then throwing out the leftovers. Instead, replace the buttermilk with soured milk made by adding 1 tablespoon of white vinegar or lemon juice to 1 cup of whole milk and letting it stand for 5 minutes.

Dried buttermilk powder is also available and can be used in place of fresh buttermilk as a baking ingredient.

Q Is it better to mix biscuit and scone dough by hand or with an electric mixer? What about biscuit dough made in a food processor?

A Although bakers will argue endlessly about the best mixing method for biscuit and scone dough, there are two things they agree on: The proper distribution of fat during mixing; and the quick and careful addition of liquid ingredients are the keys to great biscuits.

Older recipes direct bakers to "rub" chilled butter into the dry ingredients until the mixture resembles coarse meal with some larger crumbs. When the large and small pieces of butter melt in the hot oven, space is freed up for expanding gases, which help the biscuits rise. It is imperative that the butter remain cool. If it melts before it reaches the oven, its purpose as leavening aid is defeated. People with quick and cool hands like to rub the butter into the dry ingredients with their fingertips. Others (myself included) use the paddle attachment of the electric mixer, because warm hands can melt butter before it is properly incorporated. Still others believe that a few pulses in the food processor is the most surefire method.

As for adding the liquid, a few stirs by hand with a wooden spoon is all it should take to incorporate it into the flour and butter mixture. If you are already using an electric mixer, add the liquid and mix on the lowest speed until the mixture just comes together. Adding the liquid ingredients to the food processor will almost certainly lead to overmixing, so if you want to use the food processor to cut the butter into the flour, transfer this mixture to a mixing bowl before mixing in the liquid by hand.

Q What are the differences between dropped biscuits and rolled biscuits?

A The most obvious difference is that dropped biscuits are easier to make. Instead of rolling out and cutting the dough, you simply drop spoonfuls directly onto a baking sheet. The dough for dropped biscuits usually contains more liquid, which makes for a very moist and tender interior. Rolled biscuits, in contrast, have a flaky, almost layered texture, which they get from light kneading and gentle rolling (it is important not to overdo it at either of these stages). When you knead and then roll out the dough, you flatten little pieces of butter into flakes, which then melt in the oven, leaving air pockets that fill with steam.

dropping "dropped" biscuit dough

Q What is the best way to roll and cut biscuit dough?

A Overworking the dough will develop gluten in the flour and result in tough biscuits. So, as when mixing, be as gentle as possible when rolling and cutting. In fact, it's best to use the rolling pin as little as possible in getting your dough from the mixing bowl to the oven. Turn out your dough onto a lightly floured surface and very gently pat it into a ¾-inch-thick disk. Lightly roll over the dough with a floured rolling pin to even out the surface. Then use a biscuit cutter to get as many biscuits out of the disk as possible. After transferring your biscuits to a greased or parchment-lined baking sheet, don't reroll the dough. Gently push the scraps together to form a new disk, and cut with a biscuit cutter again. This second batch may not be as perfectly smooth on top as the first batch, but will have the same tenderness from your gentle handling.

SEE ALSO: How flour helps baked goods rise, page 90.

Q Why do biscuits and scones need to be baked at such a high temperature?

A At temperatures of 425°F (220°C) and above, butter melts quickly and produces steam, which lifts biscuits and scones to lofty heights. At a lower temperature, say 350°F (180°C), you'd get a less dramatic rise and a heavier product. Another benefit to high-heat baking: There is less time for moisture to evaporate, so your biscuits and scones won't dry out as they bake through. I bake my biscuits in a 500°F (260°C) oven to reap the full benefits of high heat, but take care with my scones, which have quite a bit of added sugar. At temperatures above 425°F (220°C) the sugar in the scones may burn, leaving you with blackened rather than beautifully golden pastries.

Q My scones and biscuits don't seem to rise as high as they should, even though I'm using the right amounts of ingredients, making sure my butter is chilled, mixing with a light hand, and baking in a very hot oven. Any idea what I'm doing wrong?

A First, check the expiration date on your baking powder. If it's been sitting in the pantry since the Clinton Administration, go out and buy a fresh supply.

If your biscuit cutter, chef's knife, or pizza cutter isn't sharp, or you are not cutting cleanly and incisively, your cutter's edge may be compressing your dough layers at the edges, causing them to stick together so they are unable to separate into flaky layers and rise high in the oven.

Sometimes a recipe will instruct you to glaze the tops of your scones with a beaten egg to give the scones a shiny finish. Be careful, as you would when working with puff pastry (see page 285), to brush just the tops, and not the sides of the scones. An egg wash on the sides of cut scones will dry out quickly in the oven, holding the dough back from rising to its potential height.

Q How do I tell when my biscuits and scones are done baking?

A Because these items are relatively small and bake at such a high temperature, the difference between baking them to perfection and overbaking them so that they are dry and hard is a matter of a minute or two. Don't overbake them. Chances are, if they are golden brown on the outside they will be dried out on the inside. As soon as your biscuits and scones are well-risen and just beginning to color, remove them from the oven. Let them cool on the baking sheet for 5 minutes, during which time they will continue to firm up inside from residual heat.

Q Can freshly baked biscuits and scones be frozen and reheated?

A Biscuits are best eaten fresh from the oven, and are so quick to make that you can have them on the table in less than 30 minutes from the time you start gathering your ingredients, if you are efficient and skilled. If at all possible, mix a fresh batch of biscuit dough when you need it.

Leftover biscuits may be frozen in a resealable plastic bag. Defrost them on the countertop and reheat them for a minute or two in a 500°F (260°C) oven, which will refresh them but won't restore 100 percent of their just-baked goodness. If you know you can't possibly eat all of the biscuits you are cutting, I suggest you freeze the unbaked biscuits, rather than bake and then freeze. You can bake these straight from the freezer, adding a minute or two onto your recipe's baking time, and the biscuits will taste as if you mixed the batter up that day.

CHAPTER 6

Cookies

Just because cookies are less fancy than layer cakes and require fewer steps than baking sourdough bread doesn't mean that they are undeserving of the kind of care you'd take with these bigger baking projects. Any cookie worth making is worth making well. In this chapter I aim to answer the questions you might have about making the best possible cookies.

COOKIE CATEGORIES

Here is a breakdown of the different types of cookies, from kid-simple bars to what you may have thought of as pastry chef degree–required meringues and macaroons.

Drop cookies. All in all the simplest variety, drop cookies are so called because to form them you simply drop balls of dough onto a baking sheet.

Hand-formed cookies. Instead of dropping the dough, you'll roll it or otherwise form it into balls, crescents, and other shapes, sometimes crosshatching with a fork (as with classic peanut butter cookies), sometimes leaving an impression in the center with your thumb, later to be filled with jelly or chocolate ganache. This category also includes more exotic varieties such as French tuiles and Italian biscotti.

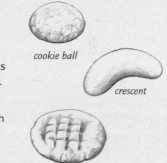

cookie ball

crescent

cross-hatched cookie

Bar cookies. Many recipes for bar cookies, including brownies and blondies, require nothing more than mixing dough and spreading it across the bottom of a baking pan. But the bar cookie category includes many layered treats, which take a bit more work. Lemon bars have a pastry crust topped with a lemon custard topping. Pecan bars have a pastry crust with a caramel and nut topping.

Rolled cookies. You'll need a rolling pin and a sharp paring knife or cookie cutters to make rolled cookies, including rolled sugar cookies and gingerbread men.

Icebox or slice-and-bake cookies.
To make these cookies, you shape
dough into logs, refrigerate or
freeze the logs, and then slice off
rounds for baking.

icebox cookie dough

Piped and molded cookies.
These include spritz cookies, which
are pressed out of a cookie gun;
a variety of cookies (such as
madeleines) baked in molds; and
cookies such as ladyfingers, macaroons, and meringues, which are
shaped by piping batter through a
pastry bag.

Filled cookies. Cookie dough
can be spread with filling and
rolled up (rugelach are a good
example) or sandwiched with filling (whoopee pies).

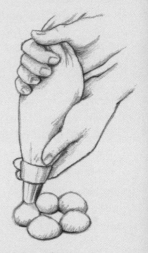

piping meringues

whoopee pie

158

Q Are there rules of thumb common to all types of cookie baking?

A Making cookies is so familiar to most people that the idea of it rarely induces anxiety. But don't get too relaxed — it's important to follow certain rules, most of them common to all types of baking, for guaranteed success.

Cookie Rules

* **Preheat the oven.** It's especially important when baking small items like cookies that the oven be up to temperature when baking begins.

* **Gather and measure your ingredients carefully.** Cookies may seem more casual and improvisational than cakes or breads, but the same scientific principles and chemical formulas that govern cake-baking and bread-baking apply to cookies. A few tablespoons of extra flour or the careless substitution of baking powder or baking soda will affect the final product. Learn what "packed" brown sugar means, master the dip-and-sweep method of measuring flour, and you will be fine.

* **Handle the ingredients properly.** If the recipe tells you to chop nuts coarsely, don't chop them finely. Sifting cocoa powder is a pain, but if the recipe specifies it, there is probably a good reason. Unless otherwise specified, liquid ingredients like milk and eggs should be at room temperature. If the recipe calls for softened butter, don't try to get away with ice-cold butter.

* **Take care to leave as much space as directed between cookies on the baking sheet.** If you don't leave enough space between cookies (2 inches is usually enough, but sometimes you'll need more), you can wind up with one big cookie in the end. Also be careful to make the cookies equal in size. When small items like these vary by even a teaspoon or two, baking time is dramatically affected. You don't want your smallish cookies to overbake before your larger ones are done.

* **Be patient and careful when removing hot cookies from a baking sheet.** Some types of cookies are very soft when they come out of the oven. It's best to let them firm up for a few minutes on the baking sheet before attempting to transfer them. When you do transfer them, use a wide spatula with a thin metal blade to get right under the cookies without damaging them. Very soft cookies may droop over a spatula that isn't wide enough to hold them, and then break. Rubber and silicone spatulas, which are thicker than metal pancake turner-type spatulas, might break the cookies as you attempt to lift them from the sheet. Spatula size is irrelevant if you line your baking sheets with parchment paper—then you can simply slide the parchment paper, with the cookies on top of it, right onto a wire rack to cool immediately. When your cookies are cool, they will effortlessly peel away from the paper.

Q What is the best way to soften butter if I'm in a hurry to bake cookies?

A Butter takes about 30 minutes to soften to a pliable but not melty stage, between 65 and 68°F (18–20°C) on an instant-read thermometer. (On a warm day this might take less than 30 minutes. If your kitchen is very cool, it will take longer.) To hasten the process, cut the butter into small pieces and lay it out on a flat surface such as a cutting board or plate. This should cut the softening time by half. The more of the butter's surface that is exposed to room-temperature air, the more quickly it will soften. Another method you might try is to grate cold butter on the large holes of a box grater. But be careful that the heat of your hands doesn't melt the butter as you grate it.

Professional pastry chefs often soften butter manually, by repeatedly pounding it with a rolling pin, when they need it to be pliable but still cold (as when making the butter packet for puff pastry, see page 278). To do this at home, cut your butter into pieces and place the pieces between two sheets of wax paper or parchment before gently pounding with a rolling pin, flipping the paper so you pound each piece once or twice on each side. Lazy bakers with a KitchenAid or other powerful mixer might consider simply cutting the butter into pieces and softening it manually by beating it with the paddle attachment before adding sugar to the bowl.

Oatmeal Chocolate Chip Cookies

This recipe calls for melted butter, which will cause the cookies to spread, rather than puff up, as they bake. Use mini chocolate chips, which work better in the flat cookies than regular-size chips.

MAKES 32 COOKIES

1 cup unbleached all-purpose
    flour
½ teaspoon baking soda
¼ teaspoon salt
14 tablespoons unsalted butter,
    melted and cooled
¾ cup granulated sugar

½ cup packed light brown sugar
1 large egg
1 teaspoon vanilla extract
2½ cups old-fashioned (not
    quick-cooking) oats
1 cup mini chocolate chips

1. Preheat the oven to 350°F (180°C). Line several baking sheets with parchment paper.
2. Whisk the flour, baking soda, and salt in a mixing bowl.
3. Combine the butter, granulated sugar, and brown sugar in a large mixing bowl, using an electric mixer on low to stir until blended. Beat in the egg and vanilla until incorporated.
4. With the mixer still on low, add the flour mixture, ½ cup at a time, until incorporated. Stir in the oats and chips.
5. Drop heaping tablespoonfuls of the dough onto the baking sheets, at least 2½ inches apart. Bake the cookies, one sheet at a time, until they are golden around the edges and just set in the centers, 12 to 15 minutes.
6. Slide the cookies, still on the parchment paper, onto wire racks to cool completely.

Q Can I substitute vegetable shortening for the butter in a cookie recipe? How will the cookies differ from cookies made with butter?

A Vegetable shortening in an equal amount will work in any cookie recipe calling for solid butter, but there will be differences in both texture and flavor. Cookies made by creaming shortening with sugar will rise higher and have a lighter texture than cookies made by creaming butter with sugar. Shortening captures more air during creaming than butter, and already contains gas bubbles which will expand during baking. But even if you prefer light, high cookies to flat, chewy ones, I would beg you to stick with butter. Vegetable shortening is neutral in flavor, adding nothing to the taste of your cookies. Butter not only adds its own fantastic flavor but also enhances the flavors of the other ingredients, making your chocolate more chocolaty and your spices more piquant.

Q I microwaved my butter to soften it, and it partially melted. Can I refrigerate it until it solidifies and then use it in cookie dough?

A I don't recommend softening butter in the microwave for exactly this reason. The risk of melting is just too high. Melting causes the milk solids and water in butter to separate from the butterfat. This separation will affect the way the butter interacts with sugar when the two are beaten together, and in the oven, will affect the structure of your cookies. Refrigerating the butter until it solidifies again will not restore it to its previous emulsified state.

So what should you do if this happens? It depends on the recipe and your taste. Many recipes specifically call for creamed butter to give the finished cookies a relatively puffy shape and light texture. If this is the case with your recipe, then set aside the melted butter for another use (put it on tonight's vegetables or make some garlic bread to go with dinner) and start over with solid butter. But melted butter doesn't necessarily spell disaster for a cookie recipe, the way it most certainly does for, say, a pound cake that relies on air trapped in the cold butter to rise. If you don't mind chocolate chip cookies that are flat and chewy (some people prefer them this way) rather than puffed and soft, then you can replace solid butter with melted butter in your recipe and enjoy the results very much.

Q My recipe calls for softened butter. Should my eggs be at room temperature, too?

A Experienced cake bakers are careful to bring all liquid ingredients, including eggs, to room temperature along with their butter. Room temperature eggs are just as important when making cookie dough. Even if your butter is properly softened and creamed to a light, fluffy state with the sugar, your batter will curdle if you then add very cold eggs. Remove your eggs from the refrigerator when you remove your butter. Or bring them to room temperature by placing them in a bowl of hot tap water for 5 minutes.

Q How do I know when my butter and sugar are properly creamed together?

chunky butter and sugar

A These ingredients go through several stages before they reach the creamed stage. At first your butter and sugar mixture will be chunky. Then it will be sandy. Soon afterward, it will look like the mixer is flattening the butter and sugar against the sides of the bowl. Then, after 2 or 3 minutes, you will notice that the butter has lightened from pale yellow to off white, and the mixture has become fluffy, due to the air that you have beaten into the butter with the aid of the sugar crystals — now it is properly creamed.

sandy mixture

fluffy, properly creamed butter and sugar

Q Is it necessary to sift the dry ingredients together before adding them to the creamed butter mixture?

A Sifting was important in the days before flour was presifted during packaging and contained lumps that needed to be broken up before using. But today's flour is lump-free, so sifting is not a concern. When I write a cookie recipe, I do direct readers to combine all of the dry ingredients — flour, baking powder, baking soda, salt — in a mixing bowl and whisk them together before adding them to the liquid ingredients. Whisking helps to evenly distribute the leaveners and salt throughout the cookie dough. I do use my fine strainer to sift cocoa powder into the bowl if it is included in the dry ingredients, because it is not presifted and often contains pesky lumps.

Q I just realized I'm out of brown sugar. What will happen if I use granulated sugar in my chocolate chip or oatmeal cookie recipe instead?

A You can replace brown sugar with white sugar. Just be aware that your cookies will be more crisp, because white sugar has less moisture than brown, and they won't have that hint of molasses flavor from the molasses in brown sugar. Likewise, you can swap brown sugar for white sugar in cookie recipes, keeping in mind that your cookies will be more moist and chewy than cookies made with white sugar alone. Also, light and dark brown sugar can be used interchangeably, with dark brown sugar giving your cookies a more intense molasses flavor.

Q I'd like to give my drop cookies a more professional look. What is the best way to shape them so they come out of the oven uniform and beautiful?

A I rely on my #40 ice cream scoop (see Resources) to make perfectly round chocolate chip, oatmeal, and other drop cookies. For extra-large cookies, I use a #16 scoop, which holds about ¼ cup of dough. Dipping the scoop into the batter and then scraping it against the side of the bowl to flatten the bottom ensures that each cookie will be exactly the same size, and each one will be perfectly rounded.

Q I underbaked my chocolate chip cookies as you suggest in your recipe (page 162), but now that they are cooled, I realize they are way too soft. Can I return them to the oven at this point?

A Absolutely. Drop cookies like these can be crisped up in the oven with a minute or two of additional baking, even after they've cooled.

Q My daughter is allergic to nuts. Can I just leave the nuts out of a drop cookie recipe and proceed?

A Nuts don't just add flavor to cookie dough — they contribute to the cookies' texture and volume, and also affect the recipe's yield. If you simply leave out the nuts, be aware that your cookies won't have the same shape (they'll probably spread a little more), and you'll get fewer cookies in the end. To maintain the recipe's balance, you can substitute an equal amount of another add-in, such as chocolate chips or raisins.

Q The last few chocolate chip cookies I portion out never have any chocolate chips. Are there any tricks to preventing this?

A Here are two tips: As you are portioning out your dough, regularly scrape down the sides of the bowl with a rubber spatula, incorporating the dough stuck to the sides (which doesn't have any chips) into the larger mass containing all of the chocolate chips. And keep a tablespoon or two of chocolate chips in reserve when adding the bulk of them to the dough, to mix into the dough you have remaining at the end.

Q Can any drop cookie recipe become a bar cookie recipe and vice versa?

A Most drop cookies can become bar cookies. It will be up to you to figure out what size pan you'll need and how long they'll need to bake. To give you an idea, a standard chocolate chip cookie dough recipe contains 2¼ cups of flour, 1½ cups of sugar, and 2 eggs. This amount of cookie dough is just right for a 9- by 13-inch pan or two 8-inch square pans. Just spread the dough evenly across the bottom of a pan lined with nonstick foil and bake until a few moist crumbs stick to a toothpick inserted into the center. You don't want to spread the dough too thin when making bar cookies, or your bars will dry out.

Adapting a bar cookie recipe to make drop cookies is a bit trickier because many bar cookie batters are just that, loose batters that will run and spread when baked as cookies. Think about your standard brownie batter, and you will understand the problem. For round, bite-size versions of my favorite bars, I prefer to portion out the bar cookie batter into mini-muffin tins to help the batter keep its shape. Depending on the size of your mini-muffin tin, these mini brownies and bars will take 12 to 18 minutes to bake, much quicker than brownies and bars in a larger baking pan, which can take upwards of 35 minutes to bake through.

Q Most recipes tell you to melt chocolate for brownies in a double boiler or in a bowl set over a pot of barely simmering water. Why can't I melt chocolate right in a pot on top of the stove?

A On its own, chocolate needs to be handled with care, because if it is overheated it will scorch and burn. When this happens, it melts into a lumpy and dull mass rather than a smooth and shiny semiliquid. To melt chocolate successfully, it is best to use indirect heat, such as on top of a double boiler. There are other indirect heating methods that you can use: Place your chocolate in a heatproof bowl and put it in an oven at the lowest setting, whisking it every couple of minutes until it is smooth. Or melt chocolate in a microwave oven, checking on it every 20 seconds or so to make sure you aren't overheating it. From personal experience I can tell you that it is much easier to ruin chocolate in a microwave than on top of a double boiler. Whichever method you choose, be sure to chop the chocolate finely and evenly before beginning. If you put uneven chunks of chocolate over even indirect heat, you risk overheating the smaller pieces that have melted first.

When you are melting chocolate with butter, as is usually the case with brownies, it's still best to heat it gently over simmering water in a double boiler, but it is possible to do so successfully directly on top of the stove if you must. Here's how: Melt the butter over a very low flame first, then add the chopped chocolate and stir until smooth. If you just throw solid butter and solid chocolate into the pot at the same time, some of the chocolate will become overheated from direct contact with the metal of the pot before the butter is able to melt and act as a protective shield.

Q My brownies taste fine, but have a cracked surface and a ridge around the outside edge. When I cut into them the surface shatters into large shards. How can I get a smooth surface that's less fragile and easier to cut?

A Take care not to beat too much air into your brownie batter. If you do this, the air bubbles will expand in the oven, only to deflate when the brownies cool, leaving you with the fallen center and cracking that you describe. A few stirs with a wooden spoon or a few seconds on low with an electric mixer should be enough to moisten all the ingredients.

Q Are there other secrets to better-looking bar cookies?

A I often line my baking pan with nonstick aluminum foil before filling it with cookie dough. So instead of having to dig out that first brownie with a spatula (and probably destroying it in the process), I just lift the foil from the pan when the cookies are cooled and slice them into neat squares.

The best bar cookies are slightly underbaked in the center. If they're not, then the bars closest to the edge of the pan will definitely be overbaked. But underbaked bars are very soft and can crumble when cut. To make neat squares, freeze the cooled but uncut cookies for 15 minutes to firm them up and then cut straight down with a sharp chef's knife rather than dragging the knife across the bars.

brownies baked on foil liner

Q What is the best way to make an even bottom crust for my bar cookies?

A After pressing the dough mixture into your pan with your fingertips, press down on it again with the smooth bottom of a juice glass. If the pastry is sticky, flour the bottom of the glass before and during the process or cover it with plastic wrap.

Q The pastry crusts of my lemon bars and pecan bars are always a little oily rather than moist and crumbly. What am I doing wrong?

A If you are melting butter to make these crusts, make sure to cool it before stirring it into the dry ingredients to avoid oiliness. If you are mixing solid butter with dry ingredients, your butter may be too soft and warm. In either case, if your crust looks shiny and oily before you bake it, put the pan into the freezer for 5 minutes to let the butter solidify.

Q What is the best way to roll cookie dough into logs to make slice-and-bake cookies?

A To form evenly shaped logs, which will become uniformly round cookies, pinch and press the dough into a rough log of the length specified in your recipe. Then transfer the log to a piece of parchment paper or wax paper and roll it inside the paper to smooth and round it. Tap each end on the counter to flatten the tapered ends.

Q Are there other tricks to getting evenly shaped slice-and-bake cookies?

A When you are ready to cut, remember to rotate the log of dough often, so that one side doesn't become flattened by the repeated pressure of the knife.

Q How long does slice-and-bake dough need to be refrigerated? How long will it keep in the refrigerator or freezer?

A Don't forget that these are also called icebox cookies. The dough needs time, at least 3 hours, to chill before it can be sliced. Unchilled dough will be squashed by your knife as you cut through it. If you are in a hurry, you can pop the dough logs in the freezer for an hour and a half, and you can freeze the dough, well-wrapped in plastic and then in foil, for up to 1 month. But don't try to slice dough straight from the freezer, or it may crumble. If your dough is frozen solid, let it soften slightly on the counter for 15 to 20 minutes before using.

Q My biscotti are as hard as rocks. What did I do wrong?

A Absolutely nothing! Traditional Italian biscotti are supposed to be very hard and dry, so they won't fall apart when dunked into sweet wine or coffee. But if you would like to bake more yielding biscotti, simply reduce the second baking time by about 5 minutes so they retain more moisture.

Crispy-Chewy
Espresso-Walnut Biscotti

Ever since my friend Jane broke a tooth on some of my peanut brittle several years ago, I've tried not to serve anything that could cause a dental emergency.

The traditional recipe for Italian biscotti includes whole almonds, which can become quite hard themselves when baked. To make my biscotti less dangerous, I use cake flour and chopped walnuts, which are more yielding, and brown sugar, which adds moisture. After slicing the cookie logs and returning the cookies to the oven, I watch them carefully, pulling them from the oven when their centers are still a little moist and soft.

If you have the time and the interest, you can place the cooled cookies on a parchment-lined baking sheet and drizzle them with melted bittersweet chocolate. Let stand until the chocolate is set before serving.

MAKES ABOUT 24 BISCOTTI

2 cups cake flour

½ cup sugar

½ cup packed light brown sugar

1 tablespoon instant espresso powder

½ teaspoon baking powder

¼ teaspoon salt

4 large eggs

1 tablespoon vegetable oil

1 teaspoon vanilla extract

1 cup walnut pieces, coarsely chopped

1. Preheat the oven to 350°F (180°C). Line a baking sheet with parchment paper.

2. Combine the flour, granulated sugar, brown sugar, espresso powder, baking powder, and salt in a large mixing bowl. Add 3 of the eggs, the oil, and the vanilla, and beat with an electric mixer on low speed until just combined. Mix in the walnuts.

3. Turn the dough out onto a lightly floured work surface and divide it in half. Shape each half into a flat log about 12 inches long and 2½ inches wide. Transfer the logs to the prepared baking sheet, several inches apart.

4. Beat the remaining egg and brush it over the dough. Bake the logs until they are firm to the touch, about 35 minutes. Remove them from the oven and allow them to cool completely.

5. Reduce the oven to 325°F (160°C). Transfer the logs to a cutting board and cut them into 1-inch-thick slices. Transfer the slices, cut-side down, to the baking sheet and return them to the oven. Bake until they are just turning crisp, about 8 minutes longer.

6. Transfer the sliced cookies to wire racks and let cool completely. These biscotti will keep at room temperature in an airtight container for 1 to 2 weeks.

Q Sticky dough covers my hands after I've shaped only a few of my hand-formed cookies. How can I prevent this so I don't have to keep running to the sink to wash my hands?

A Letting very soft cookie dough rest for 10 minutes after you mix it will give it some time to solidify, making it less sticky. Even better, refrigerate it for 10 to 30 minutes for easier handling. Longer than this in the refrigerator and the dough may become a little dry and crumbly, but it should come together when you begin to handle it. Some people like to coat their hands with flour or confectioners' sugar, but if you add too much flour or sugar to your dough this way it may affect the taste and texture of your cookies. It's better to rinse your hands in very cold tap water or ice water periodically, shaking off the excess water over the sink before proceeding. The coolness and dampness of your hands should prevent the dough from sticking.

Q When I'm coating my hand-formed cookies with chopped nuts or flaked coconut, the toppings always get clumped together with bits of cookie dough. Is there something I can do to keep the toppings fresh-looking as I work?

A You can refrigerate the shaped cookies for 5 or 10 minutes, which will make them less sticky, before rolling them in the toppings. And always place just one-third or half of your topping in the shallow bowl or on a rimmed baking sheet before beginning to roll. Using only a portion of the topping at a time will ensure that the cookies you roll last will look as fresh as the ones you rolled first.

Q Sprinkles and other decorations fall off of rolled cookies when the cookies cool. What can I do to make them stick?

A Sometimes it's enough to press the toppings lightly into the surface of the dough with the palm of your hand, so the decorations are embedded in the dough. Press your raisin buttons and red-hot eyes firmly into your ginger-bread man dough. If your dough is delicate and you are afraid your cookies will become misshapen with pressure, you could lightly brush the cookies with some beaten egg white, which will act like glue, and then sprinkle on your topping. An added bonus for some recipes, egg white will give the cookies a nice sheen.

Q I've loaded my dough into the cookie press, but when I push down nothing comes out. What can I do to soften the dough?

A Dough that is too stiff will be difficult to press through the decorative plate. The pressure of the stiff dough pressing against the plate may even break the gun. There are two reasons your dough might be too thick: First, is it very cold? Dough intended for the cookie press, unlike most other cookie doughs, should not be chilled because colder dough won't easily extrude through the decorative plate. Bring your dough to room temperature before loading it into your press. Dough that is relatively dry will be too thick and stiff to press through the plate. Thin the dough with a little bit of milk, stirring it in 1 teaspoon at a time, until it is softer and easier to press through the decorative plate.

Q When I press the dough in the cookie press it sticks to the plate and I have to scrape it off with a knife. What should I do?

A This is the opposite problem. If it's very warm in your kitchen, your dough might have become too soft. Refrigerate it briefly (4 or 5 minutes should do it), long enough to firm it up but not so long that it gets hard. Or perhaps you added too much liquid during mixing. Add some extra flour, 1 teaspoon at a time, until it extrudes smoothly from the press without sticking to the plate.

Q My spice cookie dough has a similar consistency to the butter cookie dough recommended by the cookie press manufacturer. Can I use a favorite drop cookie dough in a cookie press?

A Yes, with two caveats. Any room-temperature butter cookie dough, adjusted to pipeable consistency with the addition of some milk or flour, can be used in the cookie press. The operative word is "butter." Don't use dough made with vegetable shortening, because it will always be too soft to release cleanly from the plate. Also avoid recipes with chunky ingredients in favor of smooth doughs. Obviously, raisins, coarsely chopped nuts, and chocolate chips will block the openings of the plate, causing the dough to extrude in a mis-shapen way. Even shredded coconut and rolled oats, which might sneak through the openings, are chunky enough to make a clean design impossible. If you want chocolate in your spritz cookies, use a dough made with cocoa powder. Or you can embellish the pressed cookie dough with dried fruit or whole or halved nuts before baking the cookies.

Q I just bought some old-fashioned cookie molds. Any hints on using these successfully?

A Springerle, traditional German cookies flavored with anise, are tricky to make but worth the effort, especially during the Christmas season, when they can do double duty as tree decorations. To get the most precise impressions, flour the mold before each use. If your mold is large, with multiple impressions, roll out your dough on a lightly floured surface, press the mold firmly into the dough, and then use a sharp paring knife or pizza wheel to cut the dough apart into individual cookies at the pattern edges.

If you are using a smaller mold, the technique is different. Through trial and error, figure out how much dough your mold will hold. Then, measure or weigh portions of dough so each of your subsequent cookies will be the same size. Use the palm of your hand to press the dough into a ¼-inch-thick piece, the same size and shape as your mold; then press the dough into the mold with your fingertips, being sure it is making complete contact with the mold. Run a rolling pin over the dough to smooth out the back of the cookie. Release the cookie by tapping one side of the mold against the countertop. Don't be discouraged if your first few attempts don't take. These molds tend to release the dough more easily after they've been seasoned by use.

old-fashioned cookie molds

Individual molds make the best impressions on the dough, but for ease of use a carved springerle rolling pin can't be beat. The shaft of the pin is embossed with symbols separated by parallel grooves. To use the pin, roll it firmly over your rolled dough and then use a pizza cutter or sharp paring knife to separate the cookies from each other. To buy molds and springerle rolling pins, see Resources.

Traditional springerle recipes will direct you to air-dry the cookies overnight at room temperature before baking, to set the image in the dough. But you can use other dough in these molds. Any rolled cookie dough that holds its shape during baking will work, and the cookies can be baked immediately after molding.

Q Do you need a pastry bag to make meringue cookies?

dropped meringue

A Although professional pastry chefs use a pastry bag for beautifully shaped meringue cookies, it is easier for bakers not skilled in piping to just drop spoonfuls of meringue batter onto parchment-lined baking sheets. Not only is the drop method familiar and simple, but there is less of a chance of applying so much pressure to the bag that you deflate the meringue. Of course, dropped meringues look less neat than piped ones, but you can neaten them into cone shapes by moistening a finger with water and gently shaping each meringue mound into a peak. If you are going to use a pastry bag, use a large (½-inch) tip. Squeezing the meringue through a smaller tip will deflate the batter.

Q Why do meringue cookies bake at such a low temperature?

A Meringues are generally baked at a low temperature (about 250°F [120°C]) so they can dry out completely on the inside before they brown on the outside. A long stretch in a low oven accomplishes this, whereas a brief period in a hotter oven would result in cookies that are browned on the outside but underdone on the inside.

Q How can I prevent the sugary fillings in my filled cookies from leaking out of the cookies and burning during baking?

A Cookies filled with jam, puréed dried fruits, chocolate, and other soft, sweet ingredients can get messy when baked. Take care when filling rugelach, elephant ears, mini strudel cookies, and the like, to use fillings in moderation. Overfilling is a sure way to cause leakage. Also, while you want to roll up the cookies tightly, you don't want to roll them so tightly that there's no room for the fillings to expand a little in the heat of the oven. Chilling the cookies for 30 minutes in the refrigerator or freezer will help them to keep their shape as they bake, and hold in fillings that would otherwise ooze out. But some oozing is to be expected, and can cause a mess on your baking sheets if you don't prepare. Always bake these cookies on parchment paper, so you don't have to scrape sticky cookies and burned sugar from your baking sheets.

Q What is the best way to prevent my dough from sticking to the counter as I'm rolling and cutting?

A Different bakers prefer different methods. Mix and match from the following steps to find your perfect recipe for effortless rolling.

Rolling Techniques

* **Chill your dough.** Cold dough is less likely to stick than warm dough. Dough should be cold to the touch, but not so cold that it is difficult to roll or that it cracks under the pressure of the rolling pin. The right consistency is yielding but not squishy. If you are rolling out a large quantity of dough, cut it into pieces, refrigerating all but the piece you are rolling at the moment. If the piece you are working on gets too soft and sticky to roll, use an offset spatula to loosen it from the counter, slide it onto a rimless baking sheet, and refrigerate it for 5 or 10 minutes until it is workable again. Gently press the scraps together, wrap in plastic, and refrigerate them until they are chilled enough to roll out again.

* **Choose and prepare the rolling surface.** I'm lucky to have a marble countertop in my kitchen. Its surface stays nice and cool, keeping my cookie and pie dough from warming as I work. Still, I make sure to flour it adequately and often during rolling to prevent sticking. If your counter seems sticky, you might try spreading a pastry cloth (see Resources) over your rolling surface, which

will prevent a lot of sticking. Make sure to flour the pastry cloth as you would the countertop. Most recipes will instruct you to flour your work surface "lightly," but no matter what kind of surface you are working on, don't skimp on the flour or it won't do its job.

* **Prepare the rolling pin.** I dust my wooden rolling pin with flour before and during rolling. Some bakers swear by a cotton rolling pin cover (see Resources), which rolls over dough without sticking. A refrigerated marble or metal rolling pin will help keep dough cool during rolling. Silicone-coated rolling pins resist sticking.

* **Lift and turn the dough.** Use a large offset spatula to loosen the dough from the rolling surface after every half dozen rolls, and then gently lift and turn the dough 90 degrees before rolling again. If you roll your dough without turning it, the repeated pressure of the pin will cause it to stick to the counter. Similarly, sometimes the pressure of a cookie cutter will cause the edges of cookie dough to stick to the counter, after which you may tear the cookies when transferring them to the baking sheet. To avoid this, loosen cut cookies from the work surface with the same offset spatula.

* **Flour your cookie cutters.** For the cleanest cut, dip the edges of your cutter into flour to prevent the cutter from sticking to the dough.

* **Cut efficiently.** Cookie dough is like pie dough, biscuit dough, or any other pastry dough: The more it is

handled, the less tender the finished product. As you re-roll it, not only do you handle it more, but also you add more flour to prevent sticking. With this in mind, it's important to re-roll the dough as few times as possible. The best way to ensure this is to cut your cookies as close together as possible and with little leftover dough.

SEE ALSO: Rolling pins, page 53.

Q Some of my rolled cookies are paper-thin while others are close to a ¼ inch thick. What is the trick to rolling the dough into an even thickness so all my cookies are the same?

A Rolling out dough evenly takes some practice. It's a matter of applying even pressure on the rolling pin with your hands as you roll and avoiding pressing harder during one part of the rolling motion than another. It's also key to rotate the dough often, so that if you are applying pressure unevenly as you roll, at least you won't be applying pressure unevenly to just one or two parts of the sheet. If you need more help, there are adjustable pastry boards on the market (see Resources) with raised edges that will allow you to roll your dough only to a set thickness and no thicker. You can also improvise one of these boards: Use two thin cutting boards the same thickness as you'd like your cookies to be; position them on either side of the countertop where you are rolling. Roll dough between the cutting boards. (The flexible grip mats available online and at housewares stores make good guides; see Resources.)

Q The almond paste I was keeping in the refrigerator has some hard, dry spots. Can I still use it to make macaroons?

A If your almond paste has just begun to dry out, you can try to reverse the drying by putting it between two pieces of soft white bread and placing the "sandwich" in a resealable plastic bag. After 2 to 4 days, enough moisture from the bread will have migrated to the almond paste to soften it up. If your almond paste has hardened to the consistency of marble, there is nothing you can do but throw it away. Next time you purchase more than you can use, wrap it tightly in plastic and freeze it until you want to bake macaroons again.

Q Even when baked on ungreased baking sheets, my cookies spread more than I'd like. What's wrong?

A Make sure your butter is softened but not at the melting point. Melted butter in your cookie dough will cause your cookies to spread. If you are baking on a very warm day or in a very warm kitchen, consider refrigerating the bowl of cookie dough before portioning it out; 15 to 30 minutes in the refrigerator should firm it up. Chilled cookie dough will keep its shape longer in the oven, allowing the dough to set up before too much spreading occurs.

Q Why do some cookie recipes call for greasing the baking sheets and some don't?

A Greasing your baking sheets will cause your cookies to spread, which isn't desirable in many cases. That's why many recipes call for ungreased sheets. The dough sticks to the spot where it was placed so the finished cookies hold their shape to a degree.

This doesn't mean that cookies are guaranteed not to stick on ungreased sheets. If you suspect that your cookies might be difficult to remove from ungreased baking sheets after baking, line your baking sheets with parchment paper. Even the stickiest doughs will peel right off. Even if you are sure your cookies won't stick, consider using parchment paper anyway, for ease of clean-up.

Q What is the best way to grease a baking sheet, when it's called for?

A In my opinion, nothing beats parchment paper, which obviates the need for greasing. Nonstick aluminum foil also works well. If you don't have parchment or nonstick foil, don't try to substitute wax paper, which will smoke and sometimes even burn at 350°F (180°C) and above. Instead, use cooking spray, vegetable shortening, or butter. Don't use vegetable oil, which will smoke and burn before your cookies are baked through.

Q My baking sheets are covered with baked-on grease. How should I clean them?

A Grease on regular stainless steel (not nonstick) baking sheets can be removed with a mild abrasive, like scouring powder or baking soda mixed with water, or with a steel-wool soap pad. For thick layers of baked-on grease, you might try spraying your baking sheets with oven cleaner and then letting them stand in a well-ventilated area (outside is best) before scrubbing them clean.

Q Help! I accidentally put cooking spray on my nonstick baking sheet before baking a batch of cookies, and now the spray is baked on and I can't get it off.

A During baking, the grease bonds with the nonstick coating and it's virtually impossible to separate the two. Before throwing the baking sheet in the garbage, you might try a product like Goo-Gone, a cleaner originally developed to remove sticky, gummy residue from all types of surfaces. It may be able to lift the grease from the sheet.

Q How can I tell if my cookies are done?

A Cookies are so small that a minute or two in the oven can mean the difference between soft and moist cookies and hockey pucks. After too many batches of hockey pucks, I realized that my criteria (and the criteria in many recipes) for judging doneness was a bit off. Instead of baking most cookies until the tops are dry and golden, I now pull them from the oven when the tops are still a little bit moist. As they cool, the cookies continue to set up, so if they look a little bit underdone when you remove them, they will be perfect once they've cooled. Brownies and bars should be judged by a similar standard. If you bake them so that a toothpick inserted into the center comes out clean, the areas near the edges of the pan will be overdone. Take them out of the oven when the center is still a little bit moist. Residual heat will continue to bake the brownies so the center portion is moist but not raw.

Q Can I save time by putting two baking sheets in the oven at once?

A Unless you have a convection oven, it's best to bake one sheet of cookie dough at a time to ensure even baking. But if you are in a hurry you can bake two sheets at once, reversing their positions and rotating the sheets from back to front midway through baking to help them bake evenly. Baking two sheets at once may take a minute or two longer than the recommended baking time, so judge doneness by looking and touching as well as by the clock.

Q Do I have to cool the baking sheets between batches of cookies?

A Always place your cookie dough on a cool or room temperature baking sheet. If you don't, the dough will start to melt as you work, instead of beginning to bake properly with a hot blast of air from the oven. Some people chill the sheets between batches in the freezer or refrigerator, but I'm always afraid that a warm baking sheet will harm the cold food in the fridge or even melt the plastic shelving. I prefer to hold the baking sheet under cold running water and then dry with paper towels. It's not necessary to wash ungreased sheets with soap and water between batches as long as you wipe them dry and free of crumbs.

To get around rinsing and drying your oven-warm baking sheets, while your first batch of cookies is in the oven, lay a piece of parchment on the counter and portion out your cookie dough on the paper. Then, when you pull the baking sheet from the oven, slide the parchment with the baked cookies onto a wire rack, slide the parchment with the unbaked dough onto the baking sheet, and put the sheet right back in the oven, with no down time for cooling the hot sheet.

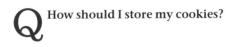

Q How should I store my cookies?

A In an airtight container at room temperature. If your cookies are soft and chewy, do what my friend's grandmother used to do to keep them that way: Place half of a piece of white bread in the container with your cookies. They'll draw moisture from the bread over the course of a few days, staying fresh. If your cookies are a little past their prime, restore their just-baked flavor and texture with a technique that my daughter brought home from the middle-school cafeteria: Wrap a single cookie loosely in a paper towel and microwave on HIGH until it is soft, 10 to 20 seconds.

Q Can I freeze cookies if I know I won't be eating them all in the next few days?

A Freshly baked and cooled cookies can be frozen in an airtight container between sheets of parchment paper. Defrost them on the counter and microwave them, if you like, as described above to restore their just-baked goodness. But consider planning ahead and freezing unbaked cookie dough if you know you have made too much.

Q Is it better to freeze cookies before or after baking?

A As a baker, it's been my particular crusade to get people to freeze some of their unbaked cookie dough every time they mix a batch. Yes, it is possible to freeze baked cookies, defrost them, and enjoy them at a later date. But freezing the portioned out dough or logs of slice-and-bake dough and then baking as many or as few cookies fresh when you want them is so much better. The advantages are multiple: While defrosted cookies are fresh-tasting enough, nothing beats the warm-from-the-oven flavor and aroma of just-baked cookies. Then there's the issue of portion control. Most people lack the self-control to keep from overindulging in just-baked cookies. If they are there, we will eat them! Freezing the unbaked dough prevents this cookie madness. The biggest bonus: Freezing cookie dough allows you to conjure fresh-baked cookies in less than 30 minutes (15 minutes to preheat the oven, and no more than 15 minutes to bake).

Q What is the best way to freeze cookie dough?

A It depends on the type of cookie you are making. To freeze drop cookies, line a baking sheet with parchment or foil and drop the dough onto the sheet. Freeze the cookie dough balls until firm, transfer them to a resealable plastic bag and place the bag in the freezer. For slice-and-bake dough, wrap the dough logs in a double thickness of plastic wrap and then a layer of aluminum foil before freezing. For rolled and cut cookies, you can roll and cut the dough and place the rolled and cut cookie shapes between layers of parchment on a baking sheet. Wrap the whole baking sheet in a double layer of plastic wrap before freezing.

Q Do I have to let frozen cookie dough defrost before baking?

A It's not necessary to let the cookie dough defrost. Place frozen cookies straight from the freezer on a prepared baking sheet and bake as directed, adding a few minutes to the suggested baking time.

Q I've had some bad experiences trying to remove hot cookies from a baking sheet. Why can't I just let my cookies cool completely on the sheet?

A There is a good reason why most recipes instruct you to remove the cookies from the baking sheet immediately or after just a few minutes out of the oven and transfer them to a wire rack. Cooling the cookies on the rack allows air to circulate all around them. If cookies cool on the hot baking sheet, moisture from the cookies will condense on the pan and seep back into the cookies, making them soggy.

Q What's the best way to remove cookies from a baking sheet?

A The most foolproof method is to line your baking sheets with parchment and simply slide the parchment from the baking sheet to a wire rack as soon as the cookies are out of the oven.

CHAPTER 7

Cakes

Nothing signals the celebratory nature of baking like cake. Whether it's the simplest snack cake received with shouts of anticipation by your children after a long day at school, a layer cake burning bright with birthday candles, or an elaborate wedding cake baked by a member of the wedding party, cakes make every occasion more special. Everyone loves cake, and to be able to bake a beautiful example and share it with family and friends is truly the baker's joy.

In this chapter, we will discuss every step on the way to this happy moment, from greasing your cake pan to whipping your eggs to the ribbon stage to filling and frosting and storing your cake until it's time to eat. When you have all the answers to your cake-baking questions, you will be ready to plan your next party with aplomb.

Q Are nonstick pans better than regular pans for cake baking?

A Shiny aluminum baking pans are fine, but for ease of use, nonstick pans can't be beat. I've recently traded in most of my old aluminum cake pans (many of which had warped after years of use) for a set of Chicago Metallic Professional bakeware with a bonded nonstick surface (see Resources). Not only do these pans guarantee an easy release, but they are easier to clean than my old pans. The one caveat is that because these pans have a darker surface than traditional baking pans, they retain heat better and tend to brown cakes faster than my old pans. For cakes that take an hour or more to bake (such as large Bundt cakes), I'll adjust my recipe by turning the oven temperature down 25°F (4°C), so that the cake crust doesn't overbrown.

Q Do nonstick pans still need to be greased?

A Manufacturers will tell you it's not necessary, but I always grease nonstick cake pans, just to be safe. Remember, this advice is for cake pans, not baking sheets. Greasing nonstick baking sheets, and especially spraying them with cooking spray, will create a sticky mess on their surface that is difficult to remove.

Q Which is the best grease for a cake pan — butter, vegetable shortening, or cooking spray?

A Some bakers prefer butter for flavor reasons, but butter can be unreliable, sometimes releasing your cake from the pan and sometimes holding onto portions of it. I use butter only when I'm greasing one of my nonstick pans, and know that I'll need just a little extra insurance that my cake will release easily. Nonstick vegetable shortening is a better bet for most pans. It's flavorless and guarantees that your cake will slide right out of any pan. Avoid vegetable oil, which can burn and can give your finished cake an unpleasant aroma and flavor.

If a recipe instructs you to grease and flour a pan, you might consider using a spray like Baker's Joy, a nonstick cooking spray with added flour, which does the job in just one step. Regular cooking spray can bead up on nonstick surfaces and will bond with added flour to form a greasy film on the surface of your cake; sprays like Baker's Joy will be invisible on the surface of your cake when it easily releases from the pan.

Q What is the best way to prepare a cake pan for baking? Is dusting the inside with flour really necessary?

A Prepare your pan depending upon what kind of cake you are baking and what kind of pan you are using. For many cakes, greasing the inside of the pan will be enough to release the cake cleanly. But if you've ever had a cake stick to the sides of the pan, you will probably want to take the precaution of greasing and flouring. It is especially important if your cake is high in sugar, because as the sugar on the surface of the cake caramelizes during baking, it will try to bond itself to the pan. The flour will form a barrier between the cake and the pan, preventing sticking.

All cake pans, whether or not they have a nonstick surface, should be greased. (There are just a couple of exceptions; see page 198, on angel food cakes.) Whether or not they should be dusted with flour, too, depends on a couple of things.

Cakes with a relatively high sugar content will be stickier and more difficult to remove from pans than cakes with less sugar, because their crusts will be more sticky from caramelization. So it's a good idea to flour pans in addition to greasing if your recipe contains a lot of sugar.

Cakes baked in pans with intricate patterns, such as specialty Bundt pans, should also be floured as well as greased, since cake batter will tend to stick to the crevices otherwise. For flat-bottomed layer cake pans, I suggest greasing, flouring, and then lining the bottom of the pan with a circle of parchment paper and greasing and flouring the paper. It is a lot easier to peel the piece of paper from the bottom of the cake than it is to scrape the bottom of the cake from the pan and reattach it to the rest of the cake.

Q Why must an angel food cake be baked in a special pan?

A Angel food cakes and most chiffon cakes are baked in a tube pan with tall sides and metal "feet" extending from the top edge of the pan. These features allow the cake to reach and maintain its full volume. The central tube of the pan distributes heat evenly, allowing the

angel food cake pan

cake to rise quickly before the egg whites can deflate. While you would grease the sides and bottom of the pan for other cake recipes, you leave the pan ungreased when making angel food cake, to allow the batter to cling to the sides of the pan as it rises, another strategy for producing a well-risen cake. Upon pulling it from the oven, you must immediately turn the cake over onto its feet, so that as it cools, gravity will prevent it from shrinking. For the same reason, you should leave the sides (but not the bottom) of a jelly-roll pan ungreased when baking a roulade. You want the batter to cling to the sides of the pan to maintain its full volume.

Q Why do cake recipes often call for ingredients at room temperature?

A Ingredients at room temperature — between 65 and 70°F (18–21°C) — will emulsify more easily than chilled ingredients. A successful emulsion will result in a cake with a light, rather than dense texture. But be sure that your ingredients aren't too warm, or they may cause the air cells in your creamed butter to dissolve, also resulting in a dense cake.

Q What is cake flour? Should it be used in all cakes?

A Cake flour is a low-protein flour made from soft wheat. It is generally treated with chlorine, which not only bleaches it a snowy white color but also breaks down proteins to inhibit gluten development during mixing, making it even softer. Because it won't develop as much gluten as all-purpose flour, it is called for in cake recipes where a tender crumb and delicate texture are desired. It's not right for all cakes, however. Batters that support heavy ingredients such as nuts and dried fruits, for example, need a sturdier structure than what cake flour will provide.

SEE ALSO: Flour and flour substitutes, page 7.

Q What is the difference between cake flour and pastry flour?

A Pastry flour has a protein content of between 8% and 10% and hasn't been chlorinated, making it softer than all-purpose flour but harder than cake flour. It generally isn't used to bake cakes, but is sometimes called for in pie dough and cookie recipes where a tender result is desired along with some crispness and structure. Pastry flour is a rarity in supermarkets, while cake flour and all-purpose flour are widely available. If you come upon a recipe requiring pastry flour but can't find it at your market, you can approximate its protein content by mixing 1⅓ cups of all-purpose flour with ⅔ cup of cake flour for every 2 cups of pastry flour called for.

Q **Are génoise and yellow cake interchangeable in layer cake recipes?**

A Although both génoise and yellow cake are generally baked in round pans, split into layers, and filled and frosted to create layer cakes, they have very different texture profiles, and require different treatments when layering. Génoise is relatively dry and light. Thus it is often soaked with a flavorful syrup and filled and frosted with egg-enriched meringue buttercream to add richness. Butter cake won't soak up any syrup, as it is saturated with moisture from butter and milk. Butter cakes are better when filled and frosted with a lighter style of buttercream made by whipping butter with confectioners' sugar or with a whipped chocolate ganache.

VARIETIES OF CAKE

Cakes can be divided into three basic classifications, with many subclassifications. Understanding the difference between foam cakes, shortened cakes, and custard-based cakes, and being able to determine which category the cake you are making belongs to, will help you understand how your recipe works.

Foam Cakes

Foam cakes have little or no fat and a high proportion of eggs to flour. They are generally leavened by the air beaten into the eggs or egg whites. In this category are:

Sponge (sometimes called biscuit). Sponge cake is made by folding together flour, egg yolks, and sugar whipped to the ribbon stage, and stiffly beaten egg whites. The recipe can be varied by adding finely chopped nuts, citrus zest, liqueurs, or extracts. Sometimes served plain, it can also be soaked with a flavored sugar syrup before being layered with whipped cream, buttercream, or fruit preserves, and frosted.

Roulade. A roulade is a sponge cake baked in a jelly-roll pan and rolled up into a cylinder while still warm. When the cake is cooled, it is unrolled and filled with mousse, ganache, buttercream, Bavarian cream, or another filling, and re-rolled.

Génoise. A slightly richer and more tender foam cake than sponge, génoise is made by whipping whole rather than separated eggs with sugar. Very often some melted butter is added to the batter for richness. Génoise is usually baked in a round cake pan and split into two layers, which can be soaked with syrup and filled and frosted in myriad ways.

Chiffon. Chiffon cakes rely on whipped egg whites and some baking powder for their rise. Dry ingredients are mixed with oil, egg yolks, and flavorings, and then whipped egg whites are folded in. Chiffon is similar to butter cake in richness and moisture content because it contains oil, but it is easier to make because there is no creaming.

Angel food. The leanest of all foam cakes, and the sweetest, it contains no oil, butter, or egg yolks and is leavened solely by egg whites whipped with sugar. The large quantity of sugar is necessary to stabilize the whites until their proteins coagulate in the heat of the oven.

Meringue. Meringue cake layers are made by whipping egg whites with sugar, piping the mixture onto parchment paper in the desired shape (rounds, squares, rectangles, hearts), and baking at a low temperature until crisp. The brittle meringues soften when layered with fruit, cream, buttercream, and other fillings.

Dacquoise. Dacquoise is meringue made with ground nuts. This term can also refer to a finished cake made by layering nut-meringue disks with buttercream or whipped cream and fruit.

Shortened Cakes

Shortened cakes contain butter or vegetable shortening and rely on a combination of creaming and chemical leaveners for their rise. The two basic recipes can be used to make a variety of related cakes, including Bundt cakes, coffee cakes, and cupcakes.

Pound cake. So named because the original recipe called for one pound each of flour, butter, sugar, and eggs. Today's recipes are slightly altered, but pound cake is still characterized by its rich flavor and dense texture.

Butter cake. The American-style butter cake evolved from pound cake, but introduced liquid, most often milk, to the recipe. The resulting cake is a little lighter than traditional pound cake, better for splitting into layers to fill and frost than pound cake, which may overwhelm these other ingredients with its density and richness.

Custard cakes

Custard cakes more closely resemble bread puddings, soufflés, and other oven-baked custards than they do foam or shortened cakes, but are included because they are baked in cake pans and sliced and served like cakes.

Cheesecake. Cheesecakes range in style from the dense and rich New York cheesecake to the light and fluffy Italian ricotta cheesecake. They get their tang from mild cheese, such as cream cheese or ricotta, and often contain sour cream or heavy cream for richness. Cheesecakes are baked custards, thickened with eggs. Like all custards (think of crème brûlée or bread pudding), they need to be cooked gently, whether that means in a water bath or at a very low oven temperature, to prevent the eggs from curdling as they cook.

Flourless chocolate cake. A very simple cake made of chocolate, butter, eggs, and sugar, sometimes flavored with liqueur. Like cheesecake, this cake requires gentle baking, preferably in a water bath, to allow the chocolate custard to set. While the large quantity of chocolate will prevent the eggs from curdling, the cake will dry out around the edges, becoming chalky and hard, if it is baked too quickly at too high a temperature.

Q My génoise recipe says "beat the egg mixture until it has reached the ribbon stage." How do I know if I've beaten the eggs and sugar long enough? What will happen if I don't beat the eggs long enough?

A The ribbon stage is just what it sounds like. When you lift the paddle or beaters up and away from your batter, it will fall back into the bowl in billowy, cream-colored ribbons. But reaching this point takes time — at least 5 minutes on medium-high with a powerful stand mixer and up to 8 or 10 minutes with a less powerful handheld machine. Egg foam beaten to this stage has large, evenly spaced bubbles and is very stable, as compared to the bubblier foams not beaten quite as long, which contain fragile air bubbles more likely to pop. Cake batters beaten to the ribbon stage will rise higher and taste lighter than cakes made with inadequately beaten eggs.

cake batter at the ribbon stage

Q I'd like to bake an angel food or chiffon cake, but am terrified of whipping the egg whites incorrectly. What is the best technique for whipping whites for these cakes, and how do I know when they are ready?

A Your concern is well placed, because the success of both of these cakes depends upon properly whipped, stable egg whites. Here are some tips that will help you get there.

For angel food cake, beat the whites on low to break them up. Add some cream of tartar and a pinch of salt, increase the speed to medium, and whip until the egg whites are cloudlike and soft. With the mixer still on, add the sugar in a slow stream (sprinkle in one teaspoon at a time) until the whites are shiny and hold soft peaks. This means that when you lift the beaters from the bowl, the peaks will flop over. Don't overwhip your whites when making angel food cake, or you will have difficulty folding in the dry ingredients without deflating them.

egg whites for angel food cake

For chiffon cake, the technique is slightly different; the whites for this cake are whipped without sugar and to a stiffer stage. Break up the egg whites as for angel food cake, and add some cream of tartar and a pinch of salt. Then beat the whites on medium-high until they are very stiff. If the whites aren't whipped sufficiently the cake will be damp on the bottom and not well risen. They won't be shiny as whites whipped with sugar are, and it's okay if they begin to clump up into dry blobs. When folding the whites into the batter, be sure to incorporate them well, gently crushing the blobs against the side of the bowl before blending them with the rest of the ingredients for a light but smooth mixture.

egg whites for chiffon cake

Q When I tried to roll up my jelly roll after baking, it resisted and cracked in places. Why did it do this and how can I make sure it rolls up smoothly next time?

A A couple of tricks, practiced together, will allow you to successfully roll up your cake. First, don't overbake it. If your cake is too dry, it will be more difficult to roll and more likely to crack. Don't wait too long before you turn your cake out of the pan and roll it up; as it cools it will become less pliable and more difficult to roll. As soon as the cake is out of the oven, invert it onto a large, clean kitchen towel (a couple of inches bigger all around than your cake), dusted with confectioners' sugar. Trim away the edges of the cake, which will be tougher than the rest of the cake. Tightly roll the cake, using the towel as a guide, into a spiral and let it cool completely.

Q I'd like to turn my chocolate roulade into a bûche de Noël for the holidays. Could you give a few simple tips to a novice cake decorator on achieving this transformation?

A You are right in recognizing that a bûche de Noël (or yule log cake) is simply a dressed-up roulade. Depending on how far you want to go, fill, roll, and chill your roulade, and then work your way down the following list to achieve the effect.

Steps to the Perfect Bûche de Noël

* **Shaping and frosting.** Trim the cake and frost it so it looks like a log. First, trim a thin piece diagonally from one end of the cake and discard. Trim a larger 2-inch-thick piece at the same diagonal angle from the other end and set it aside. Transfer the cake-log to a serving platter. Spread chocolate frosting (setting aside ½ cup) over the log and the ends. Attach the 2-inch piece about two-thirds of the way along the top side of the log, pressing lightly so it adheres. Cover the smaller piece with the reserved frosting to look like a bump on the log. Drag the tines of a fork along the length of the log, including the bump, to simulate bark.

yule log cake

* **Leaves.** For the easiest embellishment, place a few jelly candy spearmint leaves around the cake as garnish. Fresh raspberries or cranberries can stand in for holly berries. Or you could color some marzipan or fondant (see Resources) green and cut leaves freehand or using a small cookie cutter. Roll marzipan or fondant into a thin (about ⅛ inch thick) "vine" to connect the leaves.

* **Mushrooms**. Meringue mushrooms are traditional, but you can also shape uncolored marzipan or fondant into mushroom shapes. To make meringue mushrooms: Whip two large egg whites just until they hold soft peaks. With the mixer on high, pour ¼ cup of granulated sugar into the bowl until the meringue holds a stiff

peak. Sift ¼ cup more granulated sugar, ½ cup of confectioners' sugar, and 2 teaspoons of flour over the bowl and then fold the mixture into the meringue. Scrape it into a pastry bag fitted with a large (¼-inch) plain tip and pipe 1-inch-long pointed stems and 1-inch rounds onto a parchment-lined baking sheet. Bake the meringues in a 250°F (120°C) oven until dry and set, about 1 hour 30 minutes. When cool, attach the tops to the stems with a little bit of leftover frosting.

piping meringue mushrooms

Q Does nut meringue batter for dacquoise need to be prepared or handled differently from batter made with just egg whites and sugar?

A Whip the egg whites with the sugar as you would for a plain meringue, making sure your bowl and beaters are scrupulously clean and grease-free. Take care not to overprocess the nuts when grinding them in the food processor. If you do, they will release their oil, and then when you fold the oily nuts into the meringue the egg whites will deflate. Add some sugar to the bowl of the food processor with the nuts, which will help to keep them dry. For added insurance, a bit of cornstarch sprinkled in the bowl before grinding will absorb any oil that does get released and act as a barrier between the oil and the eggs.

Q What exactly is "folding" and why is it so important in cake baking?

A Folding is the process by which two substances of different densities are gently but thoroughly combined into one batter, for example, when adding whipped egg whites to a heavy batter. The point is to fold the lighter ingredients into the heavier ones without deflating the air bubbles you've worked to incorporate into either or both.

sweep the spatula along the side of the bowl, angling down to the bottom

To fold successfully, use a wide rubber spatula, which will accomplish the task in fewer strokes than a narrow one. If the difference in densities is very great, as with whipped egg whites and a much heavier flour-based batter, stir in about one-quarter of the whites to lighten the batter before folding in the remaining whites. To fold, add the remaining whites and sweep the spatula along one side of the bowl and down to the bottom. Lift it up and through the center of the batter, flipping

lift the spatula through the center, flipping and turning the batter and turning as you lift. Turn the bowl about 45 degrees and repeat, working your way around the bowl as you lift and turn the batter. Continue to fold until the whites are incorporated into the batter, which may take several revolutions of the bowl.

When folding in dry ingredients or nuts, lightening the batter is not necessary. Just proceed to the folding step, sweeping, lifting, and turning the spatula until your batter is smooth but still light.

Q What is a 1-2-3-4 cake?

A This is another name for basic two-layer yellow cake. The ingredients for 1-2-3-4 cake are so easy to remember that they don't need to be written down. To make this cake, just gather together 1 cup of butter, 2 cups of sugar, 3 cups of cake flour, and 4 large eggs (you'll also need 1 tablespoon of baking powder, ¼ teaspoon of salt, 1 teaspoon of vanilla extract, and 1 cup of milk). Whisk together the dry ingredients; whisk the milk, eggs, and vanilla; and cream the butter and sugar until fluffy. Add the dry and wet ingredients alternately, ending with the dry. Scrape the batter into two 9-inch round cake pans that have been greased, lined with parchment, greased again, and floured, and bake at 350°F (180°C) until a toothpick inserted into the center comes out clean, about 25 minutes. See? No recipe and you can have a layer cake in no time.

Q Can you give me a simple buttercream frosting recipe that's as easy to remember as the formula for 1-2-3-4 cake?

A Here's the one I use: 1 cup softened unsalted butter, one 16-ounce box confectioners' sugar, 1 tablespoon meringue powder, 1 tablespoon whole milk, 1 tablespoon vanilla extract, and a pinch of salt. I beat the butter using an electric mixer until it is fluffy, then add the powdered sugar a little bit at a time until it's all incorporated. Then I beat in the meringue powder, milk, vanilla, and salt and continue to beat on high until the frosting is fluffy, about 5 minutes.

Q What is the difference between yellow cake and white cake?

A Both are butter cakes, made using the creaming method. Both contain butter, sugar, flour, and milk. The difference is that a yellow cake contains just the egg yolks, whereas a white cake contains whole eggs.

Q The recipe for yellow cake I'm working from doesn't call for creaming. The butter is mixed with the flour and other dry ingredients and then the wet ingredients are added. How is this different from a shortened cake?

A This recipe is still considered shortened, because of the butter. But the texture will be very different because of the different mixing method, sometimes called the "one bowl" method. The cake will be less voluminous than cakes made by the creaming method, because there are no air cells created during creaming to lift it in the oven. It will also be more tender, because there is less opportunity for gluten formation once the flour has been coated with the butter, inhibiting the creation of gluten strands that form when liquid is mixed with flour that doesn't have a protective coating of fat.

Q My cake recipe calls for creaming the butter and sugar together, but then separating the eggs, whipping the whites, and folding them into the batter separately. So is this a foam or a butter cake?

A Foam cakes only contain a small amount, if any, of melted butter. Your cake is a shortened cake, because a relatively large amount of butter is creamed with the sugar, and will account for some of its rise. But the mixing method employed, sometimes called the "combination" method, borrows from foam cake recipes by folding in whipped egg whites for extra rise and lightness.

Q What is the difference between using melted unsweetened chocolate and unsweetened cocoa powder in cakes?

A Unsweetened chocolate is about 50% cocoa butter, so in addition to bringing mild chocolate flavor to a cake it also brings moisture and tenderness in the form of fat. Cocoa powder, in contrast, is fat free. It imparts a more intense chocolate flavor to baked goods than unsweetened chocolate, but can have a drying and strengthening effect, which must be offset by adding more butter or other fat, as well as by a larger amount of chemical leaveners proportionate to its dry ingredients. Some bakers like to use both types of chocolate in a cake, believing that the combination lends the cake the best qualities of both types of chocolate.

Q Why do some recipes call for mixing cocoa powder with boiling water before incorporating it into the batter?

A Not only does whisking cocoa powder with boiling water get rid of any lumps, creating a smooth mixture that will incorporate well into cake batter, but it also brings out the chocolate flavor of the powder, making for a more intensely chocolaty cake.

Double Chocolate Cake

Here is a recipe using both types of chocolate — unsweetened baking chocolate and unsweetened cocoa powder — for a rich, moist, intense chocolate cake. To make it a triple chocolate cake, frost with whipped chocolate ganache, or pour a chocolate glaze over it.

SERVES 10 TO 12

4 ounces unsweetened chocolate, finely chopped

⅓ cup unsweetened cocoa powder, not Dutch-process

1 cup boiling water

1 cup milk

3 large eggs

1 tablespoon vanilla extract

2¼ cups unbleached all-purpose flour

2 teaspoons baking powder

1 teaspoon baking soda

¼ teaspoon salt

1 cup (2 sticks) unsalted butter, softened

2 cups sugar

1. Preheat the oven to 350°F (180°C). Coat the inside of a 12-cup Bundt pan with cooking spray and dust it with flour, knocking out any excess.

2. Combine the chocolate and cocoa powder in a medium heatproof bowl. Pour the boiling water over the chocolate and whisk until smooth. Set aside to cool.

3. Whisk the milk, eggs, and vanilla in a large glass measuring cup. Whisk the flour, baking powder, baking soda, and salt in a large bowl.
4. Combine the butter and sugar in a large mixing bowl and cream with an electric mixer on medium-high until fluffy, about 3 minutes, scraping down the sides of the bowl once or twice as necessary. Add the chocolate mixture and mix on low until well combined.
5. With the mixer on low speed, add one-third of the flour mixture and beat until incorporated. Add one-half of the milk mixture. Repeat, alternating flour and milk mixtures and ending with the flour mixture, scraping down the sides of the bowl between additions. Turn the mixer to medium-high and beat for 1 minute.
6. Scrape the batter into the prepared pan. Bake until a toothpick inserted in the center comes out clean, 40 to 45 minutes. Let cool in the pan for 5 minutes; transfer to a wire rack to cool completely.

Q What is the best way to create a marbled effect in a chocolate-and-vanilla cake?

A Successful marbling depends on keeping two batters that are swirled together distinct from each other. To do this, make sure that you have proportionately more of the lighter batter, which would be the vanilla in this case, than the heavier chocolate. I like to have two parts vanilla to one part chocolate. Spread one-half of the vanilla batter across the bottom of the pan in an even layer. Spoon one-half the chocolate batter on top of the vanilla in large dollops. Repeat with the remaining vanilla and chocolate. Then, insert a butter knife into the batter perpendicularly and use it to cut a wide figure-eight pattern through the batter. If you are baking your cake in a loaf pan, one large figure eight will be suffi-cient. If you are using a Bundt or tube pan, several smaller figure eights will do the trick.

marbling a cake

Q What makes red velvet cake red?

A Red velvet cake is a chocolate cake made with natural cocoa powder, buttermilk, and vinegar. The chemical reaction that occurs when these ingredients are mixed makes the red undertones in the cocoa powder more red. But this redness is augmented considerably in most recipes by the addition of beets, jars of beet baby food, or red food coloring. Compared to devil's food cake, red velvet cake has a milder chocolate flavor because it contains relatively little cocoa powder, and a softer, more open and moist crumb from the buttermilk.

Q What is the difference between chocolate butter cake and devil's food cake?

A Chocolate butter cake is simply a chocolate version of yellow cake, made with butter, eggs, and milk, and with cocoa powder replacing some of the flour. Devil's food cake is darker in color and more intensely chocolaty, because it uses water rather than milk (milk tempers the flavor of cocoa powder in chocolate butter cake).

Q Any advice about unmolding an upside-down cake so the fruit topping doesn't stick to the pan?

A Timing is important. Let the cake cool in the pan for a couple of minutes, so that the topping begins to set, before inverting the pan onto a wire rack. This way, the brown sugar and butter mixture won't be so melty that it will slide down the sides of the cake. But don't let the cake sit so long that the caramelized topping starts to bond with the pan, or you will never get the fruit out. If I'm really worried about sticking, I'll line my pan with a parchment circle and then butter the parchment, and carefully peel the parchment away after I've unmolded the cake and it's cooled a little bit. If a few pieces of fruit stick to the pan bottom or parchment paper, it isn't a tragedy. You will easily see by the impressions left by the fruit in the top of the cake where each piece belongs, so you can carefully replace it.

Q I don't have a springform pan for my cheesecake. Can I substitute a regular cake pan?

A Yes, but be sure to line the bottom of the pan with a circle of parchment paper for an easy release, because cheesecake crusts, especially those made with graham cracker and other cookie crumbs, tend to stick.

Another consideration: Softer cheesecakes may suffer some surface damage when you invert them and re-invert them. Frozen cakes won't dent and break the way soft cakes will. Before unmolding, wrap the cheesecake, still in the pan, in plastic wrap and place it in the freezer for at least 6 hours or up to 2 weeks. A few hours before serving it, remove the plastic and run the bottom of the pan over a gas burner for several seconds to loosen the cake from the pan. If you don't have a gas burner, dip the bottom inch or so of the pan in a bowl of hot tap water for 1 minute. Run a sharp paring knife around the edges of the pan, invert it onto a platter and peel away the parchment paper, and then re-invert onto a serving platter so the cake is right side up.

Q I baked my cheesecake in a water bath as directed, and some water leaked into the pan, making the edges of the crust soggy. How could I have prevented this?

A This is a common problem with springform pans, especially as they get older and the sides don't fit as tightly against the bottom as they used to. To prevent water from leaking into your pan, wrap the bottom and sides of the pan with a sheet of heavy-duty aluminum foil, trimming the foil so that when pressed and molded tightly to the pan it comes almost to the top edge. Remove the foil before releasing the pan sides when directed.

foil-wrapped springform pan

Q What are the secrets to a smooth cheesecake?

A If the texture of your cheesecake is lumpy, then you probably didn't allow your cream cheese to soften enough or you didn't beat it enough before adding the other ingredients. It is also possible that you didn't scrape down bits of cream cheese stuck to the sides of the bowl until it was too late in the mixing process for them to be incorporated.

New York Cheesecake

Here is a simple recipe for a cheesecake that doesn't require a water bath. Baking it in an oven that cools over time will prevent the custard from curdling and prevent the top from cracking. To further ensure against cracking, run a sharp paring knife around the edge of the cake as soon as you remove it from the oven so that as it cools and shrinks slightly it won't crack from surface tension. Crush the graham crackers by giving them a whirl in a food processor or by placing them in a resealable plastic bag and rolling over them with a rolling pin.

SERVES 8 TO 10

FOR THE CRUST:
1⅓ cups graham cracker crumbs
    (from about 20 whole graham
    crackers)

5 tablespoons unsalted butter,
    melted and cooled
2 tablespoons sugar
¼ teaspoon salt

FOR THE CAKE:
Four 8-ounce packages cream
    cheese, softened
1¼ cups sugar
2 tablespoons unbleached all-
    purpose flour

¼ cup sour cream
4 large eggs, at room temperature
1 teaspoon grated lemon zest
2 teaspoons vanilla extract

1. To make the crust, preheat the oven to 350°F (180°C). Coat the inside of a 10-inch springform pan with cooking spray.

2. Combine the graham cracker crumbs, butter, sugar, and salt in a medium mixing bowl and stir until the crumbs are evenly moistened. Press the graham cracker mixture evenly across the bottom and 1 inch up the sides of the pan, packing it tightly with your fingertips. Bake until just firm, about 7 minutes. Remove from the oven and let cool completely.

3. To make the cake, increase the oven temperature to 500°F (260°C). Combine the cream cheese, sugar, and flour in a large mixing bowl and beat with an electric mixer on high speed until very smooth, scraping down the sides of the bowl once or twice as necessary. Add the sour cream and mix until smooth. Add the eggs, one at a time, and mix on low speed until combined, scraping down the sides of the bowl after each addition. Stir in the lemon zest and vanilla.

4. Put the pan containing the crust on a baking sheet and pour the filling into the crust. Transfer the baking sheet holding the springform pan to the oven and bake for 10 minutes; without opening the oven door, reduce the oven temperature to 200°F (95°C) and bake the cheesecake until the perimeter is set but the center is still a little jiggly, about 1 hour and 10 minutes longer. The cheesecake should read about 150°F (66°C) on an instant-read thermometer inserted into the center.

5. As soon as the cake is out of the oven, run a sharp paring knife around the edge of the pan to separate the cheesecake from the sides of the pan. Transfer to a wire rack and let cool completely. Wrap cheesecake in plastic, and refrigerate it for at least 6 hours or overnight before unmolding and serving. It will keep, wrapped in plastic and refrigerated, for up to 1 week.

Q Why do I have to bake my cheesecake or flourless chocolate cake in a water bath?

A Both cheesecakes and flourless chocolate cakes are baked custards, thickened with eggs. Successful custards are silky smooth. The best way to ensure this texture is to bake custards in a water bath.

The silky texture of custards depends on proper thickening of eggs, so that the web of proteins they form as they cook remains elastic and smooth. When eggs are heated too quickly and at too high a temperature, this web loses its elasticity, hardens, shrinks, and squeezes out the liquid it holds. The resulting custard becomes lumpy and weeps water. With only a few degrees of difference between thickened and curdled, it's important to control the rate of heating so that your custard doesn't cross the line before you have a chance to pull it from the oven. Baking it in a pan of water that comes halfway up the sides of your cake pan will slow the rate at which a custard heats up, allowing you to monitor its progress.

A water bath insulates the delicate mixture from the direct heat of the oven, letting it thicken without getting too hot and curdling. Even if your oven is set at 325°F (160°C), the portion of your cake that is below the water line will never rise above 212°F (100°C), the boiling point of water. It's highly unlikely, unless you completely forget about your cake, that its internal temperature will go above the curdling point, which is around 190°F (88°C), depending on how much sugar is in your cake (sugar raises the curdling point of eggs, safeguarding them a little longer).

Recipes for New York–style cheesecake use an alternate method for bringing the cake batter slowly up to temperature without curdling. The oven is preheated to a very high heat — about 500°F (260°C). The cake is baked in this hot oven for just 10 minutes, and then the temperature is turned way down to 200°F (95°C). The initial blast of heat allows the surface of the cake to brown nicely. Then the slow decrease in oven temperature to below the boiling point ensures that the custard will thicken but never to the curdling point.

Q What is the best way to remove a cake from a water bath?

A Carefully slide a very wide straight metal spatula between the water bath pan and the cake pan. With your other hand, delicately steady the pan on the spatula, holding it by its top edge using a folded dish towel thick enough to insulate your fingers from the heat but thin enough so you can feel if it is getting dangerously close to your cake.

Q Why did the top of my cheesecake crack and how can I avoid this next time?

A If the top of your cake cracked while the cake was still in the oven, you most likely overbaked it past 160°F (71°C). To prevent this from happening again, use an instant-read thermometer and pull the cake out of the oven as soon as the center reaches 150°F (66°C). The cake's temperature will continue to climb after baking.

Sometimes a cheesecake will crack after it is removed from the oven. As the cake shrinks slightly during cooling, the sides of the cake stick to the pan, creating tension on the surface of the cake and causing it to crack. To prevent this, run a sharp paring knife between the cake and the pan sides as soon as you pull the cake from the oven so it can shrink without pulling.

Q How does temperature affect cake baking? Do different types of cakes bake at different temperatures?

A Different types of cakes are baked at different temperatures, to achieve different effects. On the low end of the temperature scale are meringue layers, which are not so much baked as dehydrated in the oven at a temperature between 250 and 275°F (120–140°C). The idea is to dry the meringue mixture slowly, so it crisps all the way through without browning.

Flourless chocolate cakes and cheesecakes are often (although not always) baked at lower temperatures to avoid curdling. New York cheesecake (see page 220) begins in a 500°F (260°C) oven, but as it continues to bake, the oven temperature is reduced to 200°F (95°C) so the cake never reaches the temperature at which the custard will curdle.

Thick and dense cakes like pound cakes, tall Bundt cakes, and cakes made with lots of moist fruit are generally baked at a relatively low temperature of 325°F (160°C) to allow their centers to bake through without the risk of surface burning. Layer cakes, both génoise and butter, can be baked at 350°F (180°C) because their centers won't take as long to set up and dry out.

Small items like cupcakes and thin cakes like roulades can be baked at the relatively high temperature of 375°F (190°C). The higher temperature will promote a golden crust, whereas at lower temperatures the interior will cook through before browning on top has occurred.

Q Why did my cake rise high in the oven and then sink in the center as it cooled?

A There are several reasons why this may have happened. If you overmixed your batter, you may have whipped too much air into it. In the oven, these large air bubbles expand to a size that cannot be supported by the structure of the cake, causing the collapse as the cake cools. Or you may have used too much chemical leavener, which leads to the same sequence of events — too many expanding air bubbles for the cake's gluten structure to support. Mismeasuring other ingredients may also account for this unfortunate effect. If you skimped on the liquid, the starches in the cake may not be hydrated enough to properly gelatinize, causing the cake to fall. Or if you added too much butter or shortening it may have coated the flour to a degree that inhibited gluten development, resulting in a weak structure unable sustain the cake's rise.

Flourless Chocolate Cake for Beginners

There are many variations on flourless chocolate cake. Some will instruct you to separate the eggs and fold whipped egg whites into the batter. Some call for several different types of chocolate. For beginners, or lazy bakers, here is the simplest flourless chocolate cake recipe I know, consisting of just four ingredients including salt. The trick (as with all flourless chocolate cake and cheesecake recipes) is to bake the cake in a water bath and pull it from the oven before it is completely set. If you follow these instructions, you are sure to be pleased with the moist and creamy result.

SERVES 12

1 pound bittersweet chocolate, finely chopped
1 cup (2 sticks) unsalted butter
8 large eggs
Pinch of salt

1. Preheat the oven to 350°F (180°C). Place a large roasting pan in the oven and pour in ½ inch of hot tap water.
2. Line the bottom of a springform pan with parchment paper and spray it with cooking spray. Place the pan on a sheet of heavy-duty aluminum foil and mold the foil to the sides of the pan, but not over the top, to prevent any water from seeping in. (See illustration on page 219.)
3. Add 1 inch of water to the bottom of a double boiler or a saucepan and bring to a bare simmer over medium-low heat. Finely chop the chocolate.

4. Combine the chocolate and butter in the top of the double boiler, or in a stainless steel bowl big enough to sit on top of the pan, and set it on top of the simmering water, making sure the water doesn't touch the bottom of the double boiler or bowl. Heat, whisking occasionally, until the chocolate is completely melted and glossy. Set aside to cool until barely warm.

5. Whisk the eggs and salt in a large bowl to break up the yolks. Slowly whisk the egg mixture into the chocolate mixture until well combined. Scrape the batter into the prepared pan.

6. Carefully place the springform pan into the roasting pan of hot water and bake until the cake is set around the edges but still loose in the center, about 30 minutes. Carefully lift the springform pan from the water and let cool on a wire rack. Cover the pan with plastic wrap and refrigerate until the cake is well chilled, at least 6 hours and up to 3 days.

7. Remove the springform pan sides, invert the cake onto a sheet of wax paper or parchment, peel off the parchment paper, and re-invert the cake onto a serving platter, peeling away and discarding the wax paper. Slice and serve.

Q Why do my cake layers rise unevenly in the oven? I am placing the two cake pans on the center rack and rotating them halfway through baking.

A It is important not only to switch the pans during baking, but to pay attention to how close they are to each other and to the walls of the oven. Pans that are placed too close together will rise toward each other. Pans that are placed too close to an oven wall will rise significantly higher on the side furthest from the wall. So take into account these spatial relations as you rotate, making sure that you leave at least 3 inches between the two pans and between the pans and the walls, and that when you switch the cakes, turn them 180 degrees as well as reversing their positions.

Q Why do my cake layers rise into dome shapes? Every time I bake I wind up slicing off the domed portion before I can frost the layers.

A Some rising in the center is unavoidable, because the batter near the edges of the pan will bake through and set more quickly than the batter in the middle, which will continue to rise until set. To minimize the difference in height between the edges and the center, you can take a few precautions. Check the temperature of your oven. Is it running hot? Turn the oven down 25°F (4°C). A more moderate temperature will allow the batter near the edges to rise longer before setting. Try wrapping your pan with an aluminized cake strip (see Resources), which will keep the sides of the pan cool, allowing for a more even rise.

Q Is the toothpick test the best way to tell if a cake is done?

A It depends on what kind of cake you are baking, and how you use the toothpick. For cakes with a crumb (including pound cakes, chiffon cakes, and layer cakes), the toothpick test is reliable. First, gently touch the center of the cake with a fingertip. If it doesn't feel quite solid underneath the crust, keep baking it. If it feels firm, insert a toothpick into the center of the cake. If it comes out with batter on it, keep baking. If it comes out with a few crumbs, it's ready and you should pull it out of the oven. If it comes out perfectly clean, hope that you haven't overbaked it to a state of dryness.

Cakes that are creamy in the center rather than crumby (this includes cheesecakes and flourless chocolate cakes) should be tested with an instant-read thermometer or by following the visual clues provided in the recipe. An internal temperature of 150 to 160°F (66–71°C) for a cheesecake or flourless chocolate cake will ensure that the cake is baked all the way through while staying creamy in the center. In this temperature range, the cakes will still look a little jiggly in the center, but remember that the cake will continue to bake as it cools outside of the oven, and the center will firm up during this time.

Q When I cut into my cake it had tunnels and large air bubbles baked into it. How can I get a more even crumb next time?

A You may have overmixed your batter, beating too much air into it. Tapping the pan gently on the countertop a few times before baking will help the larger bubbles to migrate to the surface and pop before the cake can set in the oven.

Or you may have used a flour with too high a protein content. If this is the case, the air bubbles in batter with a lot of gluten will expand to a larger size than they would in batter made with a lower-protein flour. Next time, use a lower-protein flour.

Finally, an oven temperature that was too high may have caused your tunnels and bubbles. Check your oven with an oven thermometer and think about decreasing the setting by 25°F (4°C) before you bake again.

Q How can I adapt a cake recipe to make cupcakes instead?

A Most butter cake batters can be baked in cupcake liners. The tricky part is figuring out how many cupcakes your cake recipe will make. In general, a recipe calling for 2¼ cups of flour will make about two dozen cupcakes. But when portioning out the batter, fill each cupcake liner no more than three-quarters full so the batter won't rise over the top edge and just keep going. If you like your cupcakes with a flat top (better for frosting), bake them at a temperature no higher than 350°F (180°C). Higher temperatures will result in a volcanolike eruption in the center, resulting in a domed cupcake. Remember to adjust the baking time: Cupcakes take between 16 and 20 minutes to bake through.

Q How can I split my cake into layers easily?

A Place your cake on a cutting board or other flat work surface. If it has baked up with a slight dome on top, use a sharp serrated knife to slice away the domed portion for a flat surface. When doing this, it helps to crouch down so you are looking at the cake at eye level as you saw away at it with a knife. After you have done this, use your serrated knife to mark all around the side of the cake at the center point, rotating the cake on the cutting board as you mark. Finally, begin to cut through the cake, horizontally, along the mark-ings, moving the knife through the center as you rotate the cake on the counter, until you have two layers.

splitting a cake

Q Which is better, a canvas pastry bag or disposable plastic?

A I have to admit that I prefer disposable bags. Even now, I shudder at the memory of rinsing away greasy buttercream from the inside of the canvas bag I was responsible for cleaning in cooking school. I buy plastic bags by the hundreds (see Resources), and toss them when I'm finished. Another advantage: If I want to use different colors of frosting, I can keep several disposable bags filled at once.

If the idea of throwing away disposable plastic bags bothers you, buy one of the new style of canvas bags lined in plastic (see Resources). These are much easier to clean than the traditional type but are just as durable.

Q Which decorating tips do I really need to decorate a cake?

A If you are planning on going into the cake decorating business, then go for a deluxe set (Wilton sells one with 26 tips plus a coupler) that will allow you to pipe flowers, leaves, vines, pearls, shells, and other decorations in every size. But if you are just getting started, fewer than 12 tips will allow you to pipe many beautiful decorations. Remember, buttercream and whipped ganache can be piped through small tips for fine decorating, but whipped cream should be piped through large (at least ¼ inch in diameter) tips, as forcing it through smaller tips will deflate it.

Must-Have Pastry Bag Tips

* **Plain or writing.** For outlining, lettering, balls, pearls, lattice-work. Choose a smaller one (Wilton #5 or #6) for lettering and a larger one (#11 or #12) for pearls and larger balls.

* **Basket weave.** Wilton's #47 and #48 are versatile, making both smooth and ribbed stripes.

* **Closed star.** For shells, stars, and fleur-de-lis. A #27 and a #33 will give you some flexibility in size.

* **Leaf.** Leaf tips are fun and easy to use. These come in different styles, so choose a large and small in the style you like best.

* **Ruffle.** Not essential, but ruffle tips make pretty borders. They also come in different patterns, so choose a large and small that you like best.

FROSTING A LAYER CAKE, STEP-BY-STEP

To fill and frost a cake, follow these steps:

1. Split your cake into layers (see page 231 for instructions).
2. Trim the domed parts of the layers so each layer is flat.
3. Trim away about ¼ inch from the sides of each layer with a sharp serrated knife.
4. Brush the tops and sides of the layers lightly with a pastry brush to remove any loose crumbs. Clean up the work surface after you trim and brush, so there's less chance that crumbs will wind up on your frosted cake.
5. Cut out a cardboard cake circle from the bottom of a box, or use a cardboard cake circle from a baking supply shop (see Resources). The circle should be about ½ inch larger in diameter than your trimmed cake layers. Dab a tablespoon of frosting on the circle and place a cake layer on top of the frosting; this will prevent your cake from sliding around as you work. You should have between ¼ and ⅓ inch of the cardboard circle peeking out all around the bottom of the cake.
6. Spread your filling over the bottom layer. If you are using the frosting to also fill the cake, it won't matter if some oozes out the sides, but if you are using a different filling, don't spread it to the edges of the layer — leave a ½-inch border to allow it to spread without leaking out. Place the second layer over the bottom layer, trimmed-side down, so that the flat bottom is facing up. This will give you the flattest top possible.

7. Spoon about 1½ cups of frosting on top. Smooth it over the top with an offset spatula, running the spatula back and forth over the top of the cake to create a flat top and making sure that the frosting covers the entire layer.
8. Carefully pick up the cake and balance it in the palm of one hand. Working over the frosting bowl, apply a thick layer of frosting to the sides of the cake. Hold the spatula upright and against the side of the cake; run the spatula around the cake, using the cardboard as your guide, to smooth the frosting. The frosting should come just to the edge of the cardboard. Holding the spatula straight up as you rotate the cake should make the frosted sides nice and straight.
9. Run the spatula over the top of the cake to smooth the outer edges. If you are pressing any chopped nuts, chocolate, or cookie crumbs into the sides of the cake, do it now, before placing it on a cake stand or platter and before completing your decorating.

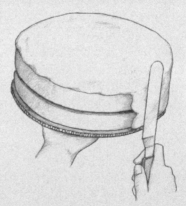

*frosting the sides
of a layer cake*

HOW TO USE A PASTRY BAG

Using a pastry bag is like other simple activities that don't come naturally until suddenly, after a lot of tries, they do — riding a bicycle comes to mind. Like most novices, I made a major mess the first few times I tried to pipe decorations onto a cake. When I squeezed the bag, frosting squirted out of the top rather than the tip. Buttercream coated the sides of the bag, making it slippery and difficult to control. I couldn't seem to apply the right amount of even pressure to create the simplest border. Some of my shells were large, some were small, some had big gaps where the pastry bag spit out air instead of frosting. Now, of course, I can pipe miles of shell border as if I were a machine, and it's hard to believe that at one time I couldn't. Follow the simple tips below and, with some practice, piping will come naturally to you, too.

1. Place the piping tip in the bag and place the bag inside a tall drinking glass. Fold the top edge of the bag over the edge of the glass. Fill the bag halfway with frosting. If you add more than this you'll have trouble twisting the bag closed without pushing excess frosting out of the top. Remove the bag from the edge of the glass and lift it out.

2. Push the frosting all the way into the bottom of the bag by holding the top of the bag closed with one

using a tall glass for stability

hand and sliding the fingers of your other hand downward. When you do this, try to compact the frosting so there are no large air bubbles. When the frosting is pushed to the bottom half of the bag, twist the empty top of the bag a few times, tightly, to seal it.

3. Hold the bag in your right hand (or left if you are left-handed), grasping it with your thumb and forefinger at the point where it is twisted to hold the bag closed. With your three other fingers, squeeze the frosting from the bag. Use your other hand only to steady and guide the tip as you move it over the cake, not to squeeze the bag. Practice your design a few times on a plate or countertop before beginning to pipe onto the cake. You can always scrape the excess frosting back into the bag later if you need it.

4. To refill the bag when you are getting low on frosting, fold down the top edge again and spoon in only as much frosting as you need, again making sure that the bag is no more than halfway full.

piping frosting

Q What does a coupler do?

A A coupler consists of a plastic base and ring. You slip the base into the pastry bag as you would a tip, then slip the tip into the ring and screw the ring onto the base. The system will allow you to change tips without emptying and washing the pastry bag. It comes in very handy when you are making different designs in the same color. But if you are making pink rosettes and green leaves and vines, you will have to use two different bags — one for the flower tip and one, fitted with a coupler, to accommodate a leaf tip for the leaves and a plain tip for the vines.

pastry bag coupler

Q What's the best way to store my cake?

A Plain, unfrosted cakes may be stored at room temperature for up to five days, wrapped tightly in plastic so they won't dry out. The exception is cheesecake, which must be stored in the refrigerator (also wrapped in plastic) for up to one week. A countertop cake keeper looks pretty and a plastic cake carrier is convenient for transporting a cake, but neither will prevent your cake from losing moisture the way that plastic wrap will.

Plain cakes, including cheesecake, can be frozen for up to two months, wrapped in a double layer of plastic and then in a layer of heavy duty foil to protect from freezer burn. Before freezing a cake, make sure it has cooled completely. Condensation from a cake that is wrapped in plastic when still warm will ruin the crust. Defrost frozen unfrosted cakes, still wrapped, on the countertop for several hours or overnight.

Frosted and filled cakes may need to be refrigerated depending on the frosting and filling ingredients. If the ingredients are nonperishable (frosting made with sugar and vegetable oil, or jam filling), then the cakes may be stored at room temperature for several days, in a cake keeper or under a large inverted bowl so as not to mar the frosting and decorations.

Cakes made with perishable frostings and fillings, anything containing dairy and eggs, must be refrigerated. Cakes frosted with buttercream can stand at cool room temperature for a day. Refrigerate these cakes unwrapped until the frosting is firm, and then drape them with plastic wrap and keep refrigerated for up to five days. Take the plastic wrap off as soon as you remove the cake from the refrigerator, when it is less likely to pull off the decorations and frosting. Bring a refrigerated cake to room temperature before serving. Freezing a frosted and filled layer cake is tricky. Butter cream frosting made with just sugar and butter freezes well, as does whipped cream. But custard, meringue, and fresh fruit fillings will shed moisture in the freezer, ruining the texture of the cake. When I want to get some work done ahead of time, I prefer to freeze unfrosted cake layers up to several weeks in advance, let them defrost completely, and then frost and decorate them.

CHAPTER 8

Pies, Tarts, Cobblers & Crisps

Pies, tarts, cobblers, and crisps represent from-scratch baking at its homiest and most friendly. Then why are so many bakers convinced that they don't have the right touch to make a flaky piecrust or a tender cobbler biscuit? This chapter will answer questions about how to make great crusts and toppings, and how to pair them with the right fillings for desserts that meet an old-fashioned ideal.

Q Which is better, a metal pie plate or a glass one?

A Glass is the clear (sorry!) choice if you want a well-browned and crisp bottom crust. Not only does it retain heat more efficiently than metal, causing superior browning, but because it is clear you can easily see how the crust is coming along, and avoid the common pitfall of pulling your pie from the oven before the bottom crust is fully baked.

Some bakers prefer metal pans because they are lighter and easier to store. If you have a choice between metal pans, dark metal is better than a light, reflective metal for heat retention and browning.

If you must bake your pie in a disposable aluminum pan, do not despair getting a crisped bottom crust. Adjust an oven rack to the lowest position and place a baking sheet on the rack when preheating the oven. Place your pie plate on the preheated baking sheet. The extra heat from the sheet will help crisp crusts baked in even the flimsiest pans.

Q Can pie recipes be made in tart pans and vice versa?

A Although pies and tarts are certainly similar in that each consists of a pastry crust and a sweet or sometimes savory filling, there are crucial differences that make pan substitutions tricky. Pies are baked in deeper (generally about 1 inch) pans with sloped sides to accommodate abundant juicy or moist fillings. While the crust is certainly an important element in a well-made pie, the filling takes center stage, flavor- and texture-wise.

Tart pans generally have straight sides no higher than ¾ inch. They hold less filling than pie pans. With tarts, the crust shares the spotlight with the filling. Tart shells are often pre-baked to a golden brown and then filled with rich unbaked fillings like pastry cream topped with fruit. A dessert made by filling a deeper pie shell with pastry cream would be overly rich and out of balance.

For a well-balanced result, it's wise to make your pie or tart in the pan recommended in the recipe. If you must substitute pans, make sure to adjust the amount of filling, keeping in mind that pie shells hold proportionately more filling than tart shells. Also adjust baking times: Thicker pies take longer to bake through than thinner tarts.

I don't recommend attempting a pan substitution in the case of a pie recipe with a double crust. Tart pans are too thin to accommodate two layers of pastry and a layer of filling.

Q Is there a difference between pie dough and tart dough?

A In general, people expect pie dough to be flaky and tender. Classic tart dough is more cookielike, with more sweetness than pie dough and either a crumbly texture like Scottish shortbread or some snap, like a classic sugar cookie.

Q I'm always afraid when removing my tart from the sides of the pan that I will drop it because the bottom of the tart pan is so slippery and unsteady on my palm. Is there a better way to unmold a tart?

A Try this: Place a 28-ounce can of tomatoes, beans, or whatever, on the countertop and set the tart on top. Gently push the ring downward and off of the tart. Then slide the tart, still on the pan bottom, onto a serving platter.

removing a tart pan ring

Q What kind of dough is best for a free-form tart? What is the best way to shape it so the fruit juices won't run onto the baking sheet and the bottom of the oven?

A Aside from being a good option when you don't have a tart pan, a free-form tart is just right when local fruit is at its peak and you want to showcase it on top of a simple pastry dough. Less formal than a tart made in a fluted pan, it is a lovely choice for casual summertime entertaining.

Dough for a free-form tart needs to be sturdy, to keep its shape in the oven without the help of a pan. Rolled out, it should be thicker than dough destined for a pie plate or tart shell, ¼- to ⅓-inch thick. Standard pie dough or pâte brisée will become tough and isn't very tasty when rolled out to this thickness. A richer and more tender dough will be able to contain the fruit and add flavor to a free-form tart. Look for doughs that have added buttermilk, sour cream, or cream cheese, which add this tenderness and flavor.

To put together the tart, roll your dough into a 12-inch circle. Place your fruit (you will need about 3 cups, sliced, tossed with 2 or 3 tablespoons of sugar, depending on how sweet the fruit is, and a teaspoon of lemon juice) in an even layer on the dough, leaving a 2-inch border. Fold a 2- or 3-inch section of the border over the fruit, and continue to fold, pleating the dough where you make a new fold, all the way around the fruit. Make sure the pleats are tight, because this is where the fruit juices are likely to leak out. Brush the border with a lightly beaten egg and sprinkle it with a little sugar to give it a nice shine. Then bake until the fruit is bubbling and the crust is golden.

Some leaking in the oven is inevitable, because there is no pan to contain the bubbling fruit juices as the tart bakes. To minimize the mess, use a rimmed baking sheet (juices will drip right off of a rimless one) and line it with parchment paper. Not only will the parchment make for easy clean-up, but it will prevent the sugary juices from burning and smoking as the tart bakes.

pleating tart dough

244

Q Is pastry cream the same thing as custard? How is it used in pies and tarts?

A Custard is a general term referring to any number of preparations made with milk and eggs and thickened by heat. So cheesecake, pumpkin pie, crème brûlée, and quiche are all considered custards, as are crème anglaise (which can be used as a dessert sauce or as a base for ice cream) and pastry cream. Pastry cream is a key component in many fruit tarts, cream pies, and cakes (such as Boston cream pie), as well as a filling for éclairs and other pastries.

The difference between pastry cream and the other items I've mentioned is that it belongs to a category of custards that contain cornstarch, which affects how quickly the custard will thicken and then curdle.

Custards made without starch, such as crème anglaise, thicken at 160°F (71°C) and curdle at 180°F (82°C). When you remember that water boils at 212°F (100°C), you will realize how easy it is to curdle an egg-thickened custard by overheating it or cooking it too long. This is why it's safest to make a custard in a double boiler, away from direct heat. Custards made with cornstarch, including pastry cream (see recipe on page 248), are much more forgiving, since they thicken at the same point that water boils, 212°F (100°C).

The method for making pastry cream is simple. Heat half-and-half or milk with sugar until simmering. Meanwhile, whisk egg yolks and cornstarch together. The proportions will vary from recipe to recipe, with two cups of liquid combining with two to six egg yolks, depending on how rich the cream needs to be. Dribble some of the hot liquid into the yolks, whisking, to temper them, then whisk the egg mixture back into the pot. Whisk the pastry cream constantly over medium heat until a few large bubbles begin to break on the surface and it thickens. Off the heat, whisk in some butter and then pour the mixture through a fine strainer. Even though it rarely curdles, you want to make sure it's silky smooth. Don't forget to press a piece of plastic wrap against the surface before refrigerating it, or a "pudding skin" will form over the top. The method for making all cornstarch-thickened custards, including custards flavored with coconut and citrus, is the same.

Once chilled, pastry cream can be spread in a thin layer on the bottom of a fully baked tart shell and topped with sliced fresh fruit.

Q What is frangipane?

A Frangipane is a rich batter made from ground almonds (or other nuts), sugar, butter, and eggs. When used as a tart filling it is spread over a partially baked tart shell and topped with fruit. In the oven, the frangipane rises to encase the fruit. Frangipane can also be used on its own as a filling for croissants, Danish pastries, or puff pastry Pithiviers.

Crustless Peach-Almond Tart

Sometimes, when I'm in the mood for a tart but too lazy to make dough, I'll just make this simple frangipane filling and spread it directly into the tart pan, top with peach slices, and bake. Try it!

SERVES 4

1½ cups (6 ounces) blanched almonds

½ cup sugar

2 large eggs

½ teaspoon pure almond extract

2 tablespoons unsalted butter, softened

2 tablespoons unbleached all-purpose flour

¼ teaspoon baking powder

Pinch of salt

1 large ripe peach, peeled, pitted, and thinly sliced

Confectioners' sugar for dusting

1. Preheat the oven to 375°F (190°C). Spray a 9-inch tart pan with cooking spray.
2. Combine the almonds and sugar in the bowl of a food processor and process until the almonds are finely ground.
3. Add the eggs and almond extract and pulse several times to combine. Cut the butter into small pieces, add to the food processor, and pulse several times to combine. Add the flour, baking powder, and salt, and pulse once or twice to combine.
4. Scrape the batter into the prepared tart pan and smooth with a small offset spatula. Arrange the peach slices on top of the batter.
5. Bake until the frangipane is slightly puffed and golden, 25 to 30 minutes. Remove it from the oven and let cool on a wire rack for 15 minutes. Remove the sides from the pan, slice the tart, dust with confectioners' sugar, and serve warm.

Pastry Cream for Tarts

This recipe will make enough cream to fill a prebaked 10-inch tart shell. Top with fresh raspberries or blueberries for the simplest late-summer fruit tart.

MAKES ABOUT 2½ CUPS

2 large eggs
½ cup sugar
¼ cup cornstarch
1½ cups milk
½ cup heavy cream
1 tablespoon unsalted butter
2 teaspoons vanilla extract

1. Whisk the eggs, sugar, and cornstarch in a medium bowl until smooth.
2. Combine the milk and heavy cream in a medium saucepan and bring to a boil. Slowly whisk about ½ cup of the milk mixture into the egg mixture. Whisk the egg mixture back into the remaining milk mixture in the saucepan and return the pan to the heat. Bring the mixture to a simmer over medium heat, whisking constantly.
3. Cook until the custard has thickened, 1 to 2 minutes. Pour the hot custard through a fine strainer and into a glass bowl. Stir in the butter and vanilla.
4. Place a sheet of plastic wrap directly on the surface of the custard and refrigerate until cold and thick, at least 3 hours and up to 1 day.

Q Is it necessary to use lard or shortening to get a flaky piecrust?

A The debate about the best way to achieve a flaky piecrust will no doubt rage on long after we're all gone and our great-great-grandchildren are making Thanksgiving dinner. Some bakers care less about flakiness than flavor and prefer an all-butter crust.

Bakers who swear by lard (rendered pork fat) claim that not only does it lend flakiness to pie dough, but it also lends its own enticing flavor. A combination of butter and lard is often recommended, because lard combined with butter has an appealingly nutty flavor while lard on its own gives the crust an overpowering aroma of pork. If health considerations and mixing meat with dessert don't deter you, try a dough made with 70% butter and 30% lard and see what you think.

Vegetable shortening will add flakiness to pie dough without adding any flavor. Because a flavorless crust is not what most bakers aspire to, shortening is often blended with butter to boost the taste. A crust made with 60% shortening and 40% butter will be flaky and flavorful in just the right balance.

But it is not just the combination of fats that determines the flakiness of a piecrust. The proper handling of the ingredients is crucial. Whether you use butter, lard, vegetable shortening, or a combination, it is important to chill the fat, which will melt in the oven and create layers of pastry separated by air pockets. This layered structure is what you are after. Using ice water rather than room temperature water is a way to help ensure that your fat will stay cold until it is time to bake.

Your mixing technique will also have an impact on the texture of your crust. Undermixing will result in a hard crust that falls into tough little pieces. Overmixing will give you a softer, crumbly crust without any prized flakiness. Again, bakers disagree on the best tools for mixing. Some people insist that cutting the fat into the flour by hand and then mixing in the ice water with a spatula is the safest way to ensure a flaky crust. Others prefer an electric mixer set on low. It is easy to see and feel how small the pieces of fat are becoming as they churn together in the mixer, although there is a danger that during the relatively long mixing time the fat will get too soft and warm. The food processor is another choice. It cuts fat into flour with lightning speed. But once ice water is poured through the feed tube it is a matter of milliseconds before the dough is overprocessed.

You may not achieve your perfect piecrust on the first try, as perfection depends on having some experience with the ingredients and techniques. Try to consider every pie-making session a leg on a journey toward a better understanding of the·dough. It helps to remember that even an imperfect homemade pie is going to taste good.

Q What are pâte brisée and pâte sucrée? What is the difference between the two?

A These are the French terms for two types of pastry dough commonly used in savory and sweet tarts and other pastries. Pâte brisée is similar to American pie dough, but always made with butter. (You can gauge from this where the French stand on the flavor-versus-flakiness debate.)

Pâte sucrée is also an all-butter dough, but with more sugar than pâte brisée and added egg or egg yolk, which gives it a cookielike crunch. The sugar and eggs make this dough similar in feel to sugar cookie dough, less crumbly, and easier to roll than pâte brisée or American pie dough.

Q Can you give me some tips for rolling out pastry dough evenly, without tearing it or having it stick to the counter?

A Temperature is the first key to an easy-to-roll dough. Cool dough is less likely to tear than warm dough, but if the dough is too cold it may crumble into pieces when you attempt to roll it. If you make your dough with chilled butter and ice-cold water as most recipes recommend, an hour or two of chilling time in the refrigerator will bring it to just the right temperature for easy rolling. If your dough has been in the refrigerator longer than this, let it sit on the counter to warm up a bit before rolling. Some recipes recommend kneading the dough a few times to soften it up, and I find that a quick kneading prevents cold dough from cracking as it rolls.

Once your dough is at the proper temperature, set it on a lightly floured countertop and press it into a rough circle by pushing down on it all over with the rolling pin before actually attempting to roll it out. It is easier to press a thick disk of dough into a thinner circle than it is to attempt rolling at this point. When you have a circle measuring 6 inches or so, lightly flour your rolling pin and use even strokes to roll the dough. After every 4 or 5 strokes, slide a large offset spatula underneath the dough to loosen it from the work surface, and rotate the dough 45 degrees. Continue to roll, loosen, and turn until you have a circle big enough to cover the bottom and sides of your pie or tart pan, with enough excess to double the edge and crimp if necessary. Although adding too much flour to the dough during rolling will result in the toughening of the crust, it is important to use enough flour on the work surface and the rolling pin to prevent sticking and tearing. Too much sticking and tearing will mean that you will have to press your dough into a ball and begin again, adding even more flour to the dough than you would have if you had been more generous to begin with.

Ideally, your rolled dough should be a perfect circle. If, during rolling, it becomes misshapen, use the side of a chef's knife to press the edges into a circle shape and continue to roll.

Q Just as I was rolling my dough into a large enough circle to transfer it to the pan, it developed a tear down the center. Can I repair it or should I start over again?

A With most pies and tarts, it is important to have a crust that isn't torn or cracking, because sugary fillings will seep through the cracks, burning on the bottom of the pan during baking and causing the crust to burn. Even if fillings are unbaked, as with pastry cream–filled tart shells, it is important to have an intact crust, as the filling will soon seep through cracks and make the bottom crust soggy.

But if your crust tears during rolling it's not necessary to re-roll. Depending on the type of dough you are using, you can simply press together the torn part, lightly flour your rolling pin, and continue to roll, or use an extra piece of dough, cut from the edge of the circle, to patch up the tear. Place the piece over the tear and use your index finger to lightly smooth its edges into the larger piece before flouring your rolling pin and continuing to roll.

Q How big should the dough circle be for a tart pan?

A To be safe, roll your dough to a diameter 2 inches larger than your pan. If you are using a 9-inch tart pan, roll the dough to a diameter of 11 inches. Fit the dough into the corners of the pan by gently pressing it with your fingertips. To trim the dough, roll a rolling pin over the top of the tart pan to cut the dough right at the pan's sharp top edge.

Q How big should my dough circle be to fit into a 9-inch pie plate?

A Roll your dough into a 12-inch circle, to ensure that you have enough pastry to make a generous edge. Once you have transferred the dough circle to the pie plate, trim away all but ¾ inch of the edge, which should be enough for crimping. If you are making a top crust, roll the second ball of dough to the same 12-inch diameter, place it on top of the filled pie, and trim the bottom and top crust edges to ¾ inch at the same time, crimping them together when you are done.

Q How do I transfer rolled dough to a pie or tart pan?

A For pliable, sturdy doughs, use a rolling pin. Loosely fold your dough circle around the pin, lift the pin, and unroll the dough over the pan. For more crumbly, delicate doughs that might crack when folded over a rolling pin, you might try rolling out your circle on a piece of parchment paper and then sliding the dough from the parchment into the pan.

Q How do I fit the dough into the pan?

A When you have transferred the dough to the pan, gently press it into the bottom and sides with your fingertips. It's important not to stretch or thin the dough when you do this or dimple it with your fingers, which may cause the dough to shrink or become otherwise misshapen in the oven. Simply make sure by touch that the dough is making contact in every spot with the pan.

Q What are pie weights and why are they necessary?

A While a pie or tart bakes, the filling acts as a weight on the pastry dough, holding it in place and preventing the sides from shrinking or parts of the pastry from bubbling up in places where air bubbles may have been rolled into the dough.

Some pie and tart recipes, however, call for the crust to be partially or fully baked before it is filled. In these cases, the crust needs to be weighed down with special ceramic or metal pellets (available in baking supply stores), or with dried beans (available in any supermarket, and reusable) before baking. *Blind baking* is the term used for baking a crust before filling.

Follow these steps when blind baking for a well-shaped and browned crust: First, prick the bottom of the shell all over with a fork to prevent air pockets from bubbling up during baking. Then cover the crust, including its edges, with a double layer of aluminum foil. Place the pie weights or dried beans on top of the foil. If you will be adding a filling that needs to be baked, as with pecan pie, remove the partially baked crust from the oven, carefully lift the foil and weights from the pan, fill the crust, and continue to bake. If you will be adding a filling that won't be baked, you'll have to remove the foil and weights and return the unfilled crust to the oven to brown once it is set and the danger of shrinking has passed.

Q How do I crimp the edges of a piecrust?

A When you have trimmed the crust all around so that it overhangs the edge of the pan by ¾ inch, tuck that extra dough underneath itself to form a double-thick edge that sits on the rim of the pie plate. Then you can mold the thick edge into one of several patterns.

Piecrust Patterns

* For a **ridged edge**, press the tines of the fork into the edge all the way around to flatten it against the rim.

* For a **fluted edge**, pinch the edge of the crust with the thumb and index finger of one hand while pressing from the inside with the index finger of the other hand, repeating all the way around the edge.

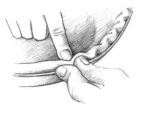

* For a **checkerboard edge**, use a scissor or paring knife to make ½-inch-deep cuts ½-inch apart into and all the way around the edge. Fold every other square over and inward to form a checkerboard pattern.

* For a **leaf edge**, re-roll the trimmed dough and use a small leaf cookie cutter or cut leaves freehand from the dough. Brush some beaten egg white onto the edge of the shell and arrange the leaves, overlapping them slightly, on the edge. Brush the tops of the leaves with more egg white.

* For a **braided edge**, roll the dough scraps into three long, thin ropes and braid them together. Brush some beaten egg white onto the edge of the shell and arrange the braid along the edge, trimming where the ends meet. Brush the braid with more egg white.

Q My pie and tart crusts always shrink during baking. What can I do to prevent this?

A Make sure that when you fit the dough into the pan you are not stretching it to the edges. If you are, it will shrink back to its original size once it begins to bake. Crusts that require blind baking (baking without a filling) will shrink if not baked with pie weights. Freezing your unfilled pie and tart shells for 30 minutes before blind baking will further prevent shrinkage.

Q What is the best type of apple for apple pie?

A Apple-pie fruit must hold its shape when baked, since part of the pleasure of eating an apple pie is in the toothsomeness of the fruit. Choose from the following list of apples that stay firm in the oven, depending on whether you prefer sweet or tart fruit and local and seasonal availability. Feel free to blend apples from either or both lists to come up with your ideal sweet-tart apple pie.

* **Sweet baking apples**: Golden Delicious, Braeburn, Fuji, Mutsu, Rome

* **Tart baking apples**: Granny Smith, Empire, Cortland, Macoun, Newton Pippin, Northern Spy, Idared

* **Sweet-tart baking apples**: Macintosh, Jonathan, Jonagold, Honeycrisp

---

Q When I make an apple pie, I fill my pie pan to the brim with apples, but they shrink in the oven, leaving a large space between the filling and the top crust, making the pie difficult to slice. Any suggestions?

A Try filling your pie shell with a precooked apple filling. If you cook your apples (and cool them, of course — hot apples will ruin your chilled piecrust), you'll preshrink them, so they'll stay the same size as they were when you placed them in the shell, with the top crust resting against them.

Precooked Apple Pie Filling

The following recipe makes enough apple filling for a 9-inch pie, and it won't shrink during baking.

3 tablespoon unsalted butter
5 pounds (10 to 12) baking apples of your choice (see page 258), peeled, cored, and cut into ½-inch chunks
¾ cup sugar
⅛ teaspoon ground cinnamon
1 tablespoon lemon juice

1. Melt the butter over medium heat in a large pot. Add the apples, sugar, and cinnamon, and cook, stirring frequently, until the apples are cooked through but are still holding their shape, about 15 minutes.
2. Use a slotted spoon to transfer the apples to a baking sheet. The apple pieces should be liberally coated with juice, but leave any extra juices in the pot to prevent your pie from becoming soggy. Spread them out in a single layer and let stand until they are cool. When they are cool, the apples can be covered with plastic wrap and refrigerated for up to 3 days.
3. Toss the cooled apples with the lemon juice before arranging them inside your pie shell.

Q Can I replace the top crust of any fruit pie with a lattice top? What is the best way to weave a lattice?

A Any fruit pie can be topped with a lattice. How tightly you weave it will depend on the fruit. Apples, which tend to dry out when exposed to the hot air of the oven, require a tightly woven lattice with just a little space between pastry strips to allow for some steam to escape but also to cover the fruit and keep it moist. Blueberries, cherries, peaches, and other very moist fruits benefit from a loose lattice with lots of exposed surface area for evaporating liquid.

Instead of weaving the strips directly on top of the pie, I prefer to cut long strips (about 13 inches long) and then weave them on top of a cardboard cake circle set on a baking sheet. When the lattice is woven, I place the baking sheet in the freezer for 15 minutes to allow the lattice to firm up. Then I slide it from the cake circle onto the pie, adjusting any strips that may have shifted during the transfer and trimming and crimping the ends into the pie's edge.

weaving a lattice crust

Q Are the vents cut into the top crust of a fruit pie decorative, or do they serve another purpose?

A Vents serve a very important purpose, providing an escape route for the steam produced by the baking fruit. Without them, steam would be trapped inside the pie, causing both the top and bottom crusts to become soggy as the pie cooled. For less watery fruit, such as apples and pears, only three or four vents are necessary. For very juicy pies, like blueberry or strawberry, cut six to eight vents to allow enough steam to escape.

Q Are thickeners like cornstarch and tapioca inter-changeable in fruit pies? Are they always necessary?

A Without a thickener of some kind, the fruit and fruit juices in a pie won't gel and your pie becomes a watery mess. With them, the flavorful juices become semisolid and add flavor to the pie instead of running off the plate. So yes, I would always use a thickener in a fruit pie, as well as in most cobblers and crisps. The type and amount varies depending on the recipe.

Cornstarch, tapioca, and flour are the most popular fruit pie thickeners. (There are other options: Some people swear by Clear-Jel, a modified cornstarch favored by commercial bakers and available at most supermarkets; when baking for Passover, many people use potato starch.) When baking fruit pies, I stay away from flour, which can get lumpy if the pro-tein in it forms gluten. Cornstarch and tapioca, in contrast, thicken without lumps because they are both pure starches without any gluten-forming proteins. Juices thickened with both cornstarch and tapioca become satiny and smooth, an appealing combination.

Each has its advantages and disadvantages. Tapioca, a starch derived from the root of the yucca plant, is flavorless and gives fruit and fruit juices a glossy shine. But it is not the best choice for lattice-top and other open-top fruit pies because any small granules directly exposed to the heat of the oven will become hard and tough instead of dissolving into the fruit as it cooks. If you'd like to make a tapioca-thickened lattice-top pie, use tapioca starch, a fine powder made of ground tapioca granules, instead of pearl tapioca. Or grind pearl tapioca to a fine dust in a spice grinder before mixing it with the fruit to prevent this from happening.

Cornstarch gives fruit a satiny, less shiny gloss than tapioca. It won't clump up and dry out when exposed to hot air, as tapioca will, so it is the natural choice for open-top baked fruit desserts. It can, in large quantities or when not cooked sufficiently, lend a slightly starchy taste to fruit fillings. And it won't work as well to thicken highly acidic fruits such as cranberries, plums, and cherries.

The quantity of thickener will depend on the water content of the fruit you are using (juicy fruits will need more thickener than relatively dry fruits) and how much sugar you are adding to the fruit (sugar itself is a thickener, so more sugar means less cornstarch or tapioca). Whichever thickener you choose, mix it with the fruit and sugar and let the filling stand, stirring occasionally, for 15 minutes before adding it to the pie shell and baking. During this time, the starch will have a chance to dissolve evenly around the fruit, resulting in an evenly thickened pie filling.

Q I'd like to make a cherry pie with fresh cherries, but I've heard that Bing cherries, the ones I usually see in the supermarket, are not good for pie. What should I look for instead?

A Bing cherries, the dark maroon ones grown in California and shipped all over the country, are wonderfully sweet when eaten out of hand, but lose their flavor when baked in a pie. Sour cherries, the bulk of which are grown in Michigan but increasingly shipped to farm markets and specialty produce stores in July when they are in season, are much preferable.

If you can't find fresh sour cherries, you don't have to resort to canned cherry pie filling, a scary concoction with a lot of red dye and not much cherry flavor. IQF (individually quick frozen) sour cherries from Michigan do make their way to some upscale markets and are available online (see Resources, but be prepared to pay a high price. Less expensive options include jarred domestic sour cherries packed in water that some American growers are distributing, and Morello cherries in light syrup imported from Europe, both of which make flavorful and juicy pies.

PITTING CHERRIES WITHOUT A CHERRY PITTER

In my opinion, even if you make a cherry pie or cobbler only once a year, it is well worth the savings in grief to invest in an inexpensive cherry pitter to help with the task (see Resources). But say you have just been given a basket of fresh sour cherries and must bake that pie tonight before they spoil. You don't have a cherry pitter. What do you do? A quick Internet search reveals that many people in a similar predicament have found clever ways to accomplish the task. Be aware that pitting cherries by any method is a messy task. Watch out for flying pits, definitely wear an apron, and consider wearing thin rubber gloves if you don't want semipermanent stains on your hands and underneath your fingernails.

conventional cherry pitter

Four Cherry-Pitting Techniques

* Use a **paring knife** to cut around each cherry from one side of the stem end to the other. Then pull the cherry apart and squeeze the pit out.

* Open a clean, unrusted **paperclip** into a skinny S shape. Push one rounded end into the stem end of the cherry, hooking the pit with it, and then pull the pit out. Or use a clean **bobby pin** (no need to open it in this case) and use the same push and pull method.

* Place a **metal pastry bag tip** on a cutting board. Push the stem end of the cherry into the tip and down toward the cutting board, leaving the pit behind.

* Remove an eraser from the **end of a pencil** and wash the end so it's clean. Place an empty beer bottle on a counter-top. Place a cherry, stem end up, on the opening of the bottle and use the metal edges of the pencil where the eraser used to be to push the pit into the bottle.

Q What is the difference between canned pumpkin and canned pumpkin pie mix?

A There is usually only one ingredient in a can of canned pumpkin — puréed pumpkin. Canned pumpkin pie mix has added sugar and spices. It's always better to be able to add as much or as little sugar as you'd like, and fresh spices will make a zestier pie than ones that have been marinating in purée, so I'd always choose canned pumpkin over the pumpkin pie mix. What to do if you've accidentally bought the wrong one and it's Thanksgiving morning? Proceed with the recipe that you'd planned on using, increasing the amount of pumpkin by half (there's less pumpkin in a can of pumpkin pie mix than in a can of pure pumpkin) and leaving out the sugar and spices.

Q How can I make a pumpkin pie with a crisp, not soggy, crust?

A The challenge with any custard pies is to get the custard to set up in the oven before it can seep into the crust and dampen it. There are a few precautions you can take to prevent this from happening.

Most pumpkin pie recipes call for blind baking the crust. Don't be timid when you do this. The crust should look dry and already be a light golden brown color before you add the filling. The more crisp it is when you add the filling, the less chance that it will become soggy later.

It also helps to time your baking so that your crust is just out of the oven when your filling is ready to go into the pie. The hot crust will help the filling start to set sooner, with less time for it to seep downward before solidifying. A lot of recipes will tell you that you can make your filling ahead of time and refrigerate it, but using ice-cold filling is a mistake because it will take that much longer for the custard to bake. Let it come to room temperature before using it, or even better, look for a recipe that calls for heating the filling before adding it to the hot pie shell for extra insurance against crust damage.

Q Is it normal to have water on top of a cooled pumpkin pie?

A A small amount of beaded water on the surface of the pie is normal. This happens with cheesecakes, too, as they cool, especially in the refrigerator. Use a paper towel to gently blot the water before slicing the pie.

If, however, your pie is watery when you cut into it, you have a more serious problem. When custard pies, including pumpkin, are overbaked they will curdle, becoming lumpy and watery. Pumpkin pie is less likely to curdle than cheesecake, because there are proportionately fewer eggs, but it can happen if you don't remove the pie when it is just a little wobbly in the center.

Q What causes the cracks in the top of my pumpkin pie?

A Pumpkin pie, like cheesecake (see page 223) and other baked custards, can crack if overbaked. Make sure to following the baking instructions and remove the pie when it is still a little wobbly in the center. Another cause of cracking is baking the pie in the top third of the oven, where the surface is exposed to more intense heat than it would be if baked in the bottom third. A "skin" may form over the filling before the rest of the pie is baked. This skin will crack as it cools and contracts. To prevent this, bake pumpkin pie in the bottom third of the oven, which will help the custard set up quickly.

Q Can I make Key lime pie with regular limes? Will a pie made with Key limes taste better?

A Key lime pie originated in the Florida Keys in the 1850s, where residents combined the juice from the local limes with newly invented condensed milk (a boon to locals, since dairy cows were scarce in the area) to make the creamy and tart dessert. The dessert's popularity spread, and eventually it became a standard in the American baker's repertoire. Originally made with a pastry crust, most Key lime pie recipes today call for a graham cracker crust. And most are made with Persian lime juice.

Key limes are smaller and rounder than the more common Persian limes sold in every supermarket. They are grown in

Florida in small quantities, and not widely available in other parts of the country. Except for the sake of authenticity, there is little reason to seek out Key limes to make a Key lime pie. Persian lime juice will give your pie the same sweet-and-tart flavor, and they are easier to juice than tiny, thin-skinned, and seedy Key limes. To get ½ cup of juice you'll need three or four Persian limes, but upwards of a dozen Key limes.

Q No matter how brown my meringue gets on the outside of my lemon meringue pie, the underside is undercooked. What can I do to prevent this?

A Spread your meringue on top of the lemon custard as soon as the custard is cooked and put the pie back into the oven to brown the meringue. The underside of the meringue, coming in contact with the hot custard, will then cook at the same rate as the top.

Q What is an icebox pie?

A Icebox pies can be filled with ice cream, Bavarian cream, mousse, custard, chocolate pudding, or any number of other creamy, cold fillings. What unites them is the fact that they aren't baked (if you don't count crisping up a crumb crust in the oven for a few minutes). A filling is simply smoothed into the pie shell and refrigerated or frozen until it is set. The pie must spend an adequate amount of time chilling, instead of baking, to achieve the proper consistency.

Q Does mincemeat pie really have meat in it?

A Mincemeat pie originated in the Middle Ages, as an effort to preserve meat by mixing it with alcohol, fruit, and spices. It is still occasionally made with beef suet and beef in England, Ireland, Brittany, and Canada. Along with plum pudding, mincemeat pie is an essential item on the holiday table in Great Britain.

Most of today's mincemeat pies, especially in the United States, eschew meat and suet for a mixture of apples, dried fruits, spices, and either butter or vegetable shortening. In spite of their name, they do not have a meaty flavor. The rich filling is more like a spicy and moist fruitcake, and is long-keeping like a fruitcake.

Q I often see recipes for crumb crusts that give only volume quantities for crumbs. How many graham crackers or wafer cookies make a cup of crumbs?

A Packaged graham cracker and chocolate cookie crumbs are now sold in the baking aisle of many supermarkets, which is probably why some recipes give quantities in cups rather than in crackers or cookies. But it is always better to take a few extra minutes to crush cookies into crumbs. Whole cookies stay fresh longer than packaged crumbs, so chances are that a crust made with crumbs from whole cookies will taste fresher than one made with precrushed cookies. Packaged crumbs tend to be crushed almost into a powder or dust. With freshly crushed cookies, your crust will have a chewier, more interesting texture. In my own icebox pie recipes, I generally use about 1⅓ cups of crumbs for a 9-inch crust.

For 1⅓ cup crumbs, you'll need	
COOKIE TYPE	NUMBER
Graham crackers	11 whole crackers (not broken along the perforation)
Chocolate wafer cookies	30
Vanilla wafers	50
Chocolate sandwich cookies	18
Gingersnap cookies	25 (standard supermarket cookies such as Sunshine or Keebler)

Q My fruit crisp topping comes out of the oven rather pale, and becomes just plain soggy as it sits on top of the warm fruit. Any suggestions?

A Recently I've seen a few fruit crisp recipes that address this complaint. They call for crisping the topping on a baking sheet in the oven before proceeding. In various versions, the precrisped topping is either sprinkled on the fruit before it is baked, or the fruit is baked separately and the topping is sprinkled on just before serving.

Q I want to make a cobbler, but it's the middle of the winter and fresh local fruit is scarce. Is it better to use fresh fruit imported from South America or frozen fruit?

A In addition to saving money, you will also wind up with a tastier cobbler (or crisp or crumble) by using frozen fruit. Individually quick frozen (IQF) fruit is picked at its peak, when it's sweetest. Fresh imported fruit, in contrast, is picked early so it can make it to distant supermarkets before spoiling. So, out of season, frozen fruit is preferable to fresh.

Don't thaw the fruit before you begin making your dessert. Just toss it with sugar, cornstarch, and whatever other filling ingredients are called for in the recipe and proceed, adding 5 to 10 minutes to the baking time.

Q Is canned fruit any good in cobblers, crisps, etc.?

A There are a lot of recipes that call for canned fruit, but I much prefer frozen fruit if fresh isn't available. Canned fruit is already very soft from processing and from sitting in liquid. When baked for a significant amount of time under a heavy layer of biscuit or piecrust, it can get mushy. Frozen fruit, in contrast, maintains its shape during baking.

The exception is canned fruit used on fruit tarts that call for poached fruit. Poaching fresh fruit is time-consuming. In addition, unless your fruit is at a perfect stage of ripeness, it can start to fall apart when it is cooled and cut, making it impossible to achieve the neat pastry shop look. Canned fruit, in contrast, just needs to be drained, patted dry, and arranged in a pretty pattern before baking. Of course, with any tart that calls for uncooked fruit, only fresh will do.

Q I've made two cherry pies and we've eaten only one. Can I freeze it and then thaw it to serve later?

A It's possible to freeze a baked and cooled fruit pie, thaw it, and reheat it to crisp the crust, but it will lose a lot of its fresh-baked flavor in the freezer. Next time, if you have any idea that you won't be needing the second pie, a better option is to assemble the pie and wrap it in a double layer of plastic and then a layer of heavy-duty aluminum foil (to guard against freezer burn) and freeze it unbaked. You can put it in the oven directly from the freezer (make sure your pie plate is safe to go from freezer to oven), adding 10 to 20 minutes of additional baking time.

Pies with baked custard fillings, such as pumpkin or pecan, cannot be frozen this way. If you'd like to do some work ahead of time, make and freeze the pie shells. They will be good for up to two months, tightly wrapped in plastic and foil.

PIE AND TART STORAGE

Most pies and tarts are best eaten soon after they are baked. Ice cream pies and many other icebox pies are exceptions. Here are answers to the questions, "How should I store my pie?" and "How long will it keep?"

Fruit pies. Cover loosely with plastic wrap and keep at room temperature for up to one day. Some fruit pies, may be edible for another day or two, but the crust will quickly soften and lose its appeal after 24 hours.

Mincemeat pie. Traditional mincemeat pie, made with beef suet, will keep, covered with plastic wrap and refrigerated, for several weeks. Newer styles of mincemeat pie, made with butter, will last only for several days in the refrigerator.

Nut pies. These pies, filled with a rich mixture of nuts and eggs, should be stored in the refrigerator, loosely covered in plastic wrap, for up to one day.

Custard pies. Pies with creamy custard fillings should be loosely covered with plastic wrap and kept in the refrigerator for up to one day.

Cream pies and cakes (including Boston cream and banana cream). Loosely cover with plastic and refrigerate for up to one day before topping with whipped cream and serving. Once the whipped cream is added, the pies must be eaten.

Meringue pies. The meringue will quickly begin to break down after the pie cools, so keep this one at room temperature, uncovered, for no more than 3 or 4 hours before serving.

Fruit tarts. Simple tarts made by topping pastry with fruit and baking can be held at room temperature for up to 6 hours, loosely covered with plastic wrap, before serving.

Icebox pies. Icebox pies made with crumb crusts generally keep longer than pastry crust pies. If your icebox pie is filled with ice cream, wrap it tightly in a double layer of plastic wrap and freeze it for up to 2 weeks before serving. Cheesecake pies will keep for up to a week, loosely wrapped and refrigerated. Pies filled with mousse or custard will keep for up to 2 days, loosely wrapped in plastic, in the refrigerator. Pudding pies, such as black bottom pie, will keep for up to 2 days. Pies topped with fresh, uncooked fruit should be refrigerated for no longer than a day before serving.

Frangipane tarts. Frangipane, a kind of cakey nut batter that is spread on top of tart dough before fruit is added, absorbs moisture from the fruit, thus keeping the crust from becoming soggy as quickly as a plain fruit tart. Loosely cover frangipane tarts and keep them at room temperature for up to one day before serving.

Pastry cream tarts. You can prebake your tart shell several days in advance and keep it wrapped in plastic at room temperature. Similarly, you can make your pastry cream several days in advance and store it, plastic wrap pressed to the surface, until ready to use. But once you assemble the tart, you should serve it within 1 or 2 hours.

Tarte tatin. This one is best served warm no more than 3 or 4 hours after it comes out of the oven.

Cobblers, crisps, and crumbles. These desserts lose their charm after several hours out of the oven, so eat them while they're hot, or at warm room temperature. You can reheat leftovers in a 350°F (180°C) oven for 10 minutes the next day to crisp up the topping.

A BAKED FRUIT DESSERT GLOSSARY

To clear up any confusion about the difference between a brown Betty and a buckle, here is a list of fruit dessert definitions.

Brown Betty. One of the simplest fruit desserts, a brown Betty is simply a sweet fruit mixture sprinkled with buttered bread crumbs and baked until the topping is crisp.

Buckle. A buckle is slightly more complicated than some of these other desserts, consisting of a cakelike batter mixed with fruit (most often blueberries), topped with streusel or crumbs.

Clafouti. A French-style dessert, for which fruit is topped with a custardlike batter and baked.

Cobbler. Although there are many variations, a basic cobbler is made by topping sweetened fruit with biscuit or cookie dough.

Crisp or Crumble. Both desserts have a crumb or streusel topping covering the fruit.

Deep-dish pie. A fruit pie with no bottom crust.

Grunt. Similar to a cobbler, with fruit on the bottom and biscuit dough on top, a grunt is different in that it is steamed, not baked.

Pandowdy. A pandowdy is made by covering sweetened fruit with pastry dough. But in contrast to a deep-dish pie, the pastry dough is cut into pieces either before or after baking, and the bubbling juices are allowed to flow over the pastry pieces, which soak them up.

Plate cake. An upside-down cobbler, in which fruit is topped with rolled biscuit dough and baked; then turned upside down onto a plate (thus the name), so the biscuit becomes a bottom crust.

Slump. Another word for a grunt.

CHAPTER 9

Layered Pastry Doughs

The pastry doughs discussed in this chapter — puff pastry, croissant, brioche, Danish dough, choux paste, phyllo dough, and strudel — are generally less familiar to American home bakers than the pie and tart doughs from chapter 8 or the bread doughs in chapter 10.

Even people who've mastered buttermilk biscuits, layer cakes, and lattice-top pies have likely not attempted from-scratch croissants or brioche. If most of your knowledge comes from sampling napoleons from a French pastry shop, then making anything from puff pastry might seem overly ambitious.

But these items really are no more difficult to produce than American-style baked goods once you understand the techniques. This chapter will answer questions about how these doughs are made and how they are used to create dozens of delicious treats.

Q Can you describe how to form the butter slab? I've never made pastry dough and I'm having trouble picturing it.

A The tricky and important thing about the butter that you are going to place inside the dough is that it has to be well-chilled but also very soft and malleable so it can be rolled out thin once placed inside the dough, folded, and rolled again without melting or poking holes in the pastry. To get chilled butter to the state where it is both cold and malleable, you must soften it manually by pounding it with a rolling pin. Most recipes will instruct you to sprinkle the counter with flour, place the chilled sticks of butter (usually between two and four depending on how much dough you are making) on the counter, and sprinkle more flour on top of the butter. Then, start to pound the butter, turning it often and sprinkling it with more flour, until it comes together into a smooth mass. What you don't want is crumbly or crackly butter. It should look like a soft, doughy square when you are through. If at any time while you are pounding the butter gets sticky or begins to melt, wrap it loosely in plastic and refrigerate it until it is cool, and continue until the butter slab is the right consistency — a cool, plastic mass. Then you can roll out your dough and place the butter slab in the center.

Q What are the similarities and differences between puff pastry, croissant dough, and Danish dough?

A Puff pastry, croissant dough, and Danish dough are all made by wrapping dough around a large slab of butter and then repeatedly rolling out and folding the packet, creating very thin alternating layers of dough and butter. When baked, the steam created as the butter melts pushes the layers of dough away from each other. The fat in the butter helps brown and crisp the layers and gives them great flavor.

They differ in their ingredients beyond butter. Puff pastry is made with just butter, flour, water, and salt. All of its flavor comes from butter and all of its rise depends on the steam created when the butter melts. Its many separate crackerlike leaves give it a crisp texture with no cakelike crumb.

To make croissant dough, the slab of butter is surrounded with a bread dough made of flour, milk, and yeast. Croissants are flaky like puff pastry, but with a soft but chewy texture from the gluten that develops during kneading and rolling.

For Danish, a briochelike yeast dough made with eggs encloses the butter. The egg protein gives Danish a more cakelike structure than puff pastry and croissant dough.

Q Is there any special equipment needed to make layered pastry dough?

A If you bake regularly you probably have all of the equipment you need. See the following page.

Pastry Equipment

* An **electric stand mixer** is necessary for the mixing and, in the case of croissant and Danish dough, the kneading of the dough, although the dough for puff pastry can also be mixed in a food processor.

* A **rolling pin** is necessary to pound the butter into a malleable mass before enclosing it in the dough packet, and then to roll the dough packet multiple times.

* A **sharp paring knife** or a **pizza wheel** is used to cut croissants into triangle shapes before rolling them up, as well as to cut out and make decorative cuts in puff pastry. Cookie cutters can also be used to cut Danish dough into decorative shapes before you top it with frangipane or fruit.

* Use a **pastry brush** to paint the surface of the pastry with an egg wash, which will give it beautiful color and sheen.

* Bake puff pastry, croissants, and Danish on **rimless baking sheets** with **parchment paper**. Not only does the parchment paper make cleanup easy (no egg wash baked onto the pan), but it also helps with removing the delicate pastries from the baking sheet to cool. Just slide the sheet, with the pastries still on it, to a wire rack and let them cool completely. It's especially important with these types of pastries that they cool on a rack, with air circulating below as well as above them, to maintain their crisp texture.

Q What is the difference between a single turn and a double turn?

A For doughs containing a butter slab, repeated rolling and folding of the dough results in a finished pastry that may have over 1,000 alternating layers of dough and butter. There are two different ways of folding the dough — single and double turns. Sometimes they are used alone, sometimes in combination.

For a single turn, the dough is rolled into a rectangle and then folded like a letter, the bottom third folded over the middle third, and then the top third folded over the first two layers. The result is a smaller 3-layered rectangle.

single turn

For a double turn, the dough is also rolled into a rectangle. The dough is folded from the top edge to the midpoint of the rectangle. Then the bottom edge is also folded to the midpoint, meeting the top edge. The dough is then folded in half, lengthwise along the midpoint, creating a smaller, 4-layered rectangle.

double turn

Different chefs have varying ideas about the type and number of turns puff pastry, croissant, and Danish dough require. Everyone agrees that puff pastry must have as many layers as possible. The classic French recipe calls for six single turns to create those 1,000 layers, but to save time, many pastry chefs will use two double and two single turns.

To give croissants their crisp leaves of pastry, the dough shouldn't be folded into as many layers as puff pastry dough.

Fewer turns will make fewer leaves that are more distinct and crackly. Croissant dough is more elastic and more difficult to roll than puff pastry dough, because it has been kneaded to develop the flour's gluten. Croissant dough is generally given single, not double, turns, because the thicker four-layer dough would be too difficult to roll out again into a larger rectangle.

Danish dough, made soft and stretchy with the addition of sugar and eggs, easily takes double turns, but doesn't need to rise as high as puff pastry. Two double turns will be enough to give it a nice flakiness without too much height.

Q Why is it so important to chill these doughs after every turn?

A There are two reasons for chilling the dough after every turn. First, and most important, is keeping the butter layers that you are creating from melting. When puff pastry, croissant dough, and Danish dough go into the oven, those layers of butter must be solid. Only when the butter is solid will it be able to do its job — melt and give off the steam that lifts the dough layers high. If the butter is the least bit melted before it goes into the oven, less steam will be created and the dough won't rise to its full potential.

Resting serves another purpose. As the dough is rolled, gluten develops, making it elastic and bouncy. Refrigerating the dough for 30 minutes to 1 hour between turns allows the gluten to relax, making the dough easier to roll into a large rectangle before turning.

Q My puff pastry tart was soggy on the bottom even though it was golden along the edges. How can I prevent this from happening next time?

A Puff pastry is characterized not only by its high rise, but also by its crisp texture. Every bit of moisture should be baked out of it to achieve ultimate flakiness. When baking puff pastry, you want to go past golden and well into brown, so that the dough underneath the crust is fully dry. You might try baking a tart with, say, sliced apples on top in the bottom third of the oven so the bottom crust is closer to the heat and more likely to crisp up along with the top edge. For all types of puff pastry try a trick I learned from former White House pastry chef Roland Mesnier, who props open the oven door slightly with a wooden spoon when the pastry has started to brown. He continues to bake it this way, so steam can escape the oven, until the pastry is a dark golden brown and completely cooked through.

Q Most of the recipes I see call for frozen purchased puff pastry. Is it better to substitute homemade puff pastry if you can?

A Making puff pastry takes hours (although much of that time is spent waiting for the dough to chill in the refrigerator) and a lot of muscle (the pounding of the butter and the rolling of the dough will give your forearms a workout). Even pastry chefs at four-star restaurants in New York and Paris use frozen purchased puff pastry to save themselves time and effort. If you are able to buy an all-butter brand such as Dufour, which is available at gourmet stores and upscale supermarkets such as Whole Foods, you may want to follow suit. The flavor of purchased all-butter puff pastry will be as good as homemade, since both are made from top-quality butter, flour, salt, and water. Not only that, but because it is rolled out by machine, purchased puff pastry will be of an even thickness and have a uniform rise, while homemade puff pastry will be only as even as your skill allows.

That said, chances are your local supermarket carries only puff pastry made with vegetable shortening. It may puff up in a similar way, but I cannot state too strongly how inferior in flavor this product is to either store-bought or homemade puff pastry made with butter. Well, you might be asking, isn't the flavor of the filling what's most important? Absolutely not! Puff pastry shouldn't be simply a medium for delivering filling ingredients. Whether it is an apple tart, a sour cherry turnover, or a napoleon filled with pastry cream and fruit, any dessert made with puff pastry relies on the way the nutty, buttery flavor of the browned pastry plays off of the flavors of the sweet or tart or creamy ingredients.

So if you can't buy all-butter puff pastry dough, I highly recommend you make some from scratch. To substitute homemade puff pastry for store-bought puff pastry in a recipe, weigh the dough and then roll it into the called-for shape.

Q Why did my puff pastry rise unevenly?

A If your knife wasn't very sharp, or you dragged it through the dough instead of cutting decisively, you may have inadvertently compressed the layers of the dough at the edges, preventing a high and straight rise. If you glazed your dough with an egg wash, and some of it dripped over the cut edges, it may have sealed the layers together in some places, preventing the dough from rising to its full height.

Q After baking, how long will puff pastry keep?

A Most items made with puff pastry are best eaten on the day they are made. Held for longer than this and they lose their delightful flakiness, becoming limp if not soggy. Store leftovers at room temperature, loosely covered with plastic wrap, for up to one day. You can crisp up leftover pastries somewhat by reheating them in a 350°F (180°C) oven for a few minutes. Of course, if the pastries contain pastry cream they should be refrigerated if not eaten several hours after assembling. The pastry cream will be good for several days, chilled, but the pastry itself will soften and eventually fall apart in the refrigerator.

Food Processor Puff Pastry

If you don't have six hours to make classic puff pastry, don't despair. Quick puff pastry made in a food processor may not rise quite as high as classic puff pastry, but it will give you plenty of flaky layers along with the essential butter flavor. The following recipe is adapted from one created by Nick Malgieri for his book How to Bake, *and uses several tricks to create layers of butter and dough without all that rolling.*

MAKES 1½ POUNDS

10 ounces (2½ sticks) unsalted butter, chilled
2 cups unbleached all-purpose flour
1 teaspoon salt
½ cup ice water

1. Use a sharp chef's knife to cut 2 sticks of the butter into ¼-inch pieces. Transfer the pieces to a plate and place the plate in the freezer.
2. Meanwhile, cut the remaining half-stick of butter into 16 pieces; transfer it to a food processor with the flour and salt. Pulse about 10 times, until the mixture resembles coarse meal.
3. Add the chilled butter and the ice water to the bowl and pulse 3 or 4 times until a rough dough just forms. Don't overprocess. You want to be able to see some chunks of butter in the dough.

4. Transfer the dough to a lightly floured piece of parchment paper and shape it into a rough rectangle. Top with another piece of parchment and roll the dough into a 12- by 18-inch rectangle. Fold the dough in thirds, like a letter, creating a 4- by 18-inch rectangle. Roll up the dough, beginning at a short end, into a cylinder. Press the cylinder into a thick square, wrap in plastic, and refrigerate until well chilled, about 2 hours.

5. The dough will keep, refrigerated, for up to 3 days, or frozen for up to 1 month. Defrost overnight in the refrigerator before using.

Q What can I do with my leftover puff pastry dough?

A Don't discard your scraps of dough. Press them together, wrap the dough in plastic, and save it for a cocktail party or dessert emergency. The ball of dough made from scraps can't be rolled into a tart shell because a sheet of dough from scraps won't have the equal, even layers of a fresh piece of puff pastry dough. But it is very good for items that don't need to rise perfectly evenly or very high, like napoleons, cheese sticks, or mini palmiers.

Uses for Leftover Pastry Dough

* **Napoleons.** To make this dessert, lightly flour a piece of parchment paper and roll out your scraps on top of the parchment into a ⅛-inch-thick rectangle measuring 16 by 5 inches, trimming the sides so they are straight and even. Prick the pastry all over with a fork. Transfer the parchment to a rimmed baking sheet and place another baking sheet on top of the pastry. Refrigerate the baking sheets for 30 minutes. Bake in a 400°F (200°C) oven for 20 minutes, remove the top baking sheet, and continue to bake until the top of the pastry is well browned, 3 to 5 minutes longer. Transfer the baking sheet to a wire rack to cool; cut the cooled pastry into two 16- by 2-inch rectangles. Cut each rectangle in half so you have four 8- by 2-inch rectangles. Layer the rectangles with pastry cream and glaze the top with vanilla or chocolate icing.

Refrigerate until well chilled and then slice into 2-inch lengths and serve.

* **Cheese straws.** Roll your leftover dough into a ¼-inch-thick rectangle. Brush the pastry with a lightly beaten egg and sprinkle liberally with grated Parmesan cheese. Use a pizza wheel or a sharp paring knife to cut the rectangle into ¾-inch-thick strips. Twist each strip into a corkscrew shape and place on a parchment-lined baking sheet, at least ½-inch apart. Bake in a 400°F (200°C) oven until golden brown, 15 to 20 minutes.

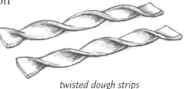

twisted dough strips

* **Mini palmiers.** Roll your leftover dough into a ¼-inch-thick rectangle measuring 9 by 12 inches. Brush the dough with beaten egg and sprinkle liberally with cinnamon sugar. Fold the long sides of the rectangle to the middle of the dough. Then fold the dough in half lengthwise along the middle line (as when making a double turn). Wrap the dough in plastic and freeze until firm, at least 1 hour and up to 2 weeks. Cut the dough into ¼-inch slices and transfer the slices, cut-sides down, to a parchment-lined baking sheet at least ½ inch apart. Bake in a 400°F (200°C) oven until golden brown, 15 to 20 minutes.

folded puff pastry for palmiers

Q In a bakery, I saw a beautiful double-crust puff pastry tart in the shape of a flower. How do pastry chefs make decorative patterns like this on their puff pastry?

A One of the most fun things to do with puff pastry is to cut it into a shape (round, square, heart) and make decorative cuts in the top. When the pastry is baked, the cuts in the dough will open up, making a beautiful design.

To get a nice, shiny crusty with a clear design, cut out your shape and then place it on a parchment-lined baking sheet. Brush it with lightly beaten egg and refrigerate it until it is firm (if your puff pastry is too soft, it will be difficult to make clean cuts). Use the tip of a sharp paring knife to lightly sketch your design on the surface of the puff pastry. Then, hold the knife at a 45-degree angle against the dough and cut into it, but not all the way through it, along the sketched lines. You can cut leaves, scallops, cross-hatching, or any other number of patterns this way.

imprinting puff pastry

To make a tart with a design on top, cut two disks and sandwich some filling between a plain one and one you've cut decoratively, sealing them together by brushing the edges of the bottom disk with beaten egg. Alternatively, you can cut and bake one disk, slice off the decorative top, fill the bottom with pastry cream and fruit, and place the top back on to cover the tart.

Q I know that croissant and Danish dough have yeast. How does this change the way they need to be handled before baking? Does the dough need to rise before it is shaped into individual pastries?

A Croissant and Danish doughs will begin to ferment slightly during the hours that they rest in the refrigerator between turns and after the turns are completed. But they do not rise at room temperature, the way bread dough does, before being shaped into individual pastries. It is only after the doughs are rolled out and shaped that the individual pastries should stand at room temperature for a few hours, loosely covered in plastic wrap. When they are puffy (they won't double in size), they can be baked.

For the best croissants and Danish pastries, don't rush them into the oven before the yeast has had time to do its work. Properly proofed (a baker's term for allowing dough to rise), croissant and Danish dough will rise high in the oven. Underproofed, they will be heavy and tough.

Q How do I cut and shape croissant dough into classic croissants?

A French croissants are on the small side, unlike the giant croissants you often see in American bakeries and markets. To make these delicate, diminutive croissants, roll your dough into a 24- by 12-inch rectangle and use a paring knife or pizza wheel to cut that rectangle into two 24- by 6-inch rectangles. Cut each strip into 10 triangles, each with a 4-inch base and 6-inch sides.

To shape a croissant, place it on a lightly floured work surface with the short base facing away from you and the point facing toward you. Gently pull each corner of the short base to stretch it to about 6 inches. Then roll the stretched edge toward you with one hand while gently pulling on the tip with the other hand. Place the rolled croissant on a parchment-lined baking sheet with the point tucked underneath. Curve the ends in slightly toward each other to make a crescent shape.

cutting and rolling croissant dough

Q How do I make pains au chocolat?

A Pains au chocolat are small rectangles of croissant dough wrapped around some bittersweet chocolate. They're easier to shape than croissants. Roll your dough into a 24- by 6-inch rectangle. Cut that rectangle into two 24- by 3-inch strips. Brush one edge of each strip with lightly beaten egg (this will prevent them from unfolding in the oven). Then spoon 1 tablespoon of chopped chocolate in a narrow line about 1 inch from the top of one of the strips. Roll the top edge over the chocolate and then fold the dough over once more to create a three-layered roll. Trim the roll away from the longer strip with a sharp paring knife and transfer the assembled dough to a parchment-lined baking sheet, flattening it slightly with your hand. Repeat with the remaining dough, and then again with the remaining strip, for a total of 16 pastries.

Q Can I freeze unbaked croissants and pain au chocolat to bake another day? Or is it better to bake and then freeze them?

A Making croissant dough takes quite a bit of effort, and it's difficult to make in small batches. Croissants definitely are best warm from the oven and will become stale within hours of baking. It would be a shame to make two dozen croissants and have to throw away even a few if there were a way to save them for another day.

If you have leftover baked croissants, put them in a resealable plastic bag and freeze them as soon as you know they won't be eaten that day. Thaw them briefly on the countertop (15 minutes will do) and then reheat them for 5 minutes in a 350°F (180°C) oven. They won't be quite as soft, moist, and fresh-tasting as when they were first baked, but you won't get too many complaints, I bet.

It is possible to freeze unbaked croissants and then bake them when you need them, but again, quality may suffer. Unlike puff pastry, which freezes beautifully, croissant dough depends in part on yeast for its rise. Inevitably, some of the yeast will not survive the low temperature of the freezer, so expect frozen croissants to rise less than freshly made ones. Transfer shaped croissants to a baking sheet and freeze them on the sheet until they are firm, about 1 hour. Then transfer them to a resealable plastic bag and freeze completely. There's no need to defrost the frozen croissants before baking. Just add a few extra minutes to the baking time.

There is a third option that I prefer when it comes to freezing croissants. This is to partially bake them until they are just turning golden, let them cool to room temperature, and then freeze them. This way, they've already taken advantage of the yeast to rise to full height, but still retain some moisture, so when they are placed in the oven right from the freezer, they don't completely dry out as they brown.

Q I've heard that Danish are not really from Denmark at all. Is this true?

A Pastries made from an egg-enriched, butter-laminated (or layered) yeast dough, are popular throughout Europe and North America, but their exact origin is debated. Danish were indeed introduced to America by bakers from Denmark, and excellent examples can be found throughout Denmark today, but food historians have traced the recipe to seventeenth-century France. From France, it is believed that the recipe spread to Italy and then Austria. Legend has it that during a baker's strike in Copenhagen, Austrian bakers arrived in the city to fill the jobs, introducing this type of pastry to

Denmark, where it became very popular under the name Wienerbrod, or Vienna bread. Danish bakers, back at work, continued to produce it, and when some of these bakers emigrated to various corners of the earth, they continued to bake, and the pastries became known as "Danish."

Q How are Danish pastries different from croissants, other than in shape?

A Danish pastries are more tender and cakelike and less crisp than croissants because the dough contains eggs. In addition to being shaped differently, Danish pastries are filled with a greater variety of fillings — fruit, pastry cream, and cheese, to name a few — and can be garnished with chocolate or white icing, candied fruit, and chopped nuts.

Q What are the storage options for leftover Danish?

A Danish, like puff pastries and croissants, are best eaten on the day they are baked. Use the guidelines on pages 293 and 294 for freezing unbaked, baked, and partially baked croissants.

Q What is choux paste?

A Although not widely used in American home kitchens as puff pastry, choux paste, or pâte à choux, also known as cream puff pastry, is one of the foundational doughs of pastry making. Éclairs, profiteroles, and classic French cakes such as Paris-Brest, croquembouche, and gâteau Saint-Honoré are made with choux paste.

The preparation of the dough is unique in that it starts on top of the stove. Flour, butter, and either milk or water are heated until the mixture resembles mashed potatoes. Off the heat, eggs are stirred in until the mixture is pastelike and soft enough to pipe through a pastry bag.

The pastry is piped into small balls or oblong shapes, and then baked until puffed and completely dry. When cooled, the pastries can be filled with pastry cream (for éclairs), whipped cream (for cream puffs), ice cream (for profiteroles), or Bavarian cream or mousse.

Although these items and the larger cakes made from choux paste may look fancy and difficult, it is actually much simpler and less time-consuming to make choux paste at home than it is to make puff pastry, croissants, or Danish.

croquembouche

Q Are there any tricks to getting cream puff pastry to puff to its maximum size?

A Follow the recipe when it tells you to "stir constantly." Stirring the dough in the pan helps develop the gluten in the flour, which will give the dough a stretchy, elastic structure and allow it to expand in the oven to its full potential. Although you can cover the bowl of dough with plastic wrap and hold it at room temperature for an hour or two, the pastry will puff up best if used immediately after it is mixed.

Q My cream puffs have little points on the ends from when I finished piping and pulled the pastry bag away. How can I get them to look round, not pointy?

A Improving your piping technique may help. Hold the pastry bag about 1 inch from the parchment paper and squeeze out a round of pastry. When it is the size you want, stop squeezing the bag before you lift it away. Applying pressure as you lift will release a pointy bit of pastry from the bag. If there is still a little point on top of some of your puffs, dampen your index finger with cold water and just smooth it into the round. The shape of your cream puffs isn't just an aesthetic concern; little peaks will burn black before the puffs are baked through.

piping cream puffs

Classic Cream Puffs

The simplest way to enjoy cream puff pastry is to pipe it into large balls, bake them, and fill them with sweetened whipped cream. Look over the following recipe, with its short list of ingredients and its easy instructions, and see if you don't agree. The most complicated step is probably baking the puffs. To dry them out sufficiently while still getting a high rise, you start them in a hot oven, then turn the heat down. When you turn off the oven, open the door a little, and let them sit in the cooling oven for 10 minutes to dry them completely.

MAKES 12 SMALL CREAM PUFFS

½ cup whole milk
¼ cup (½ stick) unsalted butter
1 teaspoon granulated sugar
¼ teaspoon salt
½ cup unbleached all-purpose flour
3 large eggs
1 cup heavy cream
½ teaspoon vanilla extract
1½ tablespoons confectioners' sugar, plus more for dusting

1. Preheat the oven to 400°F (200°C). Line a baking sheet with parchment paper. Combine the milk, butter, granulated sugar, and salt in a medium saucepan and bring to a boil over medium heat.

2. Remove the pan from the heat and stir in the flour all at once, using a wooden spoon. When the flour is incorporated, return the pan to the heat, turn it to medium-low,

and cook, stirring constantly, for 1 minute. The mixture will be thick.

3. Transfer the mixture to a large mixing bowl. Use an electric mixer on low to beat in two of the eggs, one at a time, scraping down the sides of the bowl after each addition. Do not overmix. The mixture should fall slowly from the beaters when they are lifted from the bowl, loose enough to pipe, but not runny. If it is too thick, stir in a little water until it is the proper consistency.

4. Scrape some of the choux paste into a pastry bag fitted with a large (about ¼-inch) plain tip, filling it halfway. Pipe 1½-inch mounds of pastry onto the prepared baking sheet, leaving 2 inches between each mound. Lightly beat the remaining egg and brush egg wash onto each pastry mound.

5. Bake the puffs for 15 minutes, turn down the heat to 350°F (180°C) without opening the oven door, and bake until golden brown and dried inside, about 20 minutes. Turn the oven off. Use a sharp paring knife to make a ¾-inch slit in the side of each hot puff to release any steam. Return the puffs, still on the baking sheet, to the oven and let stand for 10 minutes to dry out. Transfer the puffs to a wire rack to cool completely.

6. Whip the cream, vanilla, and the 1½ tablespoons confectioners' sugar until it holds soft peaks. Split each cream puff in half with a serrated knife. Fill the bottom half of each puff with a dollop of whipped cream and replace the top half. Dust the cream puffs heavily with powdered sugar just before serving. Filled cream puffs will keep in the refrigerator for up to 2 hours.

Q Some cream puff and éclair recipes instruct you to drag the tines of a fork through the brushed-on egg wash before baking them. Is this purely decorative or is there another purpose?

A Some cracking on the surface of cream puffs and especially éclairs (because of their elongated shape) can occur during baking. Dragging the tines of the fork along the surface will encourage the cracking to occur along those lines, making a decorative design.

Q Can I make cream puffs if I don't have a pastry bag?

A Yes. Just drop mounds of the pastry onto a parchment-lined baking sheet instead of piping them. Use your index finger, moistened with cold water, to smooth each one into an even round.

Q My cream puffs collapsed. What did I do wrong?

A If they collapsed in the oven, you may have overloaded your baking sheet. Placing the pastry mounds too close together may cause them to deflate while baking. To prevent this from happening, be sure to leave at least 2 inches of space between the puffs when you pipe them. Or you may have opened the oven door early in the baking, when the structure of the puffs wasn't yet solidified. A blast of colder air might have caused the collapse of the not-quite-set puffs.

If your puffs collapsed as they cooled, then you probably took them out too soon. Cream-puff pastry that hasn't dried completely will fall in on itself as it cools.

Q I made twelve cream puffs, and I have six left over. Can I save them?

A If you will be using them within a day, store leftover unfilled puffs in a resealable plastic bag at room temperature. Or freeze them for up to 2 weeks before defrosting them on the countertop (this will take less than an hour) and reheating them in a 350°F (180°C) oven for 5 minutes to refresh them. Then let them cool and proceed with your recipe.

Q What exactly is phyllo dough? Is it related to puff pastry?

A Phyllo (sometimes called "fillo" or "filo") is a tissue-thin dough made from flour, water, egg, and oil. It originated in Greece, thus the name, which is Greek for "leaf." Although it is possible to make it at home, it's difficult to roll out the dough as thin as store-bought. Virtually all recipes in American cookbooks call for store-bought dough, which is widely available in the freezer section of most supermarkets and at Greek and Middle Eastern specialty foods stores. Rolled up, it is packaged inside long narrow boxes like the ones that hold spaghetti.

Famous for its use in Greek dishes like spanokopita (spinach pie) and Middle Eastern specialties such as baklava, phyllo dough can be layered with melted butter and then baked to approximate puff pastry, but the differences in texture and character are significant. While a tart shell made with puff pastry is flaky, it has a yielding quality to it, a tenderness that is absent in baked phyllo dough. Phyllo, in contrast, is all crisp flakes with none of the softness of puff pastry. Although phyllo puffs slightly in the oven, due to the steam coming off of the melted butter, it doesn't reach the heights of puff pastry, with its solid butter layers.

Q What is the best way to defrost frozen phyllo dough?

A Keep phyllo dough in its package and defrost it in the refrigerator overnight. In my experience, phyllo dough that is too cold will crack when unrolled. It's a good idea to take the dough out of the refrigerator before you are ready to use it, and let it stand, still in its box, at room temperature for 30 minutes, to prevent cracking. Be aware that phyllo dough is extremely delicate, and even when handled with care it tends to break and crack. To be safe, always buy twice as much phyllo as you think you will need, so when this happens you won't be caught short.

Q When I take the dough out of the box, what's the best way to prevent it from drying out?

A Phyllo dough will dry out almost at the instant it comes in contact with air. So before you even open the box of dough, make sure that you have all of your other ingredients — your melted butter, your fillings — ready to go. Dampen two clean kitchen towels. Spread one of them out on your work surface and carefully unwrap and unroll the dough onto the towel. Quickly cover the dough with the other towel. Sandwiched this way, the dough should stay pliable. After you remove a sheet from the stack, quickly replace the towel to prevent drying.

Don't rush, but work purposefully and as quickly as you can, because time is against you when it comes to phyllo. The longer the dough sits out, even under damp towels, the better the chance that it will dry out before you are done.

Q I followed the instructions for thawing and unwrapping phyllo dough to a tee, but when I unrolled the sheets, every single one of them cracked into three or more pieces. Did I do something wrong?

A Just as important as proper handling is careful purchasing. Buy your phyllo dough at a store where you know there is a high turnover, such as a busy gourmet shop or Greek specialty foods store. Phyllo dough that languishes in a supermarket freezer for more than a few weeks will become impossibly dried out even if properly packaged and stored.

Q My equipment and ingredients are organized, my dough is unwrapped. Now what?

A Most phyllo dough recipes will instruct you to remove a sheet of phyllo from the stack, brush it with melted butter and perhaps sprinkle it with sugar and maybe some ground nuts, lay another sheet on top of this one, and repeat the process until you have as many layers as you need. The melted butter will keep the dough soft and pliable, so there's less of a worry that the dough layered this way will dry out when you start to work.

Use a soft-bristled pastry brush to brush on the butter, making sure that you butter all the way to the edges. Once the entire sheet is lightly moistened with butter, stop. If you put too much butter between the layers your finished pastry will be greasy.

Don't panic if occasionally one of the phyllo leaves develops a small crack. If you are concerned about larger cracks in the dough, brush some butter over the crack and then place a smaller piece of dough on top to patch it. Don't forget to butter the patch after you place it on top. You may find, when you unroll your dough, that each piece is cracked in the same spot. If this is the case, take care to turn the pieces as you layer them, so your finished pastry won't have a large crack running through it.

It's a good idea to work on top of a sheet of wax paper or parchment paper. Not only will it prevent the dough from sticking to the counter, but also it will help when you roll and fold the dough after it is filled, if that's called for. By lifting and shifting the paper, you'll be able to manipulate the delicate pastry without poking holes through it with your fingers.

Q If some of the sheets crack as I'm using the dough, should I discard them, or is there some use for cracked and torn phyllo dough?

A Try this: Let the dough dry completely on the counter for several hours or overnight. Then crumble it with a rolling pin or crush it in a food processor and use the phyllo crumbs instead of breadcrumbs for coating chicken breasts or fish fillets before pan-frying. You'll get a deliciously crisp and unbelievably light crust. You don't have to use the crumbs immediately, by the way. Place them in a resealable plastic bag and freeze them until you need them.

Q Can I freeze leftover phyllo dough?

A The package will tell you to rewrap and refreeze leftover dough, but in my experience refrozen dough always dries out and becomes unusable. Wrap the dough in plastic and keep it in the refrigerator for a few days if you think you will have a need for phyllo in the near future.

Q Can I freeze pastries made with phyllo dough?

A Yes — before baking. Phyllo dough pastries are perfect do-ahead desserts. Unbaked, they freeze beautifully, wrapped well in several layers of plastic wrap. To bake, just unwrap and place on a baking sheet. There's no need to defrost the pastries, just put them directly into the hot oven. If you are planning on holding the pastries just for a day or two, you can wrap them and refrigerate them instead of freezing them.

Baked phyllo dough pastries are best eaten soon after they are baked, because the crisp leaves of dough will begin to soften within hours. The exceptions are syrup-soaked phyllo pastries like baklava, which will keep at room temperature, well wrapped, for up to 10 days.

Q What is strudel, and does anyone ever make it at home?

A Strudel is a long, rectangular pastry made from many layers of very thin dough wrapped around a sweet or sometimes savory filling, sprinkled with breadcrumbs, and baked until the pastry is golden and crisp. The pastry is then cut crosswise into individual servings. Traditional strudel dough is made by mixing and kneading a dough made from bread flour (which is high in gluten), eggs, oil, and water and then slowly and carefully pulling and stretching it on all sides until the dough is paper-thin. High-gluten flour prevents the dough from tearing as it is pulled. At least four hands are needed for the project. Two bakers work together, pulling and stretching the dough over a floured table and moving frequently around the table in order to stretch the dough evenly into a very large sheet.

It is rare to find people who uphold this tradition; instead, bakers who want to make strudel at home use phyllo dough, which is widely available and very similar in taste and texture to traditional strudel dough when baked. If you are a fanatic for authenticity, it will please you to know that the strudel recipes first developed in Austria and Hungary hundreds of years ago were in fact inspired by baklava, a Turkish dessert made by layering phyllo dough with sugar, chopped nuts, and spices.

Q My strudel came out beautifully, but when I tried to slice it the pastry shattered and the slices looked terrible. Is there a way to cut this pastry so the servings are intact?

A Try lightly scoring the strudel with the tip of a paring knife, taking care not to cut through the dough, before you put it in the oven. The score marks will create weakened spots on the pastry, where you will be able to cut through it without a mess.

CHAPTER 10

Yeast Breads

Compared to recipes for cakes, pies, cookies, and even biscuits, most bread recipes have enviably short ingredient lists — in many cases just flour, water, yeast, and salt. Yet even the most avid home bakers are often happy to leave bread baking to the professionals. Some have been scared off by myths about the difficulties of baking bread successfully. Some have had a bad experience with a homemade whole-wheat bread that was heavy enough to function as a doorstop.

Many bread-baking books describe the process in scientific terms that a Nobel prizewinner might have trouble understanding. These explanations can mystify rather than enlighten. In researching bread, I often came across questions such as, "If the osmotic pressure exerted by salt does not significantly change the fermentation rate of the dough, why does the dough rise so much more slowly when salt is added?" Most home bakers, including myself, are more likely to wonder, "My Dad is on a low-salt diet. Can I leave out the salt in the bread I'm making for him?" The two questions are related, but the second one is posed in terms that are relevant to someone contemplating baking a loaf of bread at home. I sometimes felt as if my head would explode as I tried to understand bread baking in scientific terms; but in the end, I was happy to gain a better understanding of the science behind bread, because it meant I made fewer mistakes when baking.

If you don't have any interest in science, don't worry. Remember that yeast breads were being baked well before the invention of the microscope in 1674 and the subsequent discovery of yeast and friendly bacteria called lactobacilli that are responsible for bread's rise. As far back as 3000 BCE, ancient Egyptians were making leavened bread. How did they discover that the introduction of yeast into the basic flatbread formula of flour and water would result in a light, puffy, and flavorful loaf so much more pleasing than the crackerlike flatbreads baked without yeast? Historians speculate that perhaps it was the accidental discovery that dough left to sit longer than usual before baking would capture wild yeast, which caused it to rise when baked. Or the discovery might have first been made when a creative baker decided to mix some beer (which contains yeast) into flour along with or instead of water. These early bakers had no idea that microscopic organisms were causing their bread to rise. They only knew that under certain conditions or in the presence of certain ingredients, it would happen. So they learned through experience which ingredients were best for bread and how to be sensitive to bread dough through every step of the process so that it would rise well and taste good.

The questions in this chapter are not all, or even mostly, about science. Equally important in crafting a loaf of bread are experience with and sensitivity to the dough. If you don't have much experience and have not developed this sensitivity, knowing the answers to questions such as, "How do I know if I've kneaded my dough sufficiently?" and, "How do I know if my bread has proofed long enough?" will give you an idea of what to expect and what to look for as you bake.

Q What is bread flour and should it always be used in bread?

A The more protein in flour, the more gluten it will develop during mixing and kneading. The more gluten a dough has, the stronger its structure will be and the higher it will rise. While all-purpose flour has a protein content of about 12%, bread flour contains 13% to 14% protein — a much better choice when you are trying to make a dough with a lot of stretchy gluten.

But the choice of flour is actually a complicated one. It makes sense to use bread flour in recipes where a lot of gluten is important. Rye breads, for example, are made from a combination of rye flour, which has no gluten at all, and wheat flour. So the wheat flour used needs to be of the highest strength, since it will be providing all of the gluten for the dough. But a high-gluten flour is not always desirable. Though bread flour may be perfect if you want to make a crusty artisan bread with a very chewy crust and a crumb that's distinguished by large air bubbles, it may not be quite right if you want to make a softer, more yielding bread like a challah.

Bread recipes will guide you on what flour to choose, but as you become more experienced with bread baking, you might make your own adjustments. Say your pizza dough, made with bread flour, was too tough for your taste. Next time you might try substituting some all-purpose flour for the bread flour to give it a softer texture. Or maybe the sandwich bread you made with all-purpose flour lacked character. Some bread flour next time might give it a thicker crust and a higher rise.

HOW A MIXTURE OF FLOUR, WATER, YEAST, AND SALT BECOMES BREAD

The transformation of a handful of the most basic ingredients into a well-risen, tantalizingly fragrant loaf may seem mysterious, but the science underlying this transformation explains it all. In a nutshell, here is what happens to a lump of dough at different stages in a typical bread recipe.

Kneading. Mixing together your ingredients and kneading them into a smooth, elastic mass accomplishes several things at once. Mixing distributes yeast and salt evenly throughout the dough, essential for a successful rise. You may not be able to see it happening with yeast, but if you are mixing nuts, seeds, or raisins into your dough you can easily see how this happens on a larger scale. Kneading also introduces oxygen into the dough. Later on, when the dough is rising, oxygen will provide food for the yeast.

But the primary function of kneading is to develop the gluten in the dough. All wheat flour contains two types of protein, gliaden and glutenin. (See page 7 for a comparison of protein content of different types of flour.) Only when these proteins come in contact with water can they bond with each other to form a stretchy, elastic web called gluten. It is this gluten web that will provide structure (like the steel beams that hold up a building) for the bread as it rises.

Once gluten is formed, it must be strengthened through the repeated action of flattening and folding. As you knead your bread, you will feel it transforming from a rough, sticky mass into a smooth, elastic ball. This smoothness is the result of the proteins organizing themselves into a gluten web. The stronger and stretchier your gluten is, the better. A strong gluten web will be able to support a wet and heavy dough as it rises. If the web is stretchy, it will be able to rise high as the air inside the dough expands in the heat of the oven.

unbonded proteins

First rise. After you knead your dough, you will put it in a bowl or a clear plastic container (the better to judge how high it is rising), cover the container with plastic wrap or a damp kitchen towel, and

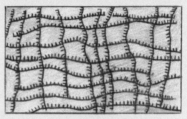

strong gluten web

let it stand until it has increased in size. Also called fermentation, this resting period is hardly one of inactivity. Yeast and bacteria in the dough hungrily feed off of the sugars in the flour, creating carbon dioxide, alcohol, and acids. The carbon dioxide, a byproduct of yeast as it feeds, is trapped in the gluten web, causing the dough to rise. You'll be able to smell the alcohol, also a byproduct of yeast (the same reaction turns grape juice into wine) as the dough ferments, but it will cook off during baking. Bread-friendly bacteria called lactobacilli are also fermenting, consuming sugars that the yeast can't digest. The byproduct is acid, which gives dough its slightly tangy taste.

Punching down. I don't love this term, because in its suggestion of violent deflation of the dough it is misleading. After the dough has fermented for a while, it has built up quite a bit of carbon dioxide. Too much carbon dioxide will begin to kill off the yeast, so it's necessary to release some of that carbon dioxide by pressing on the dough. Don't punch it! Just gently sink your fist into its center to partially deflate it. Breads that are distinguished by a large, open crumb structure (ciabatta, focaccia, pizza) should be handled even more gently. Lifting the dough out of the bowl by sliding both hands under it, letting it fold itself over your hands, and then placing the folded dough back in the bowl will expel enough gas from these doughs to safeguard the yeast while preserving the air pockets.

Dividing and shaping. When your recipe makes two or more loaves, you must divide the dough after punching it down or turning it. Do this gently, using a bench scraper or sharp chef's knife to cut cleanly through the dough and without destroying too many air pockets. You may be instructed to let the dough rest for 5 or 10 minutes after you've divided it before proceeding with shaping. This is to allow the gluten to relax, so the dough won't be so bouncy and difficult to roll or stretch into a round or a baguette.

Shaping is important not just because it determines the final look of the loaf, but because it provides one last opportunity to stretch the gluten and give the bread structure. In addition, shaping creates surface tension, tightening a "skin" around the loaf, which helps it keep its shape as it rises a second time.

Proofing. When you've shaped your loaves, loosely cover them with a floured kitchen towel or sprinkle some flour over them and loosely cover with plastic. Then let them stand, giving them time to ferment further. Proofing allows more time for the dough to develop a good, yeasty flavor as the yeast continues to feed on the sugars in the flour. Proofing also allows the loaves to increase in size.

Baking. This is perhaps the most dramatic of all of the stages. When cool dough comes in contact with a preheated baking stone in a very hot oven, several reactions occur: Gases expand, alcohol boils, yeast becomes briefly but significantly more active, and as a result of these three reactions a lot of steam is produced. If you peek through the oven window, you can almost see the loaves growing before your eyes, a phenomenon known as "oven spring."

After 15 or 20 minutes, the breads will have expanded fully. As the interior of the bread reaches 140°F (60°C), the starches begin to gelatinize and the proteins coagulate, making the bread firm and solid. At about 200°F (95°C), the moisture that has been attached to the starch molecules will begin to migrate toward the crust, a process called starch retrogradation. Even though the crust may look well browned, it is important to keep baking the bread until the crust is firm, a sign that starch retrogradation is almost complete. If you pull the bread out of the oven before this, water molecules will be trapped in the crust, making it soft and soggy rather than crackly and crisp.

Cooling. Cut into your just-baked loaf and it will still feel damp and doughy inside. But let it cool for a while to allow the process of starch retrogradation to continue, and the inside of the bread will firm up as the crust crisps.

Q What happens to dough when fat, like butter or olive oil, is added?

A There are many examples of bread dough enriched with fat: Parker House rolls, brioche, challah. Fat lends tenderness and flavor to the breads. But fats also react on a molecular level with the other ingredients in the dough. If added at the beginning of mixing, fat will coat the proteins in bread, preventing them from bonding with each other and forming a gluten web. This reaction is desirable in some baked goods — tender pie pastry depends upon fat's gluten-blocking ability — but if you want your enriched bread to rise high it is better to knead it for a few minutes first, to develop the gluten, before adding the fat.

Q My recipe gives measurements for flour and other ingredients by volume and weight. Is one set of measurements better than the other?

A Every professional baker and every serious amateur will weigh ingredients rather than measure them by volume. It is the only way to ensure uniform-quality breads, time after time. Depending on how you measure it and how much it has settled since being bagged, a cup of flour may weigh anywhere from 5 to 5½ ounces. If a typical bread recipe calls for 4 cups of flour, and sometimes you use 16 ounces while other times you use 18 ounces, your dough will feel different and your bread will bake differently every time. Of course,

flours vary in absorbency from brand to brand and from season to season, and even if you measure your flour to the last ounce every time you will sometimes have to adjust a recipe, adding a little more flour or a little more water, depending on the flour, the humidity, and other variables. But don't let weight be one of them. For tips on buying a kitchen scale for baking, see page 56.

If you don't have a scale, go ahead and measure your ingredients by volume. Use the "dip and sweep" method for measuring dry ingredients, dipping your measuring cup into the flour and then leveling off the cup with a knife. Take extra care when measuring by volume to pay attention to how your dough looks and feels as you knead it, making adjustments as necessary.

Q Is it okay to use tap water to make bread, or is bottled water better?

A If you are cultivating a sourdough starter, it's best to begin with bottled spring water, which doesn't have a high level of chlorine or minerals that may inhibit the growth of yeast. But when it comes to baking bread itself, whether you are using a well-established sourdough starter or packaged yeast, chlorine and minerals won't affect the bread's rise. You may want to substitute bottled water for reasons of taste, however. Use the same water in your bread that you regularly drink. If you don't regularly drink your tap water because it tastes terrible, chances are it will impart its off flavor to your bread.

Q **What kind of salt is best for bread-baking? Is it always necessary to bake with salt, or can I leave it out if I am on a low-salt diet?**

A Table salt will work in all bread recipes, although many experienced bakers will argue that fleur de sel and other fine sea salts give bread a better flavor.

In answer to the second question, absolutely do not leave out the salt when making bread. There are a few notable exceptions (Tuscan saltless bread being the most famous), but most breads need salt for reasons other than flavor. Salt works to dehydrate yeast, slowing down the fermentation process. While too much salt will kill the yeast, the right amount will allow time for the bread to develop a tasty amount of acid (the byproduct of yeast and bacteria production) that gives bread its wonderful flavor and aroma. It also allows time for the gluten in the flour to gain strength. While dough without salt will rise much more quickly than dough with salt, it will also more likely collapse in the oven because its gluten structure hasn't had time to properly develop.

Not only does salt give gluten time to develop, it actually aids in its development, strengthening, tightening, and compacting the network of protein strands. Thus developed, the gluten web is able to more effectively stretch and expand when the gases produced by the yeast heat up and expand in the oven, and it is able to resist collapse when those gases dissipate.

Q How does saltless Tuscan bread keep its shape?

A The recipe for saltless Tuscan bread dates back to the Middle Ages, when Tuscan bakers decided they'd rather bake bread without salt than pay a high tax on what was then considered a precious commodity. To bake successfully without salt, they developed a few techniques to help the bread keep its shape in the oven. While bread dough with salt can be kneaded and pummeled with no ill effects (in fact, strong handling will further develop the gluten), saltless dough must be handled gently so as not to destroy the fragile strands of gluten that have barely developed. Overmixing, overkneading, and rough shaping will all inhibit the dough's rise in the oven. During the dough's first and second rise, it is watched carefully. Without salt, the dough ferments quickly. As soon as it doubles in size it must be gently shaped, and as soon as the shaped loaves have fermented sufficiently they must go into the oven. Overproofing will result in a flat bread, because the underdeveloped gluten structure will collapse under the pressure of too much carbon dioxide produced by the yeast.

Q There seem to be quite a few types of packaged yeast available. Can you explain what's out there and what the differences are between them?

A When I first started baking bread as a teenager, there were just two types of yeast available at the super-market: active dry yeast, which came in a strip of three detachable packets, and fresh cake yeast, which was kept in the refrigerator section near the butter and milk. **Active dry yeast** is dehydrated yeast that becomes active when stirred into water. Although the packages display an expiration date, active dry yeast, stored properly will keep indefinitely. **Fresh yeast** (also called compressed yeast) is a moist cake that must be stored in the refrigerator and will begin to grow mold and lose its power to raise bread in a matter of days. It is more practical for professionals, who go through it rapidly, than for even an avid home baker, who is unlikely to use it up before it spoils. These two types of yeast can be used interchange-ably in recipes (one 2¼-teaspoon package of active dry yeast has the same bread-raising power as ¼ ounce of fresh yeast), although these days you are less likely to find fresh yeast in the supermarket than you are a menu of new specialty yeasts that have come on the market in recent years.

Bread-machine yeast, sometimes called **instant yeast**, was developed for use in bread machines, where there is no oppor-tunity for yeast to be dissolved in water before it is combined with flour. It works just like active dry yeast, except it does not have to be rehydrated in water. Just add it to the dry ingredients and it will become fully hydrated during kneading. I like instant yeast better than plain old active dry yeast because there is more margin for error. Even if you don't soak it, it will work.

Rapid-rise yeast should not be confused with active dry yeast or instant yeast, from which it is derived. It is a dry yeast that has been packaged with yeast foods and enzymes to accelerate fermentation. In most straight dough recipes, the bread is allowed to rise twice, once in a bowl and once after the dough is shaped into loaves. With rapid-rise yeast, the first rise can be skipped and you can proceed directly to shaping the dough, allowing it to rise just once before baking. It is certainly quicker to make bread using rapid-rise yeast, but professional artisan bakers and passionate amateurs would argue that the longer the dough is allowed to ferment, the more time it has to develop great flavor. So if you are not in a hurry, skip the rapid-rise yeast and let your dough rise twice.

Q What does "sourdough" really mean?

A Most people think that yeast for bread must come out of an envelope or jar from the supermarket, but the fact is that people had been making yeast-risen breads for hundreds if not thousands of years before the invention of packaged yeast in the late nineteenth century, and some continue to do so today.

How? The answer is sourdough, which is nothing more than wild yeast, captured from the air, and cultivated in a mixture of flour and water until it has proliferated enough to be able to raise bread. Wild yeast lives in the flour and air in your kitchen. When flour is mixed with water, it makes the starches available to the yeast in and around the bowl. The yeast feed on the starches, proliferating. As the yeast multiplies, the mixture becomes a powerful leavener, able to raise bread.

Although it is the yeast in the culture that makes dough rise, it is the friendly bacteria, called lactobacilli, that give it its name. These bacteria, like yeast, live in flour and air and proliferate if fed. When yeast feeds on the sugars in flour, it produces carbon dioxide. When lactobacilli feed, they produce acids. Depending on how wildly they are allowed to reproduce, they lend the culture a mild to strong sour flavor.

Q So what is sourdough bread?

A Contrary to popular belief, a sourdough bread is not necessarily a sour-tasting loaf, although it can be. A sourdough bread is a loaf that has been raised with a sourdough, or natural, starter. Throughout Europe, breads made with natural starters run the gamut from very mild and sweet to highly acidic, depending on how acidic the starter was, how much starter is added, proportionately, to the dough, and how long the dough is allowed to ferment. In this country, bread advertised as sourdough often does taste sour, but this is because bakers purposely ferment their breads to meet customers' expectations about flavor.

Q If sourdough is a natural starter cultivated in your own kitchen, then what is the sourdough starter sold at baking supply shops? How is it different from instant yeast?

A The item you refer to is dehydrated sourdough starter (see Resources). Instant yeast is also dehydrated, but differs from dehydrated sourdough in that it contains a single strain of yeast, bred for hardiness and reliability. Packaged dehydrated sourdough contains any number of strains of yeast, for more flavorful bread.

But the major difference is in the way the two types of yeast are used. Instant yeast is added directly to bread dough. Dehydrated sourdough starter is mixed with a small amount of flour and water, and allowed to stand until the yeast has had time to multiply and become strong enough to raise bread dough (as little as 24 hours, in comparison with the days or weeks it takes to cultivate a culture from scratch). Then a piece of this culture is mixed into dough instead of packaged yeast. The remaining portion can be fed with additional water and flour, allowed to ferment, and used again and again, the same way a homemade sourdough culture would be used.

A PRE-FERMENT GLOSSARY

A pre-ferment is a starter used in bread recipes where the dough is built in two stages. First, a small portion of dough — usually a mixture of flour, water, and packaged yeast — is mixed together and allowed to stand until the yeast multiplies. Then, the pre-ferment becomes an ingredient in the larger batch of dough, functioning in place of, or sometimes in addition to, packaged yeast to raise the bread. A pre-ferment greatly extends the fermentation time of the bread without risking overfermentation. During this long fermentation, the taste of the dough matures and flavorful acids develop, further enhancing the complex character of the bread.

There are many types of pre-ferments, coming out of a variety of bread baking traditions. The very oldest pre-ferments are sourdoughs, which require days of fermentation to properly develop. Newer pre-ferments using packaged yeast, generally called sponges, may ferment for as little as an hour before being mixed in with dough. The texture of pre-ferments ranges from dry and claylike to liquid. But all of them share the goal of slowing down the fermentation process in order to craft a more complex bread.

Here are descriptions of a few of the most common pre-ferments:

Barm. Originally, this term referred to the yeasty foam that rises to the top of fermenting malt liquors such as ale, which was used to make sourdough starter as far back as the sixteenth century in England. Today, it refers to a wet sponge made with packaged yeast or a bread raised with this type of sponge such as barmbrack, a traditional Irish tea bread.

Biga. The term used in Italy for a stiff, claylike pre-ferment made with packaged yeast that is freshly mixed and fermented for 12 hours or so before being mixed into a batch of bread. The result is a fresh-tasting, wheaty loaf with none of the acidity of sourdough breads made with longer-fermented pre-ferments.

Levain. The French term for sourdough starter. Traditionally, levain is made by kneading flour and water into a stiff dough, allowing it to capture wild yeast, and adding fresh flour and water daily to encourage yeast growth while keeping the growth of acids under control.

Pâte fermentée. A newer style of French pre-ferment, using packaged yeast. It can be made fresh, with packaged yeast, water, and flour, and allowed to ferment for a day or so before being used in bread dough, or it can be made by saving a piece of dough from one batch of dough, allowing it to ferment, and then adding the old dough to the next day's batch of bread.

Poolish. Another French-style pre-ferment, whose name is an homage to Polish bakers who brought the technique to France. Poolish is a wet mixture made from packaged yeast, as opposed to the dryer pâte fermentée. Not as powerful as pâte fermentée, it is often used in conjunction with more packaged yeast kneaded directly into the bread dough to raise it.

Sourdough. The English term for a pre-ferment employing a culture of wild yeast, maintained by the periodic addition of flour and water. It is also commonly used to refer to breads raised with such a culture.

Sponge. A wet pre-ferment made with packaged yeast, but different from a poolish in that it is generally allowed to ferment for a briefer period, sometimes just an hour. Sponges contain a relatively large amount of packaged yeast, so no additional yeast is necessary for the bread dough.

Daniel Leader's Ciabatta

This recipe was developed by baking expert Daniel Leader after studying with artisan bakers in Verona. Biga, the typical Italian pre-ferment, must be made the night before you want to bake, to allow the yeast to multiply and the flavors of the wheat to develop. In addition to demonstrating how a pre-ferment is used to add flavor and aid in the rise of the dough, this recipe also shows how the slow fermentation (between 3 and 4 hours) of the dough itself encourages the bread's beautifully large, open crumb. This is a wet dough, which makes the finished bread light and airy. But the moisture also makes it difficult to knead by hand, so use a mixer for best results.

MAKES 2 LOAVES

FOR THE BIGA:

⅓ cup (2.3 ounces) warm water

½ teaspoon (0.1 ounce) instant yeast

⅔ cup (3.5 ounces) unbleached all-purpose flour

FOR THE DOUGH:

1¾ cups (15 ounces) warm water

2 teaspoons (0.4 ounce) instant yeast

3¼ cups (17.6 ounces) unbleached all-purpose flour

1½ teaspoons (0.4 ounces) salt

1. To make the biga, combine the water, yeast, and flour in a medium mixing bowl. Stir with a rubber spatula until a rough dough forms.

2. Lightly dust the countertop with flour and knead the dough until it is smooth, 1 to 2 minutes. Transfer the dough to a lightly oiled clean bowl, cover the bowl with plastic wrap, and let stand at room temperature for 1 hour. Then, refrigerate it until it has doubled in volume, at least 8 hours but no longer than 12 hours.

3. To make the dough, scrape the biga into the bowl of an electric mixer fitted with a dough hook. Add the water, yeast, flour, and salt to the bowl and mix a few times with a rubber spatula to moisten. Mix on medium-high speed until the dough is creamy and very elastic, 10 to 15 minutes, watching the mixer at all times to make sure it does not "walk" off the counter.

4. Give the dough the "windowpane" test: Scoop up a plum-size piece of dough and stretch it until you can see the light coming through. If it does not tear, it is ready. If it does, knead it 2 to 3 minutes longer and perform the test again.

5. Transfer the dough to a large oiled bowl or clear 2-quart container. Cover with plastic wrap and let the dough rise until it triples in size, 3 to 4 hours.

6. Scrape the dough onto a lightly floured countertop and use a bench scraper or sharp chef's knife to cut it into two equal pieces. Line a baker's peel or rimless baking sheet with parchment paper and sprinkle the paper with flour.

Flour your hands and lift a piece of dough, holding an end in each hand and gently stretching the dough into an oblong shape

stretching the dough

as you transfer it to the parchment. Repeat with the second piece of dough, placing it at least 2 inches away from the first piece.

7. Pleat the parchment paper down the center, so the loaves are lying right next to each other but separated by the fold of paper (this will prevent them from rising into each other as they proof). Sprinkle the loaves with flour and then gently press your fingertips into the surface of the loaves, dimpling them all over. Lightly drape with plastic wrap and let rise until puffy, 30 to 40 minutes.

8. Place a baking stone on the middle rack of the oven and a baking pan or cast-iron skillet on the bottom rack. Preheat the oven to 475°F (240°C). Slide the loaves, still on the parchment, onto the baking stone. Stretch the parchment out flat, removing the pleat, to separate the loaves. Pour ½ cup of water into the baking pan or skillet. Bake the loaves until they are golden and well risen, about 30 minutes.

9. Slide the loaves, still on the parchment, onto a wire rack. Let them cool for 1 hour before serving.

Q Then what is San Francisco sourdough bread?

A There are thousands of known strains of yeast and lactobacilli. Different strains thrive in different climates. *Lactobacillus Sanfrancisco* is a strain found around San Francisco. Breads baked with a natural starter cultivated in the area are believed to develop a distinctive flavor because they contain this particular strain of bacteria.

You might be tempted, when visiting San Francisco, to take home a portion of local sourdough starter in the hopes of recreating this legendary bread where you live. But you should be aware that as soon as you get your "San Francisco starter" home, it will begin to trap local yeast and lactobacilli that live in your own kitchen. Week after week, as you feed your San Francisco starter with water from your tap and flour from your canister to keep it alive and healthy, it will become less like the starter it once was and more like a starter native to your area.

Q What is a straight dough?

A While doughs made with pre-ferments or a sourdough starter are mixed in two stages — first the pre-ferment or sourdough is made and allowed to ferment, and then it is mixed into a larger portion of dough — straight doughs don't employ a pre-ferment (see page 324). Straight dough relies only on packaged yeast for its rise.

Q Why do some recipes tell you to mix the ingredients briefly and then let them rest before getting down to real kneading?

A A brief (10 to 20 minute) rest before real kneading is called *autolyse* in France. It is a technique employed to maximize gluten formation while minimizing kneading time. During autolyse, the flour continues to absorb water, becoming more fully hydrated and developing gluten on its own, without kneading. So after this rest, the dough will require less kneading than it would have if you had begun kneading immediately.

Many European artisan breads get their uniquely bubbly structure and open crumb from a high percentage of water in the dough. If you were to attempt kneading a very wet dough immediately, it would be very sticky and hard to handle. Letting the flour become fully hydrated during autolyse makes the dough easier to handle.

Q What is the proper technique for hand-kneading bread dough?

A There are many ways to work the dough to fully develop its gluten. Most American bread-baking manuals will tell you to place the dough on a lightly floured work surface, flour your hands, and push downward and outward on the dough with the heels of both hands, then pull the far edge of the dough back over the top, rotate the ball, and repeat.

*push downward and
outward on the dough*

*pull the far edge back
and rotate the dough*

As you knead, scrape the dough off of the counter with a bench scraper and continue to sprinkle flour on the countertop and your hands to avoid sticking. But resist the urge to add too much flour, which will dry out your dough and inhibit its rise. As you knead, your dough will become smoother, less sticky, and easier to work with.

There are many variations on this kneading method: Using one hand instead of two, using a bench scraper to roll and press the dough inside a mixing bowl, even picking up the dough with one hand and slapping it against the countertop until it stretches into a long rope before folding it up and slapping it against the counter again. Any one of these methods will eventually develop gluten.

No-Knead Bread

If kneading develops gluten, and gluten is necessary to create the structure of a crusty loaf of bread, then how is it possible to make no-knead bread? The answer lies in autolyse, the French technique for allowing the dough to rest in order that the flour may absorb water, its proteins organizing themselves into a web of gluten as they become hydrated. Some bakers have discovered that if they employ an extended autolyse, they can skip kneading altogether. But when I say extended, I mean extended. Recipes that skip kneading often call for the bread to rest at room temperature for up to 24 hours.

Here is a no-knead bread recipe, employing master baker Jim Leahy's ingredients and some of Cook's Illustrated's techniques, that demonstrates the power of autolyse to create a loaf with a large, shiny crumb and chewy crust similar to those of artisan breads that have indeed been kneaded. The tiny amount of instant yeast multiplies many times over during the extended fermentation.

MAKES 1 LOAF

3 cups (15 ounces) unbleached all-purpose flour plus more for dusting
¼ teaspoon instant yeast
1½ teaspoons salt
1½ cups room temperature water

1. In a large mixing bowl combine the flour, yeast, salt, and water. Stir the mixture with a rubber spatula until it comes together into a rough dough. Cover the bowl with plastic wrap and let stand at room temperature overnight, or for up to 18 hours.

2. Place a piece of parchment paper inside another large mixing bowl, with its corners overhanging the edges of the bowl and spray the parchment with nonstick cooking spray. Lightly flour a work surface and turn the dough out onto it.

3. Sprinkle the dough with a little more flour and knead it two or three times, folding it over itself, flattening, and folding over again. Form a ball by gathering the edges of the dough together and twisting them into a topknot.

dough ball with topknot

4. Transfer the ball of dough, topknot-side down, to the parchment-lined bowl. Cover the bowl with plastic wrap and let the dough rise at room temperature until it has doubled in size. It will be very soft, not springy. An hour and a half into the rise, position an oven rack on the bottom third of the oven and place an 8-quart covered cast-iron or enamel Dutch oven on the rack. Preheat the oven to 425°F (220°C).

5. Sprinkle the dough with flour. Use a sharp serrated knife or a razor blade to slash an X, ½ inch deep, into the loaf. Remove the pot from the oven and remove the lid. Use two hands to carefully transfer the parchment, with the dough still on it, to the pot.

6. Cover the pot with the lid and bake for 30 minutes. Uncover and bake until the loaf is well browned, 20 to 30 minutes longer. Lift the bread, still on the parchment, from the pot and transfer it to a wire rack to cool to room temperature, about 2 hours, before serving.

Q Is it better to knead dough by hand or by machine?

A Kneading dough by hand is a good way to feel how gluten develops. But hand-kneading isn't any more effective at developing the gluten structure of dough than kneading by machine. For large batches and very wet doughs, a heavy-duty mixer with a dough hook is a godsend. Simply set the mixer to the speed recommended in your recipe and knead away, scraping down the dough hook and sides of the bowl as necessary. Don't leave the kitchen while the dough is kneading. Even the largest KitchenAid mixer will walk across the counter while working on a stiff bread dough, and you don't want it to tumble to the floor while you're not looking.

If you have a bread machine, you can use it to knead your dough even if you won't be using it to bake. Before adding your ingredients to the machine, make sure that it can accommodate your recipe.

Some bread-baking experts recommend kneading dough in a food processor. The food processor fitted with a metal blade (the plastic blade won't be able to cut through the dough) will knead your dough in seconds, not minutes, so if you are in a hurry this is a method worth considering. But keep in mind a few caveats: The standard food processor will hold only half as much dough as a mixer can; don't use the food processor for a recipe that calls for more than 3½ cups of flour. Mix the dough in two stages: First, pulse the ingredients two or three times until a rough dough forms; then let it stand in the work bowl for 5 to 10 minutes to allow the yeast and flour to fully hydrate; then pulse several times until the dough is smooth and elastic and passes the windowpane test (see below).

Q How can I tell if I've kneaded the dough sufficiently?

A After you've kneaded your dough for as long as your recipe recommends, give your dough the "windowpane" test: Pinch off a golf ball–size piece and stretch it until it is thin enough to see through. If it tears before you can stretch it enough, continue to knead, checking every two minutes or so until it can stretch without tearing.

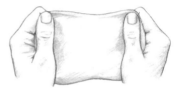

the windowpane test

Q How long should it take to rise?

A After you knead your dough, you will set it aside to allow the yeast to proliferate. Times for this first rising range widely, depending upon what kind of yeast or pre-ferment you have used, how warm or cool it is in your kitchen, how humid it is outside, and a host of other variables. Instead of going by the clock, learn to spot the signs of a properly fermented dough:

* Wheat dough will almost double in volume (loaves made with other grains, such as rye, won't grow as much).

* The dough will spring back, not deflate, when poked with a finger.

* It will be less sticky than when first mixed.

* You may be able to see air bubbles underneath the surface.

After loaves are shaped, they are set aside for a final rise, called "proofing." Most recipes will give you a ballpark estimate for how long the loaves will take to proof, but again, the same variables that affect fermentation time affect proofing. A good recipe will give you visual clues particular to the bread in question to help you decide whether it is time to bake.

Q **What will happen if I let the dough rise too long?**

A It is certainly possible to overferment and overproof your dough. This happens when the yeast exhausts its food supply and becomes weak. Dough that has been allowed to ferment or proof too long won't rise to the height it should, and the loaves will be dense and heavy with an off flavor.

Overproofed loaves may collapse. If this happens after they go into the oven, there's nothing you can do. If it happens before baking, however, you can gather up the dough, reshape it, and let it proof one more time. The yeast will be reinvigorated and will inflate the air pockets in the dough again.

Beginning bakers are much more likely to underferment and underproof their dough than to overferment and overproof, due to lack of experience combined with a lack of patience. Most wheat doughs, with their strong gluten structure, can withstand a little bit of overproofing and still rise high. (Softer doughs made with lower-protein flours need to be watched more carefully, because they don't have a strong gluten structure to rely on.) But without adequate time for the yeast to feed and produce the carbon dioxide that inflates the bread, your loaves won't rise no matter how much gluten they have. When in doubt, give them a little longer than you think necessary and your breads will probably be airier and taller.

Q I've just shaped my dough, and now I have to leave the house unexpectedly. Can I refrigerate or freeze it and bake it later?

A Freezing unbaked bread dough is risky, because at temperatures below freezing some of the yeast may die. But many shaped loaves can be refrigerated for up to 12 hours before baking. This is a technique called retarding, and not only does it give you some flexibility with baking times, but it gives many breads a more interesting flavor because of the build-up of flavorful acids during the long, slow fermentation. Many recipes specifically call for retarding the dough to give bread a particular character. The classic recipe for bagels comes to mind (see below).

To retard your loaves, place them on a parchment-lined baking sheet, sprinkle with flour, and drape the sheet with plastic wrap, completely covering the loaves. Then refrigerate them for up to 12 hours. A few hours before you are ready to bake, remove them from the refrigerator and let them come back to room temperature before proceeding with proofing.

Not all doughs can be refrigerated for such long periods. The acid build-up that is the result of retarding may compromise the less sturdy gluten structure of breads made with nonwheat flours such as rye. Keep such bread doughs in the refrigerator for no longer than an hour or two before proofing to ensure a healthy rise.

Q **Why are bagels parboiled before they're baked?**

A I have no idea what the origin of this technique is, but I can tell you that boiling gives bagels their unique look. Bagel dough is retarded in the refrigerator rather than fermented on a countertop, cooling it down to well below a standard room temperature of 70°F (21°C). So parboiling the bagels before putting them in the oven brings the interior temperature of the dough up high enough so the yeast will become active in the oven. At the same time, parboiling kills the yeast close to the surface, solidifying the crust and limiting the rise so that the bagels keep their characteristic donut shape. When you see bagels that have risen so much that they have no hole in the middle anymore, you know they weren't parboiled as they should have been. Finally, parboiling gives bagels (and their close cousins, yeast-risen pretzels) a beautiful shine by gelatinizing the starches on the surface of the dough before the bagels go into the oven. The pregelatinized starches turn shiny and golden in the oven.

Q **Is scoring the dough before it goes into the oven purely decorative or does it serve another purpose?**

A There are bakers who have made special score marks their signatures, literally signing their identities by slashing the dough in a distinctive way. But whether they slash creatively or with a plain X, they are also doing something to control the rise of the dough as it bakes. Bread dough that contains a good amount of lively yeast is going to expand one way or another in the oven. Rather than have the dough rupture at odd or weak points, so it resembles volcanic rock, bakers slash the dough at certain points to dictate exactly where the expansion will take place, and to create a pleasing pattern or design.

SHAPING BREAD

There are reasons that most bread dough isn't just thrown onto the baking stone in rough pieces, but is rather shaped into tidy rounds, logs, or loaves before being baked. Not only does shaping make bread more aesthetically pleasing, it is one more opportunity to build that gluten and so the dough will rise up instead of spreading all over the oven.

There are dozens of ways to shape bread dough, most of them based on the two most common shapes, the boule (a simple round) and the baguette. Learn these and you will be able to make a batard (a torpedo shape), an epi (sheaf of wheat), a fougasse (ladder), a couronne (a crown), and many others. No matter what shape you hope to achieve, try not to overwork the dough, or you risk bursting some of the air pockets necessary to make the dough rise. It is better to have an imperfectly shaped, awkward-looking baguette that rises well than an elegant one that is tough and small.

epi

batard

fougasse

couronne

Boule. When shaping a boule, or a round, you want to transform the dough from a rough ball into a tight, almost bouncy-looking one. To do this, follow these steps: On a loosely floured countertop, gather your dough together in a rough ball by cupping your hands around the dough and rotating it on the counter several times. With your hands still cupped around the dough, continue to rotate it as you drag it across the counter, dragging any loose bits of dough underneath the dough and forming a tight "skin" over the surface as you move it.

rotating dough for a boule

Baguette. On a lightly floured countertop, pat your dough into a rough rectangle, measuring about 4 by 7 inches. Fold the bottom third of the longer side inward toward the center of the rectangle, pressing lightly on the edge with your fingertips to seal it. Fold the top third down (as if you were folding a letter) over the other two layers, again pressing the edge to seal it. Now use the side of your hand (in karate chop position) to press a wide crevice into the center of the rectangle, lengthwise. Pinch together the dough on either side of the crevice to seal it up.

Turn the dough over so it is facing seam-side-down on the countertop. Place both hands on the dough and use gentle pressure to roll it back and forth in small motions to stretch it into a log. To taper the ends, move

folding baguette dough

your hands outward, one at each end, and use the same rolling motion, pressing a bit harder on the far ends, until the tips of the baguette are pointy.

Loaf breads. It is not just freeform loaves that need special shaping. Doughs intended for loaf pans need to be preshaped, not just plopped into the pan, for the best rise. To shape dough for a loaf pan, follow these steps: Press the dough into an 8-inch square. Roll the square into a tight cylinder and then gently roll the cylinder back and forth on the counter until it is 9 inches long. Place the bread, seam side down, into a greased 9-inch loaf pan.

*shaping dough
for a loaf pan*

Q When I dragged my knife through the bread to score it, the blade got stuck and the dough deflated slightly. How can I score more cleanly next time?

A It takes nerve, experience, and the right tool to perfectly score bread. First, the tool: Use only the very sharpest chef's knife to cut through sticky dough. Anything less than a razor-sharp blade will stick to the dough. Better than a knife is an actual razor blade or a lame, a special bread-slashing knife used by professionals and available at baking supply stores (see Resources). But even the sharpest blade will catch in the dough if you hesitate mid-slash. Use quick, decisive motions to make your cuts. And remember, the bread will taste great no matter how imperfectly it is scored. Baking the next batch will give you an opportunity to improve your technique.

Q Is a baking stone necessary for making good bread?

A For European-style kneaded hearth breads, a baking stone is absolutely necessary. It will hold heat much more effectively than a baking sheet will, giving your breads a more crisp and well-browned crust than breads baked on a baking sheet. Preheated, it will conduct heat instantly into the bottom of your loaves, allowing them to achieve maximum oven spring. Even if you are baking bread in loaf pans, it is a good idea to place a baking stone on a rack underneath your bread, or on the oven floor itself. The heat radiating from the stone will give these breads a higher rise and chewier crust than they would get from the heat of the oven alone.

Choose the largest stone that will fit in your oven (see Resources). I own a thick rectangular stone that I bought years ago and that can accommodate the largest breads. Previously I had a thin, round pizza stone, but I found it too small for long baguettes or two large rounds. In any case, it cracked down the center after several years of use, a common occurrence with thinner stones. Place the stone in the oven and preheat it for at least 30 minutes, and up to 1 hour, before baking to get the most out of it.

Q Are there tricks for slicing bread without tearing it?

A Invest in a good serrated knife with a blade that's at least 8 inches long and you will not mangle even the freshest, softest bread. I own a Viking serrated slicer (see Resources). With its super-sharp teeth it slices effortlessly through all types of bread, from thick-crusted artisan sourdough boules to challah. It does double-duty slicing poultry and meat.

When you have a good knife, practice your technique. Use long strokes to saw through the loaf, and when you are almost at the bottom crust tilt the bread so that its side, rather than its bottom crust, is resting against the cutting board, so that you don't saw at the cutting board underneath.

Q Is steaming bread necessary?

A Many bread recipes call for introducing steam into the oven when the bread goes in. The idea is that steam keeps the crust moist and supple and prevents it from hardening during the first few minutes of baking, when the bread needs to rise. Without steam, the crust is more likely to dry out, holding the dough down and preventing it from rising to its full potential.

Steaming makes the most sense for larger hearth breads. It will have little or no impact on breads baked in loaf or other pans, since the larger area of crust on these breads is protected from drying out by the sides of the pan. Small rolls may benefit a bit from steaming but not as much as larger breads, since there is a smaller dough-to-crust ratio and a full rise is accomplished quickly in comparison with larger breads. When baking pizza and other doughs that have moist toppings, even a drizzling of olive oil, steaming isn't necessary, since the topping will provide the moisture necessary for keeping the crust moist during the first few minutes of baking.

Q What is the best way to introduce steam into the oven?

A Some people use a spray bottle to spritz the bottom and sides of the oven, but there is a danger of accidentally spraying water on the oven lightbulb and shattering it. (I did this years ago and it scared me half to death.) Another downside to this method is that you don't create much steam, so you need to repeat the process several times, and every time you open the oven you lose precious heat. Some people prefer to slide some ice cubes onto the oven floor when the bread goes in. The ice cubes supply a burst of steam when they hit the hot floor, and then more steam as they continue to melt. But sometimes water can drip out of the oven and onto the floor, making a bit of a mess, especially if your oven floor isn't clean. It's neater to place a baking pan, or even better a cast iron pan, on the bottom rack of the oven when you begin to preheat. Then, when you put the dough in the oven, place the ice cubes or some water into the pan, where they will continue to give off steam while the bread rises.

Yeast can survive in the heat of the oven for only 15 minutes or so. A half-cup to a cup of ice cubes should be enough to steam your bread during this time. There's no point in adding more water or ice cubes after this first batch has melted. When the yeast has stopped working and the bread has reached its full height, you'll want the oven to dry out so the crust can crisp.

Q How do I test my bread for doneness?

A Older recipes will instruct you to knock on the underside of the bread to test for doneness. If you hear a hollow sound, your bread is baked through. But this isn't the most scientific or surest method for judging if your bread is ready to come out of the oven.

An instant-read thermometer will tell you in seconds whether or not your loaf has reached an internal temperature indicating it is fully baked. For soft breads such as white sandwich bread, dinner rolls, and challah, look for a temperature of 185°F (85°C). For crusty artisan-style breads, let the temperature go to 205°F (96°C). To take a bread's temperature, insert the thermometer into the center of the dough, which will be cooler than parts closer to the top or bottom.

When your loaf has reached the internal temperature indicating it is fully baked, take a moment to evaluate the bread's crust before pulling it from the oven. If it is firm, resisting pressure when you squeeze it (using an oven mitt, of course), then the bread can be transferred to a cooling rack. If the bread crust gives under pressure, close the oven door and let the crust dry out for 5 minutes longer before removing the bread.

Q Can I eat my bread straight from the oven?

A The aroma of freshly baked breads is almost irresistible, but remember when you pull your loaves from the oven they're not through baking. As bread cools, the process of starch retrogradation (a fancy term for the drying out of the interior of the loaf) is completed. Water molecules inside the bread migrate to the crust and evaporate. This is why if you cut into a piping hot loaf of bread, it is spongy and damp inside and difficult to slice neatly. This doesn't mean that you can't eat warm bread. Small rolls and thin baguettes will be more or less ready to eat after 15 or 20 minutes. For larger loaves, it may take up to 2 hours for the interior to finish baking.

Q **What is the best way to store bread so it stays fresh?**

A Unfortunately, once bread has cooled, starch retrogradation continues until all of the moisture has evaporated from the bread and it is dry and hard. In this late phase, starch retrogradation is a fancy term for staling.

Refrigeration hastens staling, believe it or not. With the exception of breads that contain a large proportion of oily nuts and seeds or breads that contain ingredients that may mold or spoil quickly, store breads at room temperature and not in the refrigerator. Keep your bread in a plastic bag. Its crust may get soft, but you can recrisp it in a 350°F (180°C) oven for 5 minutes. Not only will reheating bread crisp the crust, but it will also draw moisture back into the crumb, refreshing it if it has begun to stale.

Fresh-baked, cooled bread freezes beautifully. Wrap it in plastic and then foil and freeze for 2 to 3 weeks. Defrost the bread on the countertop for a few hours (thin baguettes will take less than an hour, large rounds may take up to 4 hours) and reheat in a 350°F (180°C) oven for 5 to 10 minutes to refresh before slicing and serving.

BREAD-BAKING EQUIPMENT

Here is a list of equipment necessary for making a variety
of breads at home. If you are a serious baker, or intend to
become one, gather everything on the list. If you are just starting out, purchase equipment as necessary and improvise when
you have to.

Baker's peel. Use this long-handled metal or wooden sheet
to slide breads onto a preheated baking stone. If you don't
have a peel, you can use a rimless baking sheet. Just take care
not to touch the hot stone.

Baking stone. Look for a large rectangular stone that can
accommodate the largest breads and pizzas. To avoid cracking, season a new baking stone by heating it a few times in a
350°F (180°C) oven for 30 minutes before preheating it to
500°F (260°C).

Bannetons. These willow baskets lined with canvas are traditional implements for helping dough rounds maintain their
shape. But a shallow bowl lined with a floured kitchen towel
will do just as well.

Bench scraper. This rectangular steel blade with a wooden
or plastic handle is great for dividing dough as well as for
scraping sticky dough off of a work surface.

Clear, straight-sided rising container. You can let your
dough ferment in any bowl large enough to contain it as it
rises, but clear rising containers, with measurement markings
on the side, make it easy to see when your dough has doubled.

Heavy-duty stand mixer. Many bakers enjoy kneading dough
by hand, but if you are not one of them you will need a stand
mixer with a powerful motor and a dough hook attachment to

do the job. I have used the same KitchenAid model to knead bread dough for over 20 years and it is still going strong, so I highly recommend that brand.

Instant-read thermometer. Use an instant-read thermometer, inserted into the center of your loaf, to accurately judge its doneness.

Loaf pan. A metal pan is better than ceramic or stoneware; it will conduct heat more efficiently, resulting in a crisper crust.

Parchment paper. Sometimes when shaped loaves proof directly on top of a baker's peel, they stick to the peel and become misshapen when you attempt to slide them onto the baking stone in the oven. Place your shaped loaves on a piece of parchment paper set on top of the peel (or on top of a rimless baking sheet, which works just as well) before proofing and you will never have this problem. Just slide the parchment, with the loaves still on top, from the peel to the stone.

Razor blade or lame. The best implement for slashing dough before it goes into the oven, although a very sharp chef's or utility knife will also do the trick.

Rubber spatula. Before you begin to knead, either by hand or machine, you'll need a large, strong spatula to combine your ingredients into a rough dough.

Scale. Weighing ingredients is a more accurate way of measuring them than by using measuring cups and spoons, and these days most bread books list both the weight and volume of ingredients. So if you are serious about bread-baking, invest in a good digital scale with a tare function so you can bring the display back to zero before adding each new ingredient.

High-Altitude Baking

If you usually bake at sea level but are planning to bake at an altitude above 3,000 feet, it's smart to have an idea of how your doughs and batters might behave differently up there. The air is thinner and drier at higher altitudes, and water boils at a lower temperature than it does at sea level. These conditions usually call for a 25°F (4°C) increase in the baking temperature, and occasionally a slight adjustment of ingredients, to duplicate sea level results. Sometimes a little more liquid is necessary so your baked goods don't dry out. Sometimes less leavening is better, because carbon dioxide is produced at a greater rate in the mountains. You might need to cut back on the sugar in a recipe, because at high altitudes sugars become more concentrated when they bake.

Before you start fiddling with a recipe, try it first as it is written, increasing the oven temperature. In many cases ingredient adjustments won't be necessary. If you do have one of the common problems discussed below, experiment with the small changes that are suggested, or look at a similar recipe designed especially for high-altitude baking (for a good high-altitude baking cookbook, see page 363) to see what kind of quantities and ratios of ingredients have been proven to work well in the mountains. What follows are answers to some of the most common questions.

Q My banana bread batter overflowed in the oven, causing a real mess. What can I do to prevent this from happening next time?

A At high altitudes, baking powder and baking soda quickly produce more carbon dioxide than they do at sea level. The rapid expansion of the gas bubbles in the oven can cause batter to overflow the pan. When adapting a quick bread recipe, try cutting back on the leavening by about 25 percent for a less dramatic bubbling up (and over).

Q Is it my imagination, or do my corn muffins taste overly sweet at a higher altitude?

A When muffins or any other sweetened baked goods are placed in a hot oven, liquid in the batter evaporates more quickly than it does at lower elevations, concentrating the sugars and affecting flavor. For pleasantly sweetened baked goods, reduce the sugar in the recipe by a tablespoon for every cup.

Q How can I prevent my drop cookies from spreading into brittle discs as they bake at 5,000 feet?

A Cookie dough that contains a lot of butter and sugar can give bakers a real headache at high altitudes. Because of the low boiling point, the water in the butter evaporates from the dough more quickly than at lower altitudes, before the dough has time to set. The sugar concentrates and caramelizes, resulting in overly sweet and hard cookies. To give the cookies less sweetness and more shape, cut back on the sugar (1 tablespoon for every cup in the recipe) and substitute an egg yolk for 2 tablespoons of the butter.

Q How can I make a tender piecrust at 5,000 feet?

A Just as when you are mixing and rolling pie dough at lower altitudes, be observant and sensitive to your dough as you mix and roll it. At higher altitudes you will probably need to add more liquid to the dough to compensate for the dry flour. Restrain yourself from overflouring the countertop when you roll the dough. You don't want it to stick, but you don't want to add so much flour that your dough is underhydrated, which, at high altitudes will result in tough and dry pastry.

Q My butter cake is usually moist and well risen, with a velvety crumb. Why did it bake up flat, dry, and crumbly when I made it at a high altitude? What adjustments to the recipe should I make to prevent this from happening again?

A Lower air pressure causes water to boil at a lower temperature, which causes liquid to evaporate from cake batter more quickly than it would at a lower altitude. This evaporation has a couple of consequences. A cake that will be moist at a normal altitude may taste dry when baked above 3,000 feet. Cakes that lose too much moisture in the oven may have a compromised structure, since the starches in the flour won't gelatinize and be able to support the rising cake without an adequate amount of liquid.

Slightly increasing the liquid in your recipe will help. Or you could add an egg or an egg yolk to give the cake more structure in the form of coagulating protein. But don't add egg whites on their own, as they will further dry out the cake. If your cake is very buttery, you might try cutting back on the butter, which softens a cake's structure. You could also try increasing the oven temperature by 25°F (4°C), which will allow the starches to gelatinize before too much evaporation has occurred.

Compounding the problem of structure is a cake's tendency to rise high and then collapse at a high altitude because of decreased air pressure. Cutting back on chemical leaveners will prevent this from happening.

Q Are the guidelines for baking foam cakes the same for butter cakes?

A Foam cakes rely on beaten eggs and egg whites for their rise. Because air expands more rapidly and to a greater degree at high altitudes, it is important not to beat too much of it into your eggs when making a foam cake batter. Delicate cake batters won't develop a gluten structure strong enough to support this expansion, and the result will be a fallen cake.

Q Do doughs containing yeast behave differently at high altitudes?

A Your flour will probably contain less moisture, making it necessary to add a little more liquid to your dough. Take care not to add too much extra flour to the dough during kneading, which may make your bread dry. When you let your dough rise, don't let it rise too much, which can lead to a collapse in the oven. Overproofing (see page 336) will occur more quickly and easily at high altitudes where the air expands more rapidly. To control the rise, either cut back on yeast by 25 percent, or count on a quicker rising time. It's best to avoid rapid-rise yeast when baking at high altitudes, since an accelerated rise will more quickly lead to overproofing.

Metric Equivalents

Approximate Metric Equivalents by Volume

U.S.		Metric
¼ teaspoon	=	1.25 milliliters
½ teaspoon	=	2.5 milliliters
¾ teaspoon	=	4 milliliters
1 teaspoon	=	5 milliliters
1¼ teaspoons	=	6 milliliters
1½ teaspoons	=	7.5 milliliters
1¾ teaspoons	=	8.5 milliliters
2 teaspoons	=	10 milliliters
1 tablespoon	=	15 milliliters
2 tablespoons	=	30 milliliters
¼ cup	=	59 milliliters
½ cup	=	118 milliliters
1 cup	=	237 milliliters
2 cups or 1 pint	=	473 milliliters
3 cups	=	710 milliliters
4 cups or 1 quart	=	.95 liter
4 quarts or 1 gallon	=	3.8 liters

Converting Celsius to Fahrenheit

Use the following chart to convert oven temperatures from Celsius to Fahrenheit (see this page and the next for weight and measure conversion charts).

0°C = 32°F	190°C = 375°F
100°C = 212°F	200°C = 400°F
120°C = 250°F	220°C = 425°F
140°C = 275°F	230°C = 450°F
150°C = 300°F	240°C = 475°F
160°C = 325°F	260°C = 500°F
180°C = 350°F	

Metric Conversion Formula		
When you know this	Multiply it by	To find
teaspoons	4.93	milliliters
tablespoons	14.79	milliliters
fluid ounces	29.57	milliliters
cups	236.59	milliliters
cups	0.236	liters
pints	473.18	milliliters
pints	0.473	liters
quarts	946.36	milliliters
quarts	0.946	liters
gallons	3.785	liters
ounces	28.35	grams
pounds	0.454	kilograms
inches	2.54	centimeters

Approximate Metric Temperature Equivalents					
Fahrenheit		Celsius	Fahrenheit		Celsius
200°	=	95°	375°	=	190°
250°	=	120°	400°	=	200°
275°	=	140°	425°	=	220°
300°	=	150°	450°	=	230°
325°	=	160°	475°	=	240°
350°	=	180°	500°	=	260°

Resources

Mail-Order and Online Resources for the Baker

These days, finding equipment and ingredients that aren't available locally is simply a matter of an Internet search. But even this step isn't necessary if you already know where to go. Here is a list of my favorite online purveyors of everything from buckwheat flour to cardboard cake circles, to make your shopping fun and easy.

Bob's Red Mill, *www.bobsredmill.com*
If you can't find this brand of organic flours made from buckwheat, corn, spelt, and many others in your local natural foods store, you can order from the online store.

Crate and Barrel, *www.crateandbarrel.com*
The online store has a good selection of high-quality kitchen knives, colorful mixing bowls, and an array of fun kitchen gadgets helpful to the baker. This is where I found flexible grip mats that I use as cutting boards and also to help with rolling out pastry doughs evenly.

Hodgson Mill, *www.hodgsonmill.com*
Hodgson Mill is a widely distributed brand that also sells stone-ground and certified organic grain online.

House on the Hill, *www.houseonthehill.net*
House on the Hill has an incredible selection of cookie molds and carved rolling pins for making springerle and speculaas, as well as a lot of advice about making these special cookies.

King Arthur Flour Company, *www.bakerscatalogue.com*
The Baker's Catalogue is one-stop shopping for most bakers. Almost any piece of equipment you might need is here: KitchenAid mixers, digital scales, Silpats, parchment paper by the sheet, disposable pastry bags, Kevlar and terry oven mitts, instant-read and candy thermometers.

They sell a great selection of bread-baking ingredients and equipment, including SAF yeast (the brand preferred by many professionals), dehydrated sourdough starter, baker's peels, baking stones, lames for slashing dough, bench scrapers, bannetons, and clear-sided rising containers.

The Baker's Catalogue is also the place to look for high-quality flour, including organic all-purpose and bread flour. And they sell a wonderful variety of other baking ingredients, including chocolate and cocoa powder, meringue powder, fleur de sel and Malden sea salt.

King Orchards, *www.mi-cherries.com*
Contact King Orchards to order Michigan sour cherries in water for making cherry pies and cobblers.

Smucker's, *www.onlinestore.smucker.com*
Smucker's is a division of Pillsbury, which owns and distributes White Lily self-rising flour. If you want to make traditional Southern biscuits, and can't find self-rising flour in your grocery store, order this soft, low-protein flour here.

Williams-Sonoma, *www.williams-sonoma.com*
This well-known chain sells high-quality baking and pastry tools, including a wide selection of Nordicware Bundt pans, Chicago Metallic nonstick bakeware, cookie cutters, silicone oven liners, and OXO's easy-to-use cherry pitter.

Wilton Industries, *www.wilton.com*
Here you will be able to find everything to bake and decorate a cake: specialty pans (if you are having a NASCAR- or teddy bear–themed party), aluminum cake strips, plastic-coated pastry bags, couplers, pastry tips sold individually or in deluxe 26-piece sets, cardboard cake circles, food coloring sets, and a great selection of fondant, sprinkles, sanding sugar, and other decors. There are also wonderfully detailed instructions on this website for using a pastry bag and tips to decorate cakes and cookies.

Books for Bakers

Among the hundreds of books on baking that I have in my collection, the following are the ones I turn to most often when I have a baking question or need a foolproof recipe. Without them, I could not have answered many of the questions in this book! Every one of them is a classic, and worth owning as part of your baker's reference library.

Baking Science Books

Cookwise: The Secrets of Cooking Revealed by Shirley O. Corriher (William Morrow, 1997) and her follow-up *BakeWise: The Hows and Whys of Successful Baking with Over 200 Magnificent Recipes* (Scribner, 2008). Corriher, a food scientist with a natural gift for explaining complex scientific ideas in understandable terms, reveals the science behind flaky piecrust, moist pound cake, and puffy cream puffs.

On Food and Cooking: The Science and Lore of the Kitchen by Harold McGee (Scribner, 2004). The revised and updated edition of this classic is a must-have for the curious baker. Of particular interest are the chapters on eggs, sugar, and pastry doughs.

What Einstein Told His Cook: Kitchen Science Explained by Robert L. Wolke (W. W. Norton, 2002). A question-and-answer book that is especially interesting in tackling technology and baking tools, including explanations of how a microwave oven really works and what makes a nonstick baking pan nonstick.

General Baking Books

Baking Illustrated: The Practical Kitchen Companion for the Home Baker by the editors of *Cook's Illustrated* (America's Test Kitchen, 2004). An essential reference, packed with descriptions about the many kitchen experiments leading up to the magazine's best recipes for biscuits, croissants, chiffon cake, and many more.

Dessert University by Roland Mesnier and Lauren Chattman (Simon & Schuster, 2004). Of course, I am biased, since I helped Mesnier (who was the White House pastry chef for 25 years) write this book, but I learned such a tremendous amount from him about every aspect of baking, from puff pastry to making the perfect génoise, to decorating with chocolate, that I can't help but mention it as a resource.

How to Bake by Nick Malgieri (William Morrow, 1995). One of the best clear and simple guides, by a master teacher who has trained a generation of professional pastry chefs.

In the Sweet Kitchen: The Definitive Baker's Companion by Regan Daly (Artisan, 2001). An International Association of Culinary Professionals award winner for good reason, this is an exhaustive compendium of information about ingredients, equipment, and techniques essential for good baking.

Quick Breads, Muffins, Biscuits, and Scones

Biscuit Bliss: 101 Foolproof Recipes For Fresh and Fluffy Biscuits in Just Minutes by James Villas (Harvard Common Press, 2003). The most complete guide to the subject, by an expert on Southern food.

The Best Quick Breads: 150 Recipes for Muffins, Scones, Shortcakes, Gingerbreads, Cornbreads, Coffeecakes, and More by Beth Hensperger (Harvard Common Press, 2000). An in-depth resource for making superb quick breads, with many inspiring recipes that will help you put into practice what Hensperger teaches.

Cookies

The All-American Cookie Book by Nancy Bagget (Houghton Mifflin, 2001). Bagget takes a regional and a historical approach to cookie baking, so if you are interested in how cookie baking has evolved in this country since Colonial times, but are also looking for a volume full of great contemporary recipes, this is the book for you.

Great Cookies: Secrets to Sensational Sweets by Carole Walter (Clarkson Potter, 2003). Any book by Walter is worth owning (she's also written with great authority on cakes, pies, and quick breads), but this one is my favorite, because it's the rare cookie book that takes the subject seriously enough to explain how to roll cookie dough balls into perfect spheres or argue on behalf of vegetable shortening when baking chocolate chip cookies.

Cakes

The Cake Bible by Rose Levy Beranbaum (William Morrow, 1988). After 20 years, still the definitive volume on the subject. *The Cake Bible* explains the kitchen science behind every recipe. The recipes themselves range from the simplest beginner's pound cake to large-yield recipes for elaborate wedding cakes.

The Cake Book by Tish Boyle (Wiley, 2006). Tish Boyle's reputation as a baker's baker is hard-earned (she is the longtime editor of *Chocolatier* magazine) and well-deserved. In this book, not only will you get a terrific variety of creative cake recipes, but information about cake-baking that Boyle has gleaned from years in the kitchen, including why you should toast your walnuts and almonds at different temperatures and why puréeing bananas will produce a lighter cake than mashing them with a fork. A must for the serious baker.

Pies, Tarts, Cobblers, Crisps

Pie: 300 Tried-and-True Recipes for Delicious Homemade Pie by Ken Haedrich (Harvard Common Press, 2004). The 300 recipes in this wonderful book represent the author's lifelong obsession with baking fruit pies, cream pies, nut pies, icebox pies, and many more. Haedrich devotes 50 pages to apple pie alone. Irresistible.

Layered Pastry Doughs

The Classic Art of Viennese Pastry: From Strudel to Sachertorte—More than 100 Traditional Recipes by Christine Berl (Wiley, 1998). Although written with the professional pastry chef in mind (most of the recipes yield 8 or so cakes!), this is a wonderful book full of great information for ambitious home bakers interested in classic pastry techniques for making strudel, cream puff pastry, Danish dough, and much more.

Puff: 50 Flaky, Crunchy, Delicious Appetizers, Entrées, and Desserts Made with Puff Pastry by Martha Holmberg (Chronicle, 2008). Holmberg is a veteran food writer and former editor of *Fine Cooking* magazine who has put together a terrific collection of recipes as simple to make as they are impressive to look at. If you are intrigued by the possibilities of puff pastry, check this one out.

Yeast Breads

The Bread Baker's Apprentice: Mastering the Art of Extraordinary Bread by Peter Reinhart (Ten Speed Press, 2001). This is the most thorough and absorbing exploration of bread-baking out there, with enough detailed information to interest the professional as well as the passionate amateur.

Local Breads by Daniel Leader and Lauren Chattman (W. W. Norton, 2007). Dan is a superb teacher of sourdough baking techniques. Using his clear and reassuring instructions, I successfully cultivated a wild yeast starter 5 years ago, and it's still going today! I use the recipes he has collected in his book to bake heirloom breads from Italy, France, and Germany.

High-Altitude Baking

Pie in the Sky: Successful Baking at High Altitudes by Susan G. Purdy (William Morrow, 2005). Cake expert Susan Purdy tested and retested recipes at sea level, 3,000 feet, 5,000 feet, 7,000 feet, and all the way up at 10,000 to figure out how to bake successfully at any altitude. An invaluable resource for people in need of high-altitude baking advice and recipes that work in the mountains.

Index

Page references in *italics* indicate illustrations; page numbers in **bold** indicate charts.

Other Storey Titles You Will Enjoy

101 Perfect Chocolate Chip Cookies, by Gwen Steege.
The best melt-in-your-mouth variations of the classic favorite,
selected from thousands of contest entries.
144 pages. Paper. ISBN 978-1-58017-312-4.

250 Treasured Country Desserts,
by Andrea Chesman & Fran Raboff.
A nostalgic collection of more than 250 recipes for home
bakers to rely on for all occasions.
416 pages. Paper. ISBN 978-1-60342-152-2.

Cookie Craft, by Valerie Peterson & Janice Fryer.
Clear instruction, practical methods, and all the tips and
tricks for beautifully decorated special occasion cookies.
168 pages. Hardcover. ISBN 978-1-58017-694-1.

Cookie Craft Christmas, by Valerie Peterson & Janice Fryer.
Fresh inspiration and fabulous decorating from authors of Cookie
Craft, with more than 60 new designs for Christmas cookies.
176 pages. Hardcover with jacket. ISBN 978-1-60342-440-0.

Ghoulish Goodies, by Sharon Bowers.
A colorful collection of creepy treats for celebrating Halloween
or any frightful occasion.
160 pages. Paper. ISBN 978-1-60342-146-1.